America's Modernisms

America's Modernisms

Revaluing the Canon

Essays in Honor of Joseph N. Riddel

EDITED BY KATHRYNE V. LINDBERG
AND JOSEPH G. KRONICK

Louisiana State University Press
Baton Rouge and London

Designer: Laura Roubique Gleason
Typeface: Sabon
Printer and binder: Thomson-Shore, Inc.

Grateful acknowledgment is made to the Estate of Joseph N. Riddel for permission
to publish "To Perform—A Transitive Verb?" by Joseph N. Riddel.
    "A demi-mot," by Jacques Derrida, was first published in slightly different form
as "Joe Riddel: In Memoriam," in *Emergences* (Fall, 1992), 10–15, and is reprinted
by permission.

Library of Congress Cataloging-in-Publication Data

America's modernisms : revaluing the canon : essays in honor of Joseph
    N. Riddel / edited by Kathryne V. Lindberg and Joseph G. Kronick.
        p.   cm. — (Horizons in theory and American culture)
    ISBN 0-8071-2018-9 (cloth : alk. paper)
        1. American literature—19th century—History and criticism—
    Theory, etc. 2. American literature—20th century—History and
    criticism—Theory, etc. 3. Modernism (Literature)—United States.
    4. Canon (Literature)   I. Lindberg, Kathryne V.   II. Kronick,
    Joseph G.   III. Series.
    PS217.M62A45   1996
    810.9'1—dc20   95-23249
                                                              CIP

The paper in this book meets the guidelines for permanence and durability of the
Committee on Production Guidelines for Book Longevity of the Council on Library
Resources. ⊚

Contents

Acknowledgments

We wish to express our thanks to our copyeditor, Jane Taylor, and for technical assistance in the preparation of the manuscript, we would also like to thank Susan R. Smith of Wayne State University and Terry Newgard of Louisiana State University. At LSU Press, John Easterly lent us his support and guidance throughout this project, and Catherine Landry provided expert editing and steered the manuscript through the final stages of production. We are grateful to them both.

America's Modernisms

KATHRYNE V. LINDBERG

Introduction

The following essays comprise part of a lengthy, wider, and ongoing dialogue about American literature and/or modernism—the later names the time or condition of self-canceling desires for perpetual novelty and totalization that haunt "American" culture from its shady beginnings to its still uncertain spatio-temporal borders. Each of the essayists represented here knew Joseph Riddel as teacher, colleague, and, above all, conversationalist in that strangely familiar *neo*-logistic yet *post*-modern discourse of German-nuanced, French-accented, and/or philosophically informed criticism of American texts. In place of a univocal or unified tribute to "Riddel"—man, text, or pun—this collection of original, yet necessarily and consciously inter-textual, papers testifies to the fruitful differences of style and ethos generated by reading canonical American texts *otherwise*. I use "otherwise" to name a generic skepticism about the prescribed function and exclusive provenance of such uneasily paired discursive brand names as literature and politics, history and fiction, language and Truth, reading and writing, individual actor and national cultural scene, America or the United States and Others.

Rather than a party-line or fixed oppositional platform traveling as an adjective or proper name, unified critical fields customarily classed as literature's or America's *others*—psychoanalytic, post-structuralist, feminist, phenomenological, Marxist, Lacanian, Deleuzian, Foucaldian, Derridean—

1

the criticisms herein practiced resist discursive or figurative arrest. Indeed, though every essay addresses the ethics of reading, and several offer readings of the ethics evaded or hidden beneath traditional literariness, look for no radical turn from the complexities of historicity and figuration onto the high ground of moral correction or orthodox opposition.

Reading otherwise is often more challenging than reading other texts—the texts of the privileged Other—according to canonical or canonizing fashions. Just so, do not be surprised that the following writers concern themselves with "major" figures of the sort some of our grandfathers read (even if, as in my case, in Swedish or Russian translation and as a medium of assimilation). The writing here collected fundamentally challenges shibboleths of American literature. From within the canon, borrowing tools and rigorously employing techniques borrowed from other discourses and traditions, the following essays work a critique of official literary culture and the interpretive conventions of the academic literary establishment. In various ways, each essay disrupts established protocols of American reading by interrogating assumptions about a unique and original national(ist) literature. With the de(con)structive aid of the following essays we learn, for example, that American writing is inextricable from both the nostalgic Euro-centrism and the epistemological crises of Romanticism, that American poetics and pragmatism examine—or, more accurately, *problematize*—rather than simply affirm individual agency and that *we*—informally, perhaps reluctantly, incorporated as the liberal establishment—have failed to recognize the critical thrust of the art and poetry that smudge generic and discursive definitions necessary to ground a representative art or a unified or manageably diversified culture. Rather than offering new, more acceptable versions or vistas of culture in the United States, these essays interrogate the privileged name of America and the strictly policed, once imperial now pejorated, category of Modernism.

This space or style of reading the American literary canon is both inimical and adequate to a canon that, for all its revisionary energy, remains aggressive in appropriating and renaming its sources all the while insisting—only sometimes ironically—on an American Exceptionalism with regard to European and other aesthetic, ethical, and political imperatives. Always on the threshold of knowing itself and singing or constructing, in Whitman's cryptic title, an original and originating/new and grounding Song of Myself that will stand for individual differences and a revisionary unity of culture, American writing has, sometimes despite its stated idealism, acted out a critique of subjectivity. One might ask whether the absent article is properly *A* or *The* for Whitman's "song"? This is not to say, in any case, that America and its literature have evaded metaphysics and, specifically, ethics. To the contrary, as several of the following essays, including Riddel's, indicate, American literature obsessively returns to the problematic of an ethics underwritten by questions about the priority of agency to act, truth to language, and idea to desire.

Before formally introducing the nine essays solicited for and first appearing in this festschrift, I will stop to consider a privileged American (and Joe Riddel's favorite) signature: *baseball,* a tongue-in-cheek catachresis for that distressingly delightful revisionary category, "American," which, both as adjective and noun, polemically misnames its referent. Baseball, notwithstanding its *World* Series, its Pan-American or otherwise diasporic players, and new franchises in Canada and leagues in Japan, belongs uniquely to *America*—a word that names something more and different from the fifty United States. Some—Berra and Riddel among them—would claim that baseball elegantly and covertly performs the American paradoxes of individualism and teamwork, originality and repetition; in short, an American attitude that allows for improvisation and continuity, solipsism and belonging, assimilation and diversity, expansion without resistance, and guilt without reserve. Baseball might be dangerous if its chief spokesmen, including Berra, and its obsessive armchair managers and major league wannabes, among whom Riddel numbered himself, did not temper ambition with irony. Even as he seemed to validate the American myths of individualism and honest work rewarded, Berra was also both exemplar and defamiliarizing critic of Americanism(s). With an unfailing outsider's genius, Berra transformed Franklinian moralisms into malapropisms; every one of his truisms was both an original signature or logo and, ending as it began, a misquotation of folk wisdom. "Berraism" is the proper name for a trope, examples of which might be found in, or newly coined for, the vast literature and orature of baseball. Nevertheless, one is free to coin malapropisms and/or unanswerable riddles or contexts under the signature of Yogi Berra. Such was Riddel's wont in, for example, "To Perform—A Transitive Verb?" the last essay he penned, for delivery at a conference in French-speaking Montreal.

Although I will not dwell overlong on the subject—that is, the addressee—of this festschrift or, for that matter, on the Boys of Summer, I would note that Riddel's essay, printed here for the first time, insists that one think a bit about such gaming in order to play and position herself within the modern literary and contemporary critical scenes. "To Perform— A Transitive Verb?" which plays on the Roland Barthes title "To Write: An Intransitive Verb?" examines the implications and transatlantic advent of post-structuralism's belated announcement of the inescapabilty of language and the undecidable future of concepts and history. Riddel's title and epigraphic Berraism, though not without Jacques Derrida's presiding spirit, demolish the provisional American answer to French skepticism and the apparent subversion of moral agency. Riddel invokes or quotes Berra's performance style to suggest that every performative or "speech act" (including and especially those called ethical) conforms to linguistic and larger social prescriptions of iteration and intelligibility. Not content to recuperate the truths and context of a conference he first knew as text, Riddel feels compelled to assault the serious critic with a Yogi Berra-ism—or should I write "Berraisme"? In a characteristic gesture, he memorializes the transportation of French criticism into official American literary culture with an epigraph that stands as epitaph for American innocence and French innovation or the latest wave of continental decadence. Of course, not only because there are always harbingers of change and geniuses before avant-gardists (Poe and the French Poe, for instance) Barthes's thematics and practice were always already in America—or so Riddel claims.

Permit me to ask a decidedly unanswerable question of Riddel's last essaying of America's deconstructive literature. Is Riddel's/Yogi Berra's epigraph "When you come to a fork in the road, take it" an apt epitaph for Riddel? A self-conscious and perpetually renewable marker of a dizzyingly ironic Oedipal crossroads? An ethical double-cross or at least an inappropriate and macabre chiasmus? Something, therefore, of a riddle for the condition of American literature in its originary belatedness and, perhaps more urgently, a warning for those who would abandon the anarchic byways of inquiry for the again more traveled roads of relevant, representative, ethical literature and criticism? A challenge to those who might, like good beat cops, police borders and crossings? Does Riddel mean to set Berra, himself, or us up as Laius? As Oedipus, at forked road, with forked tongue? No, but there are reasons to open this line of inquiry. Riddel suggests that Berra, aspiring poet of the common man as well as "strong" or Oedipal American reader, meant to (mis-) quote Frost's moralism in "the road not taken." The essays here published do not directly effect an Oedipal challenge, at least not to Riddel's American poetics as represented in his "major" book-length pronouncements on Stevens and Williams. Nevertheless, three of the writers go so far as to afford Eliot, his major bugbear, sustained and respectful treatment. Riddel's colleagues do, however, remain cool about the recent recovery of, say, the Frost industry and the corresponding recession in experimental Modernism. Reading a little further, and forgetting poets for a moment, one might note that Riddel's oracle of baseball, while issuing truths through, in, and about America itself, sounds a quite un-American imperative to dwell in ambiguity rather than, say, to get *it* right at the American university—Stevens said the Sorbonne—and let its truths trickle down or back around to the People. Defensively, perhaps, Riddel attacks those who would forget critique and, pivoting on the old Truth of metaphysics, simply act as though history were not a text, or a pre-text for action.

There might well be something melancholy about Riddel's gesture, the essay—epigraph or epitaph—that stands as the parting shot in his critical can(n)on. Nevertheless, it cannot be properly funereal, let alone Oedipal, and this is not only because of the status of the later text after Lacan and Derrida—or that other erstwhile founding (mis-) quoter, Freud. I could perhaps extend a far-fetched metaphor for the changing literary marketplace of ideas beyond natural half-life of Berraisms and *passing* jokes by underscoring the diversity of responses to and rejections of Riddel's riddle. One can extract many a riddle from the following revisionary readings that are cryptically addressed to various *Riddels* (intimate friend, teacher, colleague, academic adversary, conference cohort, old ally of or against a former establishment), "If you can't imitate him, don't copy him" (as Berra allegedly advised Ron Swoboda of Frank Robinson). Yet no one really ever wanted to be his intellectual son or daughter or otherwise simply to follow Joe Riddel. Riddel did not bide unquestioning filial piety any more than he could respect philosophical pieties. In passing, let me speak for myself, not for incestuous allegorical "positions" left vacant by erstwhile sons and fathers but, for the moment, as a woman represented neither by Jocasta nor Antigone. Joe Riddel, himself something of an intellectual orphan, would have balked at the piety of all such strained affiliations—even those of classic no-win situations like the Oedipal. Especially from this crowd of hard-hitting critics—even on this memorial occasion. Finally, coming from one of Riddel's adopted fathers-in-text, Derrida's *essay*, included in this collection, nicely captures, I think, the irony involved in responding to a call for papers about, in response to, or after Riddel on American literature.

A Shot, After Pound's "I Gather the Limbs of Osiris," at the Somewhat Non-Polemical Introduction

By way of general précis, and as a gesture of respect to the contributors to this volume, I will not divide the following essays according to laws of literary periodicity or schools of interpretation. Another introduction might map three groups of three essays (nineteenth-century, early-twentieth-century, and inter-epochal American authors) or extract four discrete programs from the Foucaldian re-figurings of political discourse, de Manian rhetorical criticism, deconstructive readings of national subjectivity or native (anti-) philosophical pragmatism, and post-Marxian corrections of modernist reaction and reification that underwrite these essays in recognizable ways. But, because I do not want to preempt your reading, let me offer only a provisional sketch of ways in which these essays uniquely address urgent concerns common to all of us interested—however differently—in and by modern American literature. Not quite arbitrarily, I begin my formal introductions with Henry Adams.

In "Anarchy and Perfection," Paul Bové meditates on the present role and choices of intellectuals positioned within the endless improvisational capacities of late capitalism and American invention to construct and market subjects and histories. The United States, its "oppositional critics" as well as the liberal establishment and those more readily classed as nationalists, seems called again to revise history and explain the post–Cold War world to itself. In a reading that tempers despair with ironic exposé, Bové prizes the intellectual scrupulousness of Henry Adams, the notorious American historian, novelist, man of letters, and critic, whose uncanny relationship to the origins of the nation and his discursive belatedness to statistics and such new theories as thermodynamics (except as a self-incriminating metaphorics of force and potency) leave him yet unaccommodated in America's revisionary pantheon.

According to certain proprieties of mythology and nomenclature, "Adams" might easily stand as an honored and quoted American original, scion of the founding and presidential Adamses, if not the namesake of biblical firstness. Rather than being first man, authoritative historian, or canonical writer, in any sense appropriate for nationalism or a critical pantheon, Adams still haunts discursive and political margins. He recorded his uncanny position and inadequate "education" in a book whose title and trajectory mock the privileged American genre of autobiography and, thus, the sanctity and representativeness of, let me call it, an (ethically reductive version of) Emerso-Whitmanian selfhood and the ontological priority of subjects to history. Where, Bové following Adams in refusing a fashionable moral high ground, scruples not to ask, is agency and whither ethics in Adams? Nevertheless, from the Adamsian margins of a footnote, Bové polemically silhouettes Adams' crucial yet still *untimely* (*Unzeitgemasse* as in Nietzsche's heroes and meditations) ethical stance with regard to American thought and/or Americanists: "Perhaps another reason for Adams' relative absence from current critical debates is his anti-humanist denunciation of the importance of what even or especially 'oppositional' critics call subjectivity."

After Adams, it seems appropriate to consider another American family signature, James. Whereas Bové's Adams debunks myths of origins and self-creation, the writing James brothers replace the ("Adamic"—decidedly not Adamsian) myth of American exceptionalism with an equally mythic program for what Mark Bauerlein calls the "progressive assimilation of the other." In "Henry James, William James, and the Metaphysics of American Thinking," Bauerlein recognizes the Jameses as American brothers in deed. They can be seen as cohorts in the sibling discourses of fiction and philosophy that casually overlap in American writing: Henry's novels fix on Mind "enervated by its semiotic subtleties"; William manufactures Americans. Fictional characters are maddened by metaphysics, while philosophy creates an American selfhood that will suffice for expansionist politics and technological progress. How American, one might say, this sense of relation and raging relativity! Politics, literary and increasingly global, is no exception to a liberality with regard to boundaries, assimilation, and self-aggrandizement.

Concerned with the impact as well as the ethics of America's flexible categories and fully aware of their de(con)structive advantage over the older metaphysics, Bauerlein offers a critique of pragmatism's assertion that "Mind's task is to develop fluid relativities, to domesticate otherness by forecasting it as merely yet-to-be assimilated data." While he recognizes the political implications grounding ethics and public policy in a perpetually self-revising agency, Bauerlein notes that William James, as effectively as the figures in Henry's American stories and oriental carpets, charts the reversion to an innocent Self. Hardly naïve, not an exception to, but a fragmentation and assimilation of System, what is properly but also ironically and diacritically named "American metaphysics" resists its name quite elegantly, even as it replaces an embarrassed national literature with cultural imperialism. As Bauerlein remarks, William James's philosophy "is [d]eserving [of] the predicate 'American' precisely because it eschews any such limiting, ideologically sedimented terms as 'American.'"

Henry Sussman's "At the Crossroads of the Nineteenth Century: 'Benito Cereno' and the Sublime," the fifth essay in this collection, narrates the epistemological and "identity" crises staged in Melville's juxtaposition of Hegelian dialectics and Kantian sublimity. "Benito Cereno," Sussman claims, marks the American birth—at once premature and belated—of modernism out of the contradictory claims of romanticism. Melville's characters, which must be thought to include a ship that stands for a state in ontological uncertainty and political chaos and the very name "Amasa (Delano)," an ironic dialectical epithet for a master transformed by his slave into a mask, unmask or ironize philosophical speculation and subjectivity, even as they compel characters and readers to become "exegetes of sign systems." Sussman's Melville reiterates the invitation to the serious wordplay involved in accidents of naming, quotation, and allusion. Criticism and the critique of subjectivity get more than a consolation prize for the loss of discursive mastery over the Western historical trajectory of progress. Not comfort, but awe, is the duplicitous reward meted out by and to Melville's disquieted Americans. Sussman defines the ambiguous rewards of self-knowledge and self-abnegation attendant upon the American sublime in the following terms: "As figments of original genius, post-Cartesian literary characters lead us to a certain wonder and awe that they are privileged to unearth in compensation for the constraints they are fated to endure."

Far from proving an exception or transcendence of metaphysics, Melville, in an exemplary way, frames the impasses and achievements of nineteenth-century thought, whose concepts and contradictions warn against the easy return to a history that would make alterity instrumental in the dialectical progress of Spirit an American privilege. Under the sign and by means of a reading of the ship's motto, "Follow Your Leader," Sussman demonstrates that philosophy is key to unpacking the ethical baggage of American writing. Without translating the legalistic, philosophical, and fictional language(s) that Melville had directly and indirectly from German idealism and United States civil discourse into a neo-humanism or new historicism, Sussman offers a convincing and responsible reading of Hegel's "Master Slave Dialectic" that bears comparison with the more recognizably political versions of Fanon and Du Bois.

The sixth essay, Edgar Dryden's "Mute Monuments and Doggerel Epitaphs: Melville's Shattered Sequels," also works the border conditions of literary genre and the turn of Romantic philosophy toward language. Melville, especially in *Pierre* and "Bartleby" but also in passages that expose the textual metaphors and narrative glitches in *Moby-Dick*, is Dryden's source of iconoclastic statements about epitaphs and "genre-clastic" supplements to epitaphs. Dead letters and grave markers live uncanny half-lives in "sequels" and "apocrypha" that might return to tell and, in telling, undo the inevitable story of one's own death before which writing is at once a hedge and a disclosure. While less urgently harassed by questions of ethics than some of the essayists represented herein, Dryden offers a reading of Melville's running commentary on death in—and as a precondition of—language. If, in his reading of Hawthorne, Melville proclaimed the mastery—or is it the bastardy?—of philosophy by literature, American writing is particularly doomed to borrow dead writers' figures as reminders of mortality and insurance of and a reserved seat in the (Wordsworthian) literary pantheon or boneyard.

As silent tribute to Riddel and writing, Dryden plays macabre name games with *Pierre*, the eponymous or translated name for the way literature memorializes and yet transcends the stony silence with which one faces death. Likewise and finally, and here Dryden enters into conversation with this collection's many positions with regard to subjectivity and the saying and seeing of I's, he reminds us of the embarrassing body of Bartleby, symbolic somehow of Melville's corpus, and more generally, the whole tribe of scribblers and scriveners: "The shiver that the corpse sends through the living body as the 'I' closes the lifeless 'eyes' confirms the text's specular structure as the narrator is brought face to face with his own mortality."

The haunting and forever current question of literature's—especially modernism's—alleged evasion of ethics, politics, and death, any of which might be disguised as totalization, surfaces most cunningly in Michael Beehler's essay. His essay surprises by characterizing Eliot, the very signatory of High Modernism's questionable politics and artistic autonomy, as an exemplar, if not a precursor, of the self-transcendence and embrace of alterity that Levinas privileges as the post-ethical (or existential), which, by renouncing the dream of closure and the illusion of timeless truth, remains critically engaged in metaphysics and theology. It seems fitting that his reading of Riddel—who never lost an opportunity to tag Eliot the moral coward—is at once viciously funny and generously respectful.

At Riddel's expense, and piggy-backing on more than one original misquotation or misprision, Beehler carries out a serious program of recuperating Eliot's moral outrage at the solipsism, morbidity, and skepticism of Poe and Valéry. Let me say that Riddel, always free with his mis-spelled signature, would have endorsed this expense or investment, whether or not he would have appreciated the returns. Rather than (Riddel's) Eliot escaping his scriptive fate by an embrace of religious, aesthetic, political orthodoxy, we get an Eliot who, especially in *Quartets* and the late plays, continually abjures the narcissistic joys of self-reflection and the consolation of the Church of England. I don't want to spoil the punch line more than to say that "'Riddle the Inevitable': Levinas, Eliot, and the Critical Moment of Ethics" presumes to re-sign Riddel's text with a quotation from Eliot, wherein "inevitability" names the unknowable ravages of time, and the forks and detours in roads that still lead inexorably to death.

Margot Norris' "The Trace of the Trenches: Recovering Modernism's World War I," while attending more closely to Ezra Pound and Wyndham Lewis than to Eliot, covers some of the same ground by interrogating the modernist ethics—and ethos—of reading and writing. She arrives at far different judgments and solutions than Beehler, as she hopes to put an end to ever more elegant interpretations by exploring the empirics of canonicity and the discursive investments of its formalist proponents. In Norris' reading, which is no more reverent to Riddel than Beehler's (and therefore faithfully unfaithful), the likes of Pound, Yeats, and Eliot become the means by which the realities of war are reified into personal struggles for artistic purity and market share in the culture industry. Not only did their own poetry re-figure the war out of history, but also as poet-critics these writers, followed and enabled by academic readers, managed to banish from Poetry proper such pejorated writing as "trench poetry," which is, for Norris, the authentic voice of suffering.

Following Norris, one certainly does wonder how and why the High Modernists policed—or have been made to police—their discourse so effectively; Norris elaborates a recent use of their ideological (in)utility, in the U.S. "police action" in Vietnam. Recalling that Eliot and Conrad were the presiding spirits of *Apocalypse Now,* a movie that mythologizes American individualism and mystifies the real conditions and economic preconditions of a colonial war, Norris shows how, despite its authors' elitism and resistance to instrumentality, the text of modernism gets re-tooled for mass consumption. She says, for example, that "[A]s ideological inter-text of a mass medium, modernism is allowed to reproduce itself in Coppola's film with a complex set of differences." Exploring the degree to which especially Lewis recognized the aestheticization of politics and war before World War I, and how this potential critique was turned instead into a glorification of a macho and metaphoric struggle of art against the masses, Norris exposes the ongoing culture—and literal "war crimes" of High Modernism, a poetic canon fixed in Yeats's 1936 *Oxford Book of Modern Verse*. Deftly, and presumably not without irony, she too uses the tools of Anglo-American modernism against itself—Coppola's fissured self-reflecting camera being just one of these.

Charles Altieri also returns to a modernism that might have been, if Eliot and the others had picked up the ethical ball dropped by modern philosophy rather than falling into "a radically individualist aestheticism." "A Tale of Two Modernisms, or Richard Rorty's Philosophy as Trojan Horse" attempts to chart the ways Richard Rorty repeats the modernist dilemma (*i.e.*, for Bauerlein's Jameses, the American *advantage*) of working from an ethics free of foundational claims and in a discourse—philosophy—that has lost the license to dictate truths for life and art. Altieri charges that Rorty, having misused the potential of Russell's and Wittgenstein's speculations about and in figurative language, has reduced ethics and value statements to the equally unattractive alternatives of irony, which can be dangerous and destructive, and solidarity, which works only provisionally and contingently.

More explicitly, perhaps more polemically, than most of the essayists here, Altieri stages a pitched battle between literature and philosophy, roughly between figurative expression and totalizing system. Ultimately, he argues, Eliot and other modern writers betrayed both the ethical potential of lyric constructions and the vestiges of decency left to modern philosophy in the form of secular liberalism. In the face of uncertainty about the power of poetry to author truth and effect change, Eliot turned to political authoritarianism. Altieri, by warning that this path is still open at least in the micro-politics of academic disciplines, calls upon Rorty's critique of philosophical vocabularies to do more; that is, to describe but also to create—to poetically re-figure—an ethical poetics, a poetic ethics. In sum, against what he characterizes as the reductive analysis of philosophy, Altieri reaffirms his belief in the positive force and beneficent power of poetry.

From a different position in the poetry wars, but also as a reader of war poems, John Carlos Rowe limns "Whitman's Body Poetic" as a "utopian vision [that] comprehends the equality of the labor of the poet and the mechanic." Resisting an Emersonian idealism (something of a "straw man" in its reifying redundancy) that abstracts or transcends history, Rowe claims for Whitman a representative status and a figurative language that achieves physical effects, if not full presence. This Whitman can hardly escape unscathed the dangers of aspiring to the status of poet/god transforming pain into historical mission, even as he puts his body on the line as witness and nurse. Rowe suggests that the problem and the solution are one: Whitman's self-assertion that the poet speaks *for* the nation—a dangerous abstraction, especially in Civil War America—rather than *as* worker and citizen engaged in the struggle to bring the United States into line with "the original revolutionary purpose of the nation." Rowe's Whitman is surrounded on all sides by idealizing abstractions, as he hardly resists transforming the carnage of war into a nationalistic chant that forgets the life and deaths it would remember.

In "Jameson's Hyperspace, Heidegger's Rift, Frank Gehry's House," John Johnston recognizes the crucially therapeutic violence of interpretation from which post-modernism and post-structuralism retreat at the risk of political complacency. For Johnston, Frank Gehry's literal house, a doctored and textualized 1930s fragment of an old American tract Dream, effects both an address to the "neighborhood" of everyday life and to the critical tradition that would go through language to truth. This house, which functions as a reading of American "life-style" and an abusive quotation, repeats in aesthetically embarrassing terms Heidegger's problematics of the rift (*der Riss*); that is, of art that at once abolishes grounding terms and initiates a critique of its own desire for closure. Johnston's reading of the rift exacerbates and profits from problems of translating from architectural to written art and criticism.

Johnston implies that Gehry's buildings, especially the parasitical/paraciting dwelling that haunts Santa Monica, achieve a disruptive Art (anti-art works, irreducibly theoretical objects?) interesting enough to stand up to the advances in phenomenological critique and post-structuralist discourse that some critics have abandoned in despair. Metal corrugation enwraps and unwraps—or "raps" with—the house in the cross-town/inner-city urban scene its neighborhood would deny; glass surfaces open it to the world for which the family manse usually represents protection. What must be called "the Gehry house" resists being a "home," the name by which real estate agents and bourgeois moralists might package it. And more important for Johnston, this structure resists Fredric Jameson's Marxist allegories. Post-modernism, added to all the rest of the baggage modernist artistic autonomy wanted to throw over, has yet to be got beyond. Just as a history of criticism is written in contemporary art and public culture, so do all the following essays engage an ongoing critique from which America—historical and mythical—has never been exempt.

If I have been rather too coy or cryptic an introducer in leaving you to stitch together recurrent themes of American subjectivity, literary and critical ethics, and discursive wars, I hope that I have made clear, never leaving a pun un-turned or a trope un-taken, that obsessive play with the great names of American culture and their signatures marks—some might say mars—nearly all of these essays. This is serious play, though; play that, departing from Freud's observations about jokes, destabilizes patronymics and ideologies that usually travel as truth and tradition. In exposing life and art to the alterity of time and being(s), performing or exposing ones's argument to accidents of language that force change and choice to jolt dead metaphors to life, critics can open and remain open to criticism. In this sense, we are always and again approaching what Riddel's Berra referred to as "a fork in the road." This does not involve only a simple turn from language to action, pure art to real history. Perhaps not at all, since only someone vain to the point of madness or otherwise beyond the reach of time and death could fail to recognize—and at the same time deny—the extent to which events and decisions are scripted and overdetermined.

JOSEPH N. RIDDEL

To Perform—A Transitive Verb?

When you come to a fork in the road, take it.
—Yogi Berra

It very possibly never occurred to that consummate speech actor, Yogi Berra, that his words of instruction might locate or site the condition of a certain modernity or post-modernity, the chiasm and aporia of a discourse that performs the future rather than predicating it. Precisely because that discourse, as act, is never, in another Yogism, "over 'til it's [that is, the speech act's] over." Which is indeterminable, even considering the perlocutionary success. Suppose one takes, or has taken, the fork, has chosen, as Yogi states, not one way or another, but simply chosen, acted. What, then, is the meaning, the ethical implications and consequences, of the choice, except the act itself? And what, to echo Heidegger on the "thing," is an act—choice, promise, direction, proclamation, etc., or a citation, quotation, in general, performative utterances? Is a performance a thing, event, fact, or even meaning, in sum, a reality that is either genitive (thus a subject or intention) or the productive issue of a subject, that is, an object? Is the act intransitive, as Roland Barthes questions of the verb or infinitive "to write," or transitive? And what is the difference?

I ask these questions in the words of speech act theory and in the ordinary language of an extraordinary performer, an act that would probably offend those theorists who might find in Berra's mono-neologisms something non-serious or etiolated, or at least one-liners that could be either spontaneous non-sense or scripted act. For isn't there more wisdom and ethical scrupulosity in Berra's utterance than in Frost's nostalgic meditation on

14

"the road not taken"? The latter's liberal caution in insisting on the heroism of choosing the harder, less traveled but nonetheless already created way disguises his fear of fate, of being condemned to repeat one thing or another; Berra exalts in the strange freedom of repetition. Frost's dogmatic voice does not act but instructs us to be as original as we can be, which is not original at all. Berra's instruction acts, and sets aside the consequences. But is one more ethical than the other, more instructive?

My title, most of you will recognize, cites another one much more familiar to recent consumers of theory than any single speech act communiqué, though Barthes' famous essay may now seem to have receded into the rhetorical background of poststructural discourse and to belong to a road, path, or way (to language) we who are enticed by "theory" have long since taken, a way with many crossings and bypaths none of which come out at the same site. But I want to return along one of those ways a way in order to recall what was at stake at the "fork," and why it may still be at stake today, despite our claims to have gone beyond the "word" (or language) to culture and history and all the consequent realities they signify. Have we advanced, to ask another question, from "writing" as a certain intransitivity to performance, from "to write" to "to perform," or simply come face-to-face with the aporia between constative and performative—the space of the "trans-word," of the old verb itself? What is transitivity? and why is it the most suggestive "name" for modern theory, or for that which seems to link, in an unhappy coalition, metaphysics and cybernetics, that is, a certain physics, the word (logos) and the word processor. Let us return to the site, Baltimore, 1966, of a certain performance of "theory" that might now be recalled as an inaugural moment, though of course it was only a repetition of something that had been going on a long time.

Roland Barthes' justly celebrated essay can certainly not be limited to this, his intervention at the Johns Hopkins conference, even if that were its first performance. Nor to its place in what has been called theory's "turn toward language," a troping long before if not always already begun. But this context or site does provide a certain indelible marking of the return. Barthes' gesture in displacing the priority of thought with language, as one of his respondents protested, was somewhat upsetting even to those long since accustomed to the reversal, and who recognized its significance in Heidegger as well as in the structuralist revolution. It was not so much a question of re-siting thought in language as determining where in language that situating occurred that surprised his auditors. Extrapolating from the linguistics of Emile Benveniste, Barthes had focused upon the question of "voice" as tense in order to question the place and function of the subject in certain kinds of productive activities. Thus, the verb "to write," either a transitive or intransitive verb, locates a kind of genetic scene. Barthes' argument that writing is not simply the vehicle or record of thinking, or the phonetic inscription of idea, focuses not upon writing as an act of a subject, but as the act of language, that which is already taking place in discourse. Thus Benveniste's notion of the "middle voice" and the neutralized subject allow Barthes to highlight something that structural linguistics and its semiotics had regularly claimed, the production of meanings in binary structures that preceded the explanation of intentionality or consciousness; the primacy of agency is accorded to language, not the subject, as a kind of zero degree discourse. Barthes did not acknowledge, or perhaps recognize, that his new centering of utterance in the "middle voice" anticipated the question of "speech act," for his concern was to return a sense of "time" to language that he found excluded in either philology or linguistics. Discourse itself was agent.

Neither did he acknowledge the performative effect of his own intervention, even down to the site of his delivery (something that Derrida, one might recall, does not forget in his equally notorious essay on speech acts, "Signature, Event, Context"). This conference on the "Human Sciences" in Baltimore, later given a collective title, "The Structuralist Controversy," is generally regarded as the moment in which the viral (and parasitic) discourse of poststructural Europe was posted to what would become its most supportive host or culture. Whether or not Poe's Baltimore is or was the after-scene of his Gallic ricorso is a question for critical/theoretical history, or whether the occasion was only another repetition of intercontinental and intertextual randomness is a moot point. But evidently something happened in Baltimore, some "event," even some things that have yet to be read.

Let me focus, then, on a marginal moment of that marginal "scene of writing," long since available in the archives or records of the proceedings and, in a peculiar sense, as unverifiable as a Poe reference. I refer to the "Discussion" sessions that follow each essay in that text, and of which I know, thanks to the explanation of old friends who organized the event, to be supplementations or comments "enhanced" by their speakers long after the conference was adjourned, by the need of the editors to provide a kind of logic and grammar to recorded voices that often appeared to be "white noise." But to recall the text—one is impressed by the detail of the respondants to the distinct positions of the essays, and the fullness of reply, like American philosopher Jay Loewenberg's essay question to Jean Hyppolite. For example, the first response to Barthes' presentation raised the issue on which Barthes had concluded with emphasis and flourish. The elevation of "language" to the universal problematic, which is to say, to the center of the thinking of structurality, while at the same time suspending the originary or intentional function of the speaking subject, perplexed the phenomenological critic, Georges Poulet, and Poulet responded to Barthes that where the structuralist speaks of language, the critic of consciousness hears "thought." Barthes, perhaps evoking Heidegger and phenomenology against his questioner, restates the semiotic principle of the essay, averring not only the primacy of the signifier and of a discourse, Benveniste's "middle voice," but that "man" (or subject) "does not exist prior to language either as species or as an individual."[1] Writing, then, is Barthes' name for a discourse that has long since begun; and "Discourse," he continues, is not an accumulation of sentences but "one great sentence." Open and endless, without beginning, discourse hosts consciousness and is not commanded by it. Man, intention, subject, and finally meaning arise within the larger temporal structure of enunciation itself, and not the other way around.

But the most provocative and (given the literary example he uses) perverse intervention to this session (which included a text on semiotics by Todorov) is Jacques Derrida's interlocution. After acknowledging the significance of Barthes' reversal, Derrida offers a characteristic codicil to the notion of writing's rhetorical "will to power," its capacity to produce a "person" in the grammatical position where one did not previously appear. Derrida's example (literary) is the notorious utterance of Poe's M. Valdemar, the assertion that "I am dead," which becomes for Derrida meaningful not only because of being pronounced in a literary space but because it characterizes one of the fundamental possibilities of language, to mean even when it speaks nonsense—that is, it abides by the laws of grammaticality and repeatability, enunciating logically an I or "je" that does not exist except within the conventions of linguistic structure. This "I," says Derrida, cannot refer to a particular or originary consciousness or self and thus is, in its position in a sentence that is otherwise senseless, understandable as a function of the sentence structure, that is, of language's iterability: "If the repetition is original," he notes of Poe's sentence, "that means that I am not dealing with the new in language." "A true act of language"—note the word "act" here, which Derrida may or may not have used—he continues, is necessarily situated in the conditions that allow for a sentence to be true when false, or to make sense when it speaks "*contre-sens*" (*SC,* 156). Thus, "I am dead" is "not nonsense," but an act that locates a scene of writing that both unsettles and reinscribes the classical function of the subject: "That means that the power of language is, to a point, independent of the possibility of its object"; and thus Valdemar's utterance is not only a possible proposition for a fictional character to make, "it is the very condition for a living person to speak."

In later remarks, which respond to challenges to his own primary intervention at the conference, the programmatic essay "Structure, Sign, and Play in the Discourse of the Human Sciences," Derrida makes the now better known but rarely admitted claim that his argument for a decentering writing, so easily elided with a Nietzschean nihilism or, more pejoratively, with an irresponsible and non-cognitive aesthetics of "play," does not "destroy the subject; I situate it." "The subject," he says, "is absolutely indispensable," but not necessarily as the old psychological or grammatical subject, the sentence's motor or the self located at the origin of perception, nor even in Barthes' "middle" and neutralized voice (271).

Looking back over the situation or scenes of these dialogues, we might notice something other than the one accomplishment usually credited to deconstruction, for better or worse—the deconstruction of the subject, which has disturbed so many recent questioners of Derrida's homocidal and even geneacidal writing acts. For it is clearly his resistance to such ends of deconstruction (the destruction of the subject) that he stages in this "rap" with Barthes. Deconstruction or decentering is never rid of the subject, nor of language, though both names now do not refer either to essences or things. In short, Derrida's remarks upon Barthes and others are performative, performances upon performances: "I do not destroy the subject; I situate it," says this "I" who has just explained why it can be said, "I am dead," why this possibility is the very condition of living speech. Deconstruction could not have emerged as the name for a kind of writing without some thinking of the performative, with or without Austin's particular formulations of speech act theory as a distinct yet marginal philosophy of language. And performatives, we hasten to add, cannot brook the negative, cannot advance a nihilistic philosophy—except perhaps against the negative, as deconstruction does in its engagement of the dialectical. One might argue then that the problem of dealing with so-called deconstructive discourse within the brief "history" of poststructuralism is that those who would describe it have had to do so in the language of cognition (even when emphasizing its situating itself in rhetoric and a kind of power language) or conation, as a set of declared positions or concepts, albeit a negative logo-theology, rather than in the language of performatives. But that, of course, is inescapable, as Austin's theoretical utterances reveal. Even when organized by others, students and so on, or especially when incorporated by Searle, Austin's formulations encounter the double-bind of all theory, and especially a theory of pragmatics or acts, the limit, as Derrida would put it, of something (language) being employed to account for or analyze itself (language). The inextricability of cognitive and performative is the already doubled epicenter that precludes the one from explaining the other, and vice versa. Writing is never separable from *act,* then, and this is why Derrida names all acts writing. Even the writing of philosophy is act and actionable, working upon the very concepts that it is employing; so that Heidegger's example of overwriting metaphysics can never so much get "beyond" metaphysics as repeat that endless act Barthes calls the sentence of discourse. Heidegger's "call" is both a performative displacement of classical concepts of Being and the provisional name of a "new" concept that is deferred. This is why literature, once disengaged from its classical definition of closed or self-reflexive "work," is another word for writing, and performative.

But having established the obvious, that a certain notion of performative has been fundamental to deconstruction from its uncertain beginnings, before it began to turn up in the terminology or even, as in Derrida's writings on Austin and Searle, as the "object" of interrogation, it is necessary to remark that the word no longer carries the same sense or force it bears in speech act theory. For Derrida, the performative is like writing generalized to the point of an indeterminate function and force, as that which inhabits all discourse. One could, for example, trace this increasing awareness of the performative in Derrida's writing from his earliest considerations of the sign in Husserl's *Origin of Geometry,* through *Of Grammatology* and *Speech and Writing,* or in other words that writing which had the earliest and most enduring impact on American critical writing, before the appearance of the essay on Austin in *Glyph,* six or so years after its initial delivery here in Montreal, and the subsequent notorious engagement or miscommunication between Derrida and Searle in *Limited Inc.* Indeed, a history of Derrida's (not deconstruction's) "development," could it be written with any authority as an intellectual history, might emphasize the role of the performative as the one constant concept of any grammatology. But, of course, it does not function as a concept for Derrida, who is not writing a grammatology, and the emphasis on praxis or act in Derrida is so different from that in Austin's theory that one wonders why the former is so parasitic of the latter's terminology, and why Derrida eventually writes the name of the "laws" of this writing as "pragrammatology." Performatives, as Derrida shows of Austin's *How to Do Things with Words,* resists exhaustive description or systematization, even explanation by the old linguistic laws, as the proliferation of endless examples that never quite exhaust the case reveal.

In short, the crucial notion of performatives that is reinscribed everywhere in deconstruction from 1970 onward, and often in different ways and to different purposes, takes its name from Austin, but in an active way that displaces the commonsense, practical formulations and exempla that Austin and Searle had proposed to complement linguistics. Now, the use of a familiar established word-concept in an unfamiliar and often neologistic sense is one of the signature characteristics of deconstructive writing, and one of the symptoms of its viral effects on contemporary discourse. The instance of "differance" written with an *a* is only the most famous, as is "supplement"; and it is still not always acknowledged today that "writing" or "*écriture*" function in a Derridean text in a generalized and not literal sense, even when their erasure retains both a literal and conceptual element, the simulacrum of script and idea. The maintenance of old word-concepts not as simulacra of the stabilities they putatively govern, but as overdetermined functions that recall and split the old concepts, transforming them into functions rather than concepts, Derrida calls paleonymics (see, for example, in passing, *Positions* and *Dissemination,* especially "Outwork," and the section entitled "Signature" in "Signature, Event, Context," on the strategy and "risk" of "putting old names to work" or leaving them "in circulation" in deconstruction, particularly the "risk" of "regressing" into the system being deconstructed). In the essay "Fors," writing of Nicholas Abraham's theory of "anasemia," an account of what occurs when, as in Freud, a phenomenological terminology is retained within a physiological terminology as a way of newly mapping "consciousness" for the developing science of psychoanalysis, Derrida notes that the words not only change sense but begin to produce distinct erratic effects even when, as Abraham argues, Freud's new terms displace their philosophical etymology into a vocabulary that makes sense only in the terms' new relations with each other. The phenomenological concepts, displaced into Freudian theory, are tropes for a mapping of the terrain of consciousness different from philosophy mapping, and, as tropes, take on meaning only in their serial relations (*The Post Card* traces the errata of this Freudian and Lacanian reconstruction). Derrida accentuates the destabilizing and transforming "effects" of the "new" terms; the paleonyms function neither in the same nor in a radically different way within the developing but incomplete new system, and thus preclude that system's closure. To account for these paleonymic inscriptions, then, requires one to forgo etymology for another theory of transformation or slippage, a "theory of errata," the laws of which cannot yet be written not simply because the effects never restabilize but because of the structural limit always encountered in transformational systems. Freud's theorizing, then, inscribes an "act" or "acts" that cannot be accounted for by naming Freud as intentional subject, author, or creator of a new system. Freud and Lacan resituate the subject, but cannot rid it of the old metaphysical residue.

It might occur to us that paleonymics is something we as writers and, in a certain sense, critics of whatever must assume as our condition or situation. Even our histories of ideas are subject to the deformations of conceptual transactions, the most obvious occurring in those very moments when we consider ourselves masters of a tropological sequence, recorders of the march of human spirit through a "tradition"—for example, Meyer Abrams in *Natural Supernaturalism* with its seamless unfolding narrative of the self, imagination, and humanist self-overcoming from Plato through Wordsworth, Hegel, and Nietzsche to Wallace Stevens, through both philosophy and literature as symmetrical pairings of the one truth of the human. To write this story, one has to suppress the paleonymic obstacle of certain governing terms, say, imagination in the employ of this or that poet, in the manner in which Derrida traces the erratic banishment and return of "spirit" in Heidegger (*De l'esprit*).

If all writing, both in the literal or idiomatic as well as in the generalized sense, involves paleonymics, the deployment of old words in new situations, deconstruction can only be a different kind of writing in degree, not in kind. Disseminative, translative, performative writing, or simply "acts," is not a new writing deliberately chosen by the poststructural critic as "subject." "To perform" or act is not synonymous with Barthes' "to write," not an intransitive act or an act in the middle voice that neutralizes the classical authority of the subject, any more than it is a transitive act in the sense of Barthes' linguistic model. It does not "destroy" the subject exactly, but neither does it leave the old sense or position of the subject intact. Barthes' neutralization of the writing subject in the middle voice represents the ultimate gesture of structuralism against phenomenology, inverting it but not intervening in its own totalizing program. Derrida's strategic "situating" of the subject involves another strategy. To put it another way, "to perform" is not a word or verb, as it is in speech act theory, or as "to write" is, for Barthes, the name of an act or event in language, even though it evokes something taking place in "words," an activity otherwise called "force" that cannot be designated by grammatical, syntactical, or semantic rules, but only by the "marks."

Readers of the Derrida-Searle debate in *Limited Inc* will recall what baffled Searle about the other's reading or misreading of Austin in "Signature, Event, Context," its "abuse" as Searle viewed it of Austinian systematics and pragmatics, his commonsense and philosophical seriousness. Austin's elaboration of "speech act" as a complement, and not a supplement, to philology was in Searle's view the opening up of virtually a new subdivision within the philosophy of language, and thus marked the inauguration of a discipline, meaning that the performative could now be studied as discrete from the conative of which it was nevertheless an integral part. Derrida had revealed how integral, or how, indeed, the assumed whole of language could not be complemented without producing supplementary (that is, performative) effects, and that any "theory" of language that anchored its subject matter in the unity or univocality of the word while seeing that unity capable of producing two discrete operations was blind to the splitting and doubleness that originarily inhabits that "word." In short, language had never been divisible into cognitive and performative, nor the one reducible or subordinated to the other. The two functions were originary grafts, bifurcating but not separating the word, and it was possible to deal with the two as distinct, if not hierarchical, only by positing a prior unity in the subject, or in intentionality. Thus, Austin's pragmatism, as it were, reinscribed the very metaphysical structure it assumed to complete, repeating if in a different mode Condillac's philology and Husserl's phenomenology, the history and philosophy of language that remained bound by the very logocentric tradition they would amend.

But Austin's blindness was not for Derrida an error of thinking; it marked precisely the double-bind of "theory," as inevitable for deconstruction as for all the "human sciences." The subject remains "indispensable," as he reminded those questioners of his decentering habits. The subject can never be banned from the game, nor neutralized, but neither can it be definitively positioned. To "situate" it is to mark its over-determination. Just as he had reminded Barthes' audience in Baltimore that the "I" in language can never be "new" or unique in an utterance because the elemental structure of language requires the possibility of iteration or repeatability, "I am always already absent from my language" and thus from the experience of "singularity." Austin's theory posits the uniqueness of each performative, as "event," and thus the uniqueness of an intentional subject even though the act is tied to the grammatical rule of repetition. For Derrida the clearest evidence that Austin must ignore this irreducible crux is his exclusion of certain secondary or "parasitic" acts, like speech acts performed from the script of a play, because they are "etiolated" and unoriginal, imitations of an originary intention. But the structure of iterability requires each such act to be parasitic and iterable, thus marking the literary performance as the originary model, the singular repetition. (There is no time here to consider Searle's inconsiderate misunderstanding of Derrida's remarks on the excluded example.) What marks the uniqueness of the performative for Austin, Derrida notes, is its "force," not its meaning, and force cannot be accounted for by the laws of grammar that regulate repeatability. Force cannot be read in the words. Nor is it ever singular. We might recall this argument from "Différance," where Derrida amplifies Deleuze's reading of Nietzsche's power as the clash of equivocal forces. Thus speech act theory, which wishes to remain within the conservative restraints of an ethical pragmatics, making possible, we might remind ourselves, our escape from theory and thus the development of a literary criticism "Against Theory" which assumes that the written work bears its singular intention along the way and remains the coherent instance or "event" of that intention—speech act theory allows us to discard or ignore the problematics of "reading" and reclaim a community of understanding.

Deconstruction cannot let this go. It is not a matter of choice or performance to go beyond the problematics, because the structure of "theory" inscribes this double-bind as a limit. This is evident in Austin's attempts to write his "theory" in a sufficient number of examples, and to account for an exhaustive catalogue of types and exclusions. One such example of the problematics of the exemplary (the examples would be constative statements representing illocutionary performances, since he who coins them is only imitating the act-event they would produce if intentionally uttered) is Austin's distinction between spoken and written utterances and the charge of parasitism that, Derrida notes, has always been laid upon writing in the metaphysical tradition, the argument in Austin's words that writing is not "tethered" to its sources (subject, intention) in the sense that speech is. But the structural necessity of all utterance, repeatability, recalls that all utterance is a kind of citation of the rules of repetition, and thus any performative utterance "splits and dissociates from itself the pure singularity of the event." All events are untethered, as it were, and thus not singular. If they were pure or "new," they could not be understood, read, or commented on—communicated across a distance. All acts are kinds of citation, translation, quotation, echo, and so on.

That is what gives them a certain significance. At this point Derrida can provide a kind of name for this repeated original event, a name for this newly situated subject-force. He calls it "signature," summoning up all the echos of sign, writing, gesture, mark, proper name and simulacrum, and so on, even including the belief in an ordinary and natural language, a sign tethered to nature and death contained by life. The signature, in both the literal and figural sense, stands for and displaces the idea of the living subject or authorizing intention. It precedes the subject and guarantees, as it were, the possibility of communication at a distance, a certain determination of authority, a force of meaning in the absence of the author. But it also marks the possibility of counterfeit, of a repetition that itself produces possibilities (say, in reading) not determined in the mark. The signature is at once mimetic and supplementary, is and is not phonetic writing, is repeatable yet may authorize an action or series of actions (say, perlocutionary acts) it cannot determine. Like quotation marks it may incorporate one event in another, but not without producing the question of all corporate appropriations, the uncertain relation of inside to outside, of one text to another, say, which no longer stands on the priority and privilege of tradition, mastery, intention. Citation carries away the unity of the citing act as event, splits and doubles it, without either subordinating or submitting to the authority of the cited. It undoes the host-parasite paradigm, and a certain common-sense. But it does not dispense with meaning in nonsense. This is the privilege Derrida accords literature, not the classical sense of literature as totalized work, but literature as performative force, as an "event" already an original repetition and therefore bearing the signatory power to insert itself within any discourse, a subject-like position that is restless and thus never identifiable as position. The literary, the always already secondary, then, is originary and primary force, overdetermined in its originality. It cannot be productive of the random or of nonsense. It does not permit us to interpret or read as we choose, but marks those acts of ours as based on the same repeatability that structure language. It does permit, however, through its signatory, the possibility of yet another signature, a repetition with a difference we call writing; and thus it makes possible certain transitiveness of the transitory one who signs. I would say that literature is critical or analytical, then, rather than representational, knowing that Derrida would reject these terms because of their privileged place in the discourse of rational authority, their tendency to divide, decide, and conquer. But can they not now be reclaimed as paleonyms, and as performatives, as acts and therefore transitives though not verbs?

That question is not precisely answerable. The performative has its laws, but they cannot be theorized except in examples that effect the law's stability. Writing rewrites. It acts and stages its action, amending like the parasite the rules it inhabits, thus altering its site and marking the limits of theory. It is not radical or revolutionary, then, in the sense deplored and decried by literal and conservative critics alike, who see it as a threat to the humanist reign of the subject or a return to elitist mastery in the guise of terrorist subject, even when this is a retreat from politics and history into textuality and aesthetics. In two senses, then, deconstructive performances are politically incorrect, because they declare no position and tend to occupy several, and because they question positionality itself by taking, as it were, a "fork in the road" and having their own way. So be it.

JACQUES DERRIDA

A demi-mot*

Aujourd'hui, j'aurais tant aimé me trouver là-bas, je veux dire ici, parmi vous, près des amis de Joe Riddel. Permettez-moi de vous le dire très simplement.

A Los Angeles et dans son université, où, avec la générosité que nous lui connaissons, il m'avait plus d'une fois accueilli, aidé, guidé j'aurais donc voulu dire moi-même, ici, maintenant, et ma tristesse et combien j'aimais et admirais Joe. Et dire aussi pourquoi je le ferai toujours, pourquoi c'est à un grand ami que je dis adieu, pourquoi j'aurai encore besoin de lui, irremplaçablement.

Tout est allé trop vite: comme dans une course à la mort qui nous laisserait juste le temps de nous croiser et de nous saluer, d'une automobile à l'autre, avant l'accident fatal. Nos rencontres furent rares, je les trouvais déjà trop rares, et toutes vouées à cette espérance incrédule qui hante sans doute nos amitiés les plus intenses, la promesse de nous revoir plus tard et plus souvent, de parler enfin sans fin et d'être ensemble, interminablement. Cette promesse à la fois interrompue, d'un coup brisée mais indestructible, je la crois infiniment renouvelée par la mort même, et je resterai tourné vers lui, vers la mémoire si vivante que je garde de lui, vers ce que j'ai entrevu de lui, si vite, trop vite, et vers ce qu'il nous laisse à lire et à penser.

*Composed October 17, 1991, and delivered on behalf of the author October 24, 1991, at a memorial service held at UCLA. Translation begins on p. 32.

26

Jamais n'a été plus vive en moi cette certitude désespérée mais aussi lumineuse: pour ce qu'on appelle "être-ensemble," et quand avec ceux qu'on aime on *appelle* les rencontres, la proximité des corps, les jouissances du jour partagées (un diner avec Joe et d'autres amis à Los Angeles ou à Irvine, par exemple, un éclat de rire complice en plein colloque, ici même, il y a moins de deux ans, une promenade un soir d'été dans Paris), eh bien, nous savons que toutes les singularités inoubliables de ces moments ne seront jamais remplacées par quoi que ce soit, pas même par ce qu'elles promettent ou gardent en réserve—elles sont irremplaçables et c'est là le désespoir—mais nous savons aussi qu'elles ne seraient rien, ou pas grand'chose, sans la riche intensité de cette réserve même. Bénis furent pour moi les moments que j'ai vécus près de Joe, à Irvine, à Los Angeles, à Paris, dans l'université et hors de l'université. Mais je sais que si de tels moments ont eu la force et la profondeur qu'ils gardent encore dans mon coeur, c'est que, si brefs qu'ils fussent, hélas, et si rares, ils étaient, de façon à la fois silencieuse et prolixe, habités ou traversés par les poètes et les philosophes que nous lisions, d'une certaine manière, *ensemble,* et qui à l'amitié—car ils n'étaient là, je le crois toujours, que pour servir l'amitié—, donnaient son sens, son rythme, sa respiration, je dirais aussi son inspiration, même si ce n'était pas toujours les mêmes philosophes, les mêmes poètes, les mêmes oeuvres que nous approchions, pas les mêmes lieux, les mêmes titres et les mêmes noms, au même moment et de la même manière.

Dans la précipitation de ce que j'appelais la *course à la mort,* ces moments, ces lieux, ces noms et ces noms de lieux, nous avions à les reconnaître mais ils nous reconnaissaient d'avance, il étaient comme pré-occupés par la puissance (à la fois la virtualité et la force, la *dynamis*) des écrivains du passé ou celle des fantômes à venir qui se parlaient entre eux à travers nous, nous provoquant à parler à notre tour, à les faire ou laisser vivre en nous, nous prenant à témoin à chaque virage de la course, à travers les questions, les débats, les délibérations sans fin, les pensées risquées, les accélérations ou les coups de frein, les routes ou les apories d'écriture dans lesquels ils nous jetaient, nous engageaient et prédisaient nos rencontres, et jusqu'à cette manière que nous avions en commun, malgré la différence des langues et des histoires, de nous orienter dans cet héritage en nous comprenant très vite, à demi-mot. Je devrais dire à demi-mort car la mort, nous le savions aussi, parfois d'un gai savoir (étrange gaîté de Joe, gaîté que je sentais inquiète, blessée, mais où je pressentais aussi le pari et le défi), la mort, donc, guettait à chaque tournant, s'annonçait entre les lignes et prédestinait chaque nom.

Et Joe m'a appris à m'orienter, je dirais presque à conduire: non seulement dans une certaine littérature américaine (Poe, Melville, Pound et Stein, Stevens et Williams), une littérature américaine dont il est, je crois, un des très grands lecteurs de ce siècle, de ceux, très rares, au fond, qui ont su mettre les enjeux les plus graves et les plus inédits de la philosophie ou de la théorie de ce temps à l'épreuve de votre littérature en ce qu'elle a de plus singulier. Mais Joe, l'auteur de "Reading America/American Readings" (*MLN*, XCIX [1984]), m'a aussi aidé à m'orienter, tout simplement et rien de moins, dans la culture américaine. Peu à peu, j'ai compris que, s'agissant de la culture américaine, et en particulier de l'institution académique, ses jugements sur les idées et sur les êtres, sur les écrits et sur les paroles, ses prises de parti avaient cette lucidité solitaire, oui, je crois, assez solitaire, au fond, rigoureuse et tranchante, courageuse, ironique et sereine à laquelle il vaut mieux, je le crois, toujours se fier. Et j'avais confiance en lui, en sa solitude même, une certaine solitude intellectuelle, j'avais confiance dans le choix qu'il faisait d'une certaine rareté du petit nombre, disons, en des lieux déterminés de l'université, sur les routes les moins fréquentées, sur les trajets les moins faciles, les moins normalisés de la pensée, de la lecture et de l'écriture. J'avais confiance en lui et la confiance qu'il m'a témoignée de son côté a toujours été l'un des encouragements qui ont le plus compté pour moi dans ce pays. Dans les secousses et les conflits qui, surtout depuis une ou deux décennies, torturent notre paysage historique, politique ou académique, il m'est souvent arrivé de me régler implicitement, surtout pour les choses américaines, sur le jugement et sur les positions de Joe. Sans lui demander littéralement conseil (j'ai dit que nous nous voyions et nous parlions assez peu) je me rassurais en le lisant, en cherchant des signaux lumineux dans ses propres mouvements, évaluations, choix, dans sa manière de conduire, en somme, qui m'a toujours paru des plus nécessaires même si ou parce qu'elle était aussi très risquée, justement: bref, il me paraissait plus juste, et je le crois encore, d'être de son côté, *à son côté*, même si c'était par moments, en apparence, le côté le moins sûr de la route, le côté le moins confortable de la solitude ou du bord accidenté.

Je ne revenais jamais en Californie, au printemps, sans espérer revoir Joe et mes retours seront désormais assombris. Je devrai faire comme si—mais comment y croire?—notre amitié n'avait plus besoin de rencontre, comme si elle avait toujours été destinée à respirer à travers l'appareil du livre et de la lettre en souffrance, comme elle le fit pendant plusieurs années, tout au début. Permettez-moi de rappeler à mon tour une histoire que Joe aimait à raconter publiquement chaque fois qu'il me recevait dans cette université. Je l'entends encore, je vois son sourire, et j'ai l'impression de dire ce que je vais dire à travers lui, j'ai même envie de prononcer, j'ai envie que vous entendiez, vous, cette histoire de sa propre voix, par sa bouche, comme on peut avoir envie de manger de la bouche même d'un ami mort—et j'aimais aussi la façon sensuelle dont Joe aimait manger, et j'aimais partager cette jouissance aussi avec lui. C'était donc en 1975, je crois, nous ne nous connaissions pas encore. De Buffalo, à la suggestion de Hillis Miller ou de Eugenio Donato, Joe m'avait envoyé *The Inverted Bell*. Déjà ce livre, qui fraya tant de voies nouvelles, jouait gravement et puissamment avec le nom propre, c'est-à-dire avec la mort, et c'est une des choses, parmi d'autres, qui aussitôt m'impressionnèrent. Car de quoi, de qui, à qui parlons-nous, ici, maintenant, en son absence absolue, sinon du nom et au nom de Joe Riddel? Au cours de la vie même, de notre vivant, comme du vivant de Joe, nous le savons et le savions déjà: le nom signe la mort et marque la vie d'une ride à déchiffrer. Le nom court à la mort plus vite que nous qui croyons naïvement le porter. Il nous porte à une vitesse infinie vers la fin. Il est d'avance le nom d'un mort. Et d'une mort précipitée qui nous arrive en lui, par lui, sans être jamais proprement la nôtre. Sans attendre, Joe suivait chez Williams, comme il le fit souvent ailleurs, le passage fatal de son propre nom. Une lettre en chemin doublant l'autre, la permutation de deux lettres suffisait pour jouer avec tout ce qui se cryptait déjà joyeusement et tragiquement dans le chiffre de son nom, R.I.D.D.E.L., d'un nom devenu assez commun pour que d'autres, dont moi, dans leur propre patronyme, y trouvent *littéralement,* je veux dire à la lettre, quelque chose d'essentiel à partager: une sorte de concurrence irrésistible dans la course à la mort. Je me rappelle bien certaines pages dans "Poem and City: The Sarcophagus of Time." Par exemple, pour annoncer une citation de Williams, Joe écrivait ceci, qui annonce ce qu'il intitulera plus tard "The Hermeneutical Self—Notes Toward an 'American' Practice" (*boundary 2,* [1984]): "The world is a 'riddle' for the Puritan, a riddle only partly decoded by an original Word or Text, the Bible. Even man in a state of grace is condemned to interpretation. Characteristically, Williams concludes the Mather section with the following remark: 'Unriddle these Things'" (*The Inverted Bell,* 157).

Puisque nous parlons de la survivance du nom qui, annonçant notre mort, s'efface donc lui-même, dé-nomme ou se dé-nomme lui-même dans le nom commun, emporte d'avance celui-là même qui proprement le porte, *Unriddling these things* me rappelle aussi ce que Joe décrivait ailleurs, à savoir ce que je décrirais comme un certain *unnaming effect* de la nomination elle-même. Joe y voyait tout simplement le privilège de la poésie. Je dirai qu'il s'agit encore de patronymie. Dans "Juda Becomes New Haven," en 1980, à propos de *The Auroras of Autumn,* de Wallace Stevens, il écrivait: "The naming that erases, that unnames, is reserved, however, for poetry, a privilege it putatively claims only by undermining the status of ephebe or son" (*Diacritics* [Summer, 1980], 29).

Quelque temps après avoir lu *The Inverted Bell,* donc, en 1975, et pour lui dire mon admirative reconnaissance, j'envoyai à Joe une lettre. A son adresse de Buffalo. Il n'était plus là, je ne le savais pas encore. Déjà il n'était plus là. Cette lettre aurait pu ne jamais lui arriver et cette course rester sans fin—ou vouée à ce sort des "dead letters" où se retire l'énigme de tous les Bartleby's du monde, nos frères impossibles ("On errands of life, these letters speed to death. Ah Bartleby! Ah humanity!").

Des mois plus tard, peut-être plus d'un an après, je ne me rappelle plus toutes les étapes et combien de détours, ni combien d'universités elle a parcouru, à travers combien de mains amies elle a voyagé, ma lettre enfin est parvenue à Joe, là-bas, c'est-à-dire ici, en Californie où je n'étais encore, moi, jamais venu. Joe racontait souvent cette histoire, ici même. J'y ai beaucoup repensé, plus tard, surtout en lisant ce qu'il avait écrit, toujours avec la même verve, cruelle et grave, de la *Purloined Letter,* des noms propres et des noms de lieux dans son merveilleux texte de 1980, "The 'Crypt' of Edgar Poe," une crypte qu'il compare au centre de la pyramide de Melville, dans *Pierre; or, The Ambiguities* ("By vast pains we mine into the pyramid; by horrible gropings we come to the central room; with joy we espy the sarcophagus; but we lift the lid—and no body is there!—"). Cette pyramide ou ce cénotaphe, n'est-ce pas aussi un "memorial"—et ce lieu-ci dont le vide aujourd'hui nous aspire plutôt que nous ne l'occupons?

Ainsi, à notre première rencontre, quelques années plus tard, je l'avais déjà beaucoup lu, nous avions d'avance fait beaucoup de chemin ensemble, littéralement, par lettres, sans nous rencontrer; nous avions de l'avance et beaucoup couru ensemble, une étrange familiarité nous rapprochait déjà, que j'ai tout de suite aimée et qui ne fut jamais contradictoire, entre nous, avec la distance, l'absence, la discrétion pudique, le silence, l'ignorance même de ce que pouvaient être nos vies, d'autre part, l'autre part de nos vies, la région la plus invisible et la plus exposée, la plus dangereuse de nos courses respectives. Comme si nous ne savions pas, comme si nous savions sans savoir, et c'est l'énigme, comme si nous n'avions pas besoin de savoir ce que nous ne savions pas l'un de l'autre. Comme si nous le savions trop pour avoir besoin d'en savoir plus—et c'est pourquoi on ne séparera jamais l'énigme du crible (a riddle from a riddle, if you want), et l'interprétation de la sélection. Comme si dans l'accélération de cette course si brève, nous savions d'avance que nous n'aurions jamais le temps de voir et de savoir tout de l'autre. Il fallait conduire très vite, de plus en plus vite.

Pourquoi nommer ici la course avec tant d'insistance, pourquoi tant de courses de voitures et de voitures de course? A cause de la vitesse, sans doute, et de la cruauté d'un temps qui manque, mais aussi à cause des accidents et de la mort qui nous guette à chaque virage. Et puis aussi parce que j'ai de Joe un autre souvenir, qui me hante et me tient à cœur. Ce fut un instant furtif, l'échange d'un regard sans durée, un incident léger à la fin d'une journée californienne. Ce souvenir m'obsède depuis des années et je voudrais le partager avec vous. C'était peu après la mort d'Eugenio Donato, notre cher et vieil ami commun, chez qui nous nous étions d'ailleurs rencontrés pour la première fois, et qui entretenait un culte savant et raffiné pour les automobiles de grande noblesse, pour ces machines nerveuses comme des chevaux de course, celles qu'on conduit, si je puis dire, à la main, sans embrayage automatique. Moins d'un an après la mort d'Eugenio, donc, j'ai revu Joe, en avril 1984, à Irvine. Je venais d'évoquer dans une conférence la mémoire de Paul de Man et d'Eugenio Donato, tous deux morts à quelques mois d'intervalle. En sortant de l'université, je raccompagne Joe jusqu'au parking et il me demande, avec un sourire complice, en me montrant sa voiture et en guettant d'un oeil malin ma réaction: "Regardez. Qu'est-ce que vous en pensez? Elle vous dit quelque chose?" J'ai aussitôt reconnu la voiture d'Eugenio. Joe avait fait ce qu'il fallait, il l'avait sans doute achetée pour la garder après la mort de notre ami, pour l'habiter, la conduire, la laisser courir encore jusqu'à sa propre fin—et je suis sûr qu'à cette seconde, en avril 1984, nous étions au moins trois fous, deux ou trois amis, à aimer ce geste. Un geste signé "Riddel" qui jouait fidèlement avec la vie et la mort comme avec l'énigme d'un changement de vitesse, comme la lettre du poème sur la route ou dans la ville.

Je voudrais, pour finir, rendre ou laisser la parole à Joe, la sienne. Avec la conscience du sacrifice, je découpe ceci encore, précipitamment, dans "Poem and City: The Sarcophagus of Time" (*The Inverted Bell,* 158):

As Williams puts it in *Paterson,* a "riddle (in the Joyceian mode— . . .)" which holds the enigma of death at its center:

What end but love, that stares death in the eye?

. . . .

Sing me a song to make death tolerable, a song
of a man and a woman: the riddle of a man
and a woman.

I would have so much wished to be there today, here that is, among you, friends (colleagues, students) of Joe Riddel. Allow me to say that to you as simply as possible. In Los Angeles and at his university, where, with the generosity that we all knew, he more than once welcomed me, helped and guided me, I would have liked to have been able myself to express, here and now, both my sadness and how much I loved and admired Joe. And also to tell you why I will do so forever, why it is a great friend to whom I bid farewell, and why I will still need him in the future, why to me he is irreplaceable.

Everything happened too quickly: like a race to death that left us only enough time to pass and wave to each other, from one automobile to another, before the fatal accident. Our meetings were rare, too rare I had begun to think, and all were dedicated to that unbelieving hope that haunts just our most intense friendships: the promise that we would see each other more often later on, that in the end we would speak without end and be together, interminably. This promise now interrupted, broken all of a sudden, and yet still indestructible, I take it to be infinitely renewed by death itself, and I will remain turned toward him, toward the so vibrant memory of him that I have, turned toward the glimpse that I was granted of him so rapidly, too rapidly, and turned toward what he leaves us with, to read and to think.

Never has this desperate but radiant certainty been more alive in me: what we call "being together," and with those that we love we *call* encounters, the physical proximity, the shared joys of the day (a dinner with Joe and other friends in Los Angeles or in Irvine, for example, a complicitous burst of laughter in the middle of a colloquium, right here, less than two years ago, a walk one summer evening in Paris)—we know that the unforgettable singularity of such moments will never be replaced by anything else, not even by that which they promise or keep in reserve—they are irreplaceable and that is precisely the reason for despairing—but we also know that they would be nothing, or not very much, without the rich intensity of this very reserve. Blessed were the moments that I lived in Joe's vicinity, in Irvine, Los Angeles, Paris, in the university and outside of the university. But I know that if such moments had the force and depth that they still retain in my heart, it is because, as brief as they were, alas, and as rare, they were inhabited and traversed, in a manner that was both silent and verbose, by the poets and philosophers that we read, in a certain way, *together,* and who gave friendship—for they were there, I remain convinced, only to serve friendship—[who gave friendship] its meaning, its rhythm, its breath, I would even say its inspiration, even if they weren't always the same philosophers, the same poets, the same works that we approached, nor the same places, the same titles, and the same names, at the same time and in the same manner.

In the haste of what I called the *race to death,* these moments, these places, these names, and these names of places, which we had to recognize and which also recognized us in advance,—all were as though pre-occupied by the power (both the potentiality and the force, the *dynamis*) of the writers of the past, or of the ghosts to come who spoke to each other through us, in turn provoking us to speak, to make or let them live in us, taking us as witness to each curve in the race, through the questions, the debates, the deliberations without end, through risky thoughts, accelerating or slamming on the brakes, through the roads or the aporias of writing into which they cast us, led us and predicted our encounters, down to the very manner that we had in common, despite the difference of languages and histories, of orienting ourselves in this heritage while understanding each other very quickly, with scarcely a word, *à demi-mot* as we say in French. *Demi-mort,* half-dead, is what I should say because death, we also knew from a gay science (strange, that gaiety of Joe's, in which I felt the worry, the wound, but in which I also sensed the gamble, the challenge, and the provocation)—[because] death, in short, lay waiting at every turn, announcing itself between the lines and predestining each name.

And Joe taught me to find my way about—I would almost say to drive—not only in a certain American literature (Poe, Melville, Pound and Stein, Stevens and Williams), an American literature of which he is, I believe, one of the very great readers of this century, one of those, very rare when you think of it, who have known how to put the gravest and most inventive stakes of the philosophy or theory of the time to the test of your literature in its greatest singularity. But Joe, author of "Reading America/American Readers" (*MLN*, XCIX [1984]), also helped me to orient myself, quite simply and nothing less, in American culture. Little by little I understood that where American culture was concerned, and in particular the academic institution, his judgments on ideas and on persons, on writings and on discourses, his political decisions (*prises de partie*) had that solitary lucidity—yes, quite solitary, I believe, in its rigor, incisiveness, courage, irony, and serenity—upon which it is preferable, I am convinced, always to rely. And I had confidence in him, in his solitude itself, a certain intellectual solitude, I had confidence in the choice he made of a small number, of a certain scarcity let us say, in particular places in the university, on the least-traveled roads, on the least-easy routes, the least-normalized [avenues] of thought, of reading and writing. I had confidence in him, and the confidence that he in turn demonstrated in me was always one of the encouragements that counted the most for me in this country. In the shocks and struggles which, particularly in the last decade or two, have tormented our historical, political, or academic landscape, I often found myself implicitly getting my bearings, especially where things American were concerned, from Joe's judgment and positions. Without literally asking his advice (I said that we saw each other and spoke relatively little), I drew reassurance from reading him, looking for bright signals in his own movements, evaluations, choices, in his manner of conducting himself—of driving, if you will—which always seemed to me to be one of the most necessary courses of conduct, even if, or precisely because it was full of risks: in short, it seemed to me more apt and equitable to be on his side, *at his side,* even if at times it seemed to be the side of the road that was least safe, the least comfortable side of solitude or of the precarious edge.

I never came back to California, in the spring, without hoping to see Joe, and when I return in the future there will be a shadow. I will have to act as though—but how can I believe it?—[as though] our friendship did not require meetings any more, as though it had always been destined to breathe through the apparatus of books and dead letters, as it did for several years, at the very beginning. Permit me to recall a story that Joe liked to tell publicly each time he welcomed me to this university. I hear him even now, I see his smile, and I have the impression that what I am about to say is spoken through him; I would even like to tell you this story in his own voice, through his mouth, just as one can have the desire to eat from the mouth of a dead friend—and I also loved the sensual way Joe loved to eat, and I loved to share that joy with him. It was in 1975, I believe—we didn't know each other yet. From Buffalo, Joe, at the suggestion of Hillis Miller or of Eugenio Donato, had sent me *The Inverted Bell.* Already this book, which opened up so many new avenues, played gravely and powerfully with the proper name, which is to say, with death, and it is one of the things, among others, that impressed me immediately. For of what, of whom, to whom are we speaking, here, now, in his absolute absence, if not of the name and to the name of Joe Riddel? Even during the course of life, of our lifetime as of Joe's lifetime, we know this and knew it already: the name signs death and marks life with a fold to be deciphered. The name races toward death even more quickly than we do, we who naïvely believe that we bear it. It bears us with infinite speed toward the end. It is in advance the name of a dead person. And of a premature death that comes to us in it, through it, without ever being properly our own. Without waiting, Joe followed in Williams, as he often did elsewhere, the fatal passage of his own name. One letter doubling the other along the way, the permutation of two letters sufficed to play with everything that encrypted itself already, joyously and tragically, in the cipher of his name, R.I.D.D.E.L., a name that had become common enough (as noun) for others, including myself, to have found *literally,* and I mean down to the very letter, in their own patronyms, something essential to share: a sort of irresistible competition in the race to death. I remember well certain pages in "Poem and City: The Sarcophagus of Time." For example, to introduce a Williams citation, Joe wrote the following, which announced what he would later entitle "The Hermeneutical Self—Notes Toward an 'American' Practice" (*boundary 2,* [1984]): "The world is a 'riddle' for the Puritan, a riddle only partly decoded by an original Word or Text, the Bible. Even man in a state of grace is condemned to interpretation. Characteristically, Williams concludes the Mather section with the following remark: 'Unriddle these Things'" (*The Inverted Bell,* 157).

Since we are speaking of the survival of the name which, in announcing our death thereby effaces itself, de-nominates or de-nominates itself in the common name (or noun), carrying away in advance the person who bears it properly—(since we are speaking of this survival), *Unriddling these Things* reminds me also of something Joe described elsewhere, and what I would call a certain *unnaming effect* of nomination itself. In this Joe saw quite simply the privilege of poetry. I will say that what is involved here, once again, is patronymics. In "Juda Becomes New Haven," in 1980, concerning *The Auroras of Autumn,* he wrote: "The naming that erases, that unnames, is reserved, however, for poetry, a privilege it putatively claims only by undermining the status of ephebe or son" (*Diacritics* [Summer, 1980], 29).

Some time after having read *The Inverted Bell* then, in 1975, in order to let him know of my admiring recognition and gratitude, I sent Joe a letter. To his Buffalo address. He wasn't there any longer, something I didn't yet know. Already he wasn't there any more. This letter might easily never have reached him, this race might have remained without end or condemned to the fate of those "dead letters" wherein is buried the enigma of all the Bartlebys of the world, our impossible brothers ("On errands of life, these letters speed to death. Ah Bartleby! Ah Humanity!"). Months later, perhaps more than a year later—I don't remember any more all the stages, nor how many detours or universities it passed through, or how many friendly hands—finally my letter reached Joe there, or rather, here, in California, where I for my part had not yet set foot. Joe often told this story, in this very place. I frequently thought of it, later, above all while reading what he had written, always with the same verve, cruel and grave, on "The Purloined Letter," concerning proper names and place names, in his marvellous text of 1980, "The 'Crypt' of Edgar Poe," a crypt he compares to the center of the pyramid in Melville's *Pierre; or, The Ambiguities* ("By vast pains we mine into the pyramid; by horrible gropings we come to the central room; with joy we espy the sarcophagus; but we lift the lid—and no body is there!—"). This pyramid or this cenotaph, is it not also a "memorial"—and this place here, whose emptiness today sucks us in rather than our breathing it.

Thus, at our first meeting, several years later, I had already read much of him; we had in advance gone a long way together, literally, by letters, without meeting each other; we were ahead of ourselves and had already done much racing together; a strange familiarity already brought us closer, something I loved right away and which was never contradicted between us by distance, absence, modest discretion, silence, even ignorance of what our lives could be, on the other hand, [ignorance] of the other side of our lives, the most invisible and most exposed, most dangerous part of our respective races. As if we didn't know, as if we knew without knowing, and most enigmatically, as though we didn't need to know what we didn't know about each other. As if we knew too much to need to know any more—and this is why the enigma will never be separated from the sieve, a riddle from a riddle, if you like, and interpretation from selection. As though in the acceleration of this very brief race, we knew in advance that we would never have time to see and know everything about each other. We had to drive very fast, faster and faster.

Why name here the race with such insistence, why so many car races and racing cars? Because of speed, to be sure, and the cruelty of time that is lacking, but also because of accidents and of death, which await us at each curve in the road. And then also because I am obsessed by another memory of Joe, close to my heart. It was a fleeting instant, a furtive exchange of looks, a slight incident at the end of a California day. For years this memory has haunted me and I would like to share it with you. It was shortly after the death of Eugenio Donato, our dear and old common friend, at whose place, moreover, we first met, and who cultivated a scholarly and sophisticated taste for cars of great distinction, for those machines which are as nervous as racehorses, those which you drive, if I may say so, by hand, without automatic transmission. Less than one year after Eugenio's death, then, I saw Joe again, in April of 1984, at Irvine. I had just evoked, in a lecture, the memory of Paul de Man and of Eugenio Donato, who had died a few months apart. In leaving the university, I accompanied Joe to the parking lot and he asked me, with a smile of complicity, pointing toward his car and eyeing my reaction: "Take a look. What do you think of it? Does it remind you of anything?" I immediately recognized Eugenio's car. Joe had done what had to be done; he had undoubtedly bought it to keep after the death of our friend, to live in, to drive, so that it could go on racing until the very end—and I am certain that at that moment, in April, 1984, there were three of us at least, friends, who were crazy enough to love this gesture. A gesture, signed "Riddel," which played faithfully with life and death as with the mystery of a shift in gears, as with the letter of a poem on the road or in the city.

To conclude, I would like to leave or give back the word to Joe—his words. With the awareness of sacrificing, I detach once more, hastily, this, from "Poem and City: The Sarcophagus of Time" (*The Inverted Bell*, 158):

As Williams puts it in *Paterson*, a "riddle (in the Joycean mode— . . .)" which holds the enigma of death at its center:

What end but love, that stares death in the eye?
. . . .
Sing me a song to make death tolerable, a song
of a man and a woman: the riddle of a man
and a woman.

Translated by Samuel Weber

PAUL A. BOVÉ

Anarchy and Perfection:
Henry Adams, Intelligence, and America

Although Henry Adams has been called the "most intelligent man in the nineteenth century," he has had no major critic and rather only a marginal position within American Studies.[1] Unlike Emerson, Hawthorne, Melville, or James, for example, and, more recently, unlike Douglass, Harriet Jacobs, or Zora Neale Hurston, Americanists rarely claim Adams as either the key to America, its values, and its psyche, or as a representative embodiment of its critical and oppositional movements. He has, until now, never been made suspect by success.

Adams never had a central position within the Americanist canon nor a great Americanist critic because his work uniquely analyzes the American system and its place in the world. Unlike the major canonical figures, he is concerned to understand the United States materialistically, that is, in terms of its forces of production; and unlike many others whom academics value for the "subject positions" that "situate" them "outside" the canon, he has a rigorously global perspective on the United States that specifically cannot be assimilated to either the statist project of American Studies or its recent reformist incarnations. There is no other U.S. writer of his time who, for example, takes seriously the existence of such forms of knowledge as statistics. Adams studies statistics both to apply it to the society that creates it—on the assumption that the society must need it to understand something about itself, or to organize itself—and to understand what can be learned about the society that creates it by the mere fact of its existence as opposed to its nonexistence in an earlier form of society. Adams is, if you will, interested in the double perspective of looking at the society through its tools and of comparing that society through its tools with other earlier societies in order both to understand the present and, when appropriate, to develop a critical perspective on it.

Adams' thought is rigorously materialistic without being pragmatic; he writes that when he was a student the only form of contemporary knowledge that would have been helpful to him later in life would have been Marxism; and that he precisely never once heard Marx's name mentioned while he was at Harvard—nor that of Auguste Comte. And not for ideological reasons but for reasons of ignorance: the university could not be contemporary with its own age.[2]

I came to the study of Henry Adams out of an interest in the role of intellectuals in capitalist societies; I set myself a specific problem around Adams, a uniquely American problem that nonetheless has consequences for much of the world in this century. I want to know two things: what happens to a domestic society at the time when a state becomes imperialistic, and what roles might intellectuals play in the production of such a society. Essentially, I have a historical interest in how the U.S. state built a social structure that would support its imperial ambitions, all the while insisting that the United States is not an imperial or interventionary power. I intended to examine Adams' work and context to investigate this problem because Adams, more than any other U.S. intellectual of the late nineteenth and early twentieth centuries, represents and investigates the broad range of intellectual, political, and economic transformations within U.S. capital that necessitate the imperial project and earn it support among the domestic population. Indeed, Adams himself sometimes actively encouraged U.S. imperial ambitions, particularly in the Caribbean; he encouraged the war against Spain, the revolt in Cuba (which he helped finance contrary to U.S. law), and recommended at various times the seizure of other islands and of Canada.

As interesting and important as this set of problems has been, I have found it impossible to deal with Adams on the historical level that this little narrative of an investigation suggests. There are two reasons for this: one is that Adams' work makes mockery of any idea of historical investigation, this despite the fact that he is the author of a monumental nine-volume study of the history of the United States and was president of the American Historical Association (an appointment he mocked by never once attending a meeting); a second is that Adams' work is more valuable a way to help think through more complex problems that must be treated analytically and theoretically, which come, as it were, prior to any historicist formulation of the importance of his work.

American literary and intellectual history offers few examples of analytic work as comprehensive, rigorous, and devastatingly critical as Adams'. That he has been a figure marginal to the canons of American literature is not accidental, for his work is in the end a massive critique of Americanism, that is, of the forms of capital peculiar to the United States and to the modes of knowledge and discourse as well as political and social organization produced by that system. He is useful both to thinking through problems posed by Americanism and as an example of the kind of work a critical intellectual should attempt to carry out.

The Education often appears as a major autobiography in American literature, albeit a very troubling example of the genre.[3] To discuss this book as an autobiography seems to me patently silly. There are, I think, reasons why it appears as an example of this genre: It can be more easily psychologized in the form of old pragmatic or existentialist clichés. Treating the text as autobiography allows critics to acknowledge its aesthetic accomplishments and to avoid its implications by absorbing Adams' work into one of three categories: psychological study of person; positivist corrections of the supposed "facts";[4] or theoretical discussions of the nature and limits of the genre autobiography itself, particularly around the tiresome question: What's unique about American autobiography. More important, however, U.S. critics could not satisfy their task as hegemonic intellectuals were they to take seriously Adams' devastating criticisms of Americanism, capitalism, and the forms of knowledge associated with them—and so the forms of knowledge identical to or underlying those practiced by the critics themselves. The "autobiography" category—no matter how argued—is an avoidance of these issues.

Adams can help us think through two related problems: how to understand Americanism in the United States and in the world; and how to act as critical intellectuals in the face of the increasingly rapid transformations of national and global structures brought about by capital. I want to treat both problems at once because Americanism is a challenge to critical intellectuals and once again in two ways: first, because of the success of U.S. hegemony in this century—the hegemony of America should not be confused with U.S. political, economic, or military dominance; second, because the increasing globalization of capital will require of critical intellectuals a response not unlike in kind that exemplified in Adams' work on America. *The Education* can be made to work as a key text here because it embodies analytic work of the theoretical sort needed to take up the task of thinking America or thinking globalization and because it follows, almost in a Gramscian sense, the forces that left traces in Adams as he moved to understand America, its place in the world, and the intellectual resources needed to engage it critically and politically.[5]

Adams is a polymath. He has had no great critic, in part because no U.S. critic has been able to extend far enough across disciplines, orders of knowledge, historical periods, genre, and wandering preoccupations to follow his traces—and I cannot hope to do so here, nor perhaps anywhere. There are, however, basic features of Adams' intellectual procedure that can and should be stressed.

Adams is an anarchist. He shows repeatedly how efforts to form a U.S. nation-state are bound to fail; in other words, he shows how the United States is neither a nation nor a state—albeit there are political and economic forces that tend to produce both. Adams' anarchism is radically materialist and atomist; this means that he is not a dialectician; that he does not credit evolutionary theory; and that he is a productivist.[6] At the same time, he believes futilely in intelligence, even as he discovers everywhere its absence and its inadequacy. He studies science, but learns from it what it does not know. He studies government to show it does not work, or is not allowed to work by the men placed by productive forces to assure its failure. He does not believe in uniformity or unity; nor does he believe in multiplicity as the opposite and alternative concept. He believes instead in chaos and in the second law of thermodynamics, that is, in entropy, both of which concepts he opposes everywhere to American beliefs in perfectibility, order, efficiency, and directed or controlled force.

He opposes the capitalist, Americanist present to the past and to other societies. He creates erudite, theoretical, and imaginative narratives of different societies and the various forces that make them in order to denaturalize the present and sharpen its analysis by contrast.[7] The most extended and powerful example of this method is the book *Mont-Saint-Michel and Chartres*, in which Adams reconstructs a Gothic universe driven by what he calls the force of the Virgin, a power that compels the production of culture, and a power absent from Americanism, unremembered by capital, and radically disconnected from the order of society that Americanism has established—a society that, from this point of view, has no culture, but only an infinitude of transformations and relations defined by the mediations of capitalist production.

Adams is a materialist. His interest in the various fields of knowledge—from finance, to geology, to evolution, to thermodynamics, to nuclear physics, to history, etc., etc.—is never abstract. By that I mean, he is not interested in what we might call the history of ideas, and above all he is never interested in whether or not the knowledge produced within these various fields is "right" or "correct." As he says repeatedly, he is not concerned with the "truth" of science as correspondence, and he is not expert within the fields—although when he writes on finance, geology, or Gothic architecture he makes himself expert. He is concerned rather with two facets of knowledge: what work does it get done? can it direct mass in motion? that is, can it counteract or is it a form of chaos;[8] also, is it explanatory of its own first principles. For example, he would ask Newton, "What is gravity" or he would ask Darwinians such as Walcott to prove, not assume, their basic concepts (*Education*, 1084 ff). When the knowledge systems cannot answer these questions to the satisfaction of a student seeking education, he concludes that to understand the world as it is and as it is changing, he can only draw on and transform the knowledge these systems offer, taking them, if you will, as symptoms of the age to be read rather than as convincing acts of reason. The most famous example of this effort in *The Education* is the repeated questioning of evolutionary disciplines such as geology and paleontology. Equally important, however, especially in the later pages, is Adams' interest in physics.

From his student days at Harvard, Adams insists that an adequate education would provide him with several languages and mathematics. He acquired none of what he needed at Harvard, having to study German in a *Gymnasium* before attending lectures at Berlin. His desire to know mathematics had to do with his hope to use statistics both as guide to the future—he wanted to know if he could project the transformative effects of Americanism—and as a prism, an invention to be looked at in itself as peculiarly essential to the productive functions of capitalist society, especially in England, Germany, and the United States. Later in life, his need for mathematics recurs in his desire to know physics. He attaches himself to Langley, a leading physicist and director of the Smithsonian. Langley teaches him about the dynamo, about thermodynamics, and about radiation. Langley cannot teach him much about the latter and, of course, teaches nothing about magnetism nor gravity, lapses that discourage Adams' regard for mathematical physics (1066 ff).

Adams himself established the terms in which his fascination with physics is normally taken. He treats the matter at length in a chapter entitled "The Dynamo and the Virgin," set in the Paris Exhibition of 1900, which could just as easily have been entitled "Continuity and Discontinuity," or "Culture and America," or "Chaos and Anarchy." The opposition has been treated, in the style of T. S. Eliot, as a contrast between organic and nonorganic societies, between art and industry, between the auratic original and mechanical reproduction.[9] All of these have some place in the discussion. More recently, it has been available to feminists as an example of masochism within Western discourse, the assignment of suffering and cultural production to the woman.

I have a somewhat different interest in Adams' chapter. He begins it with a reference to Francis Bacon's *Advancement of Science* and what it taught, "that true science was the development or economy of forces" (*Education*, 1066). In one sense, all of *The Education* is an effort to understand and act upon this dictum. Thinking this concept Adams works to powerful critiques of Americanism as mass and motion without intelligence, of capitalism as endless transformation of society and subjectivities, and of intellectuals as insufficiently materialist and caught within the process of substitution and transformation. The American semiotic, ideological efforts to assert, produce, and maintain a national unity—which is at best an approximate unity of market—are failures. What Adams' materialism reveals is the succession of different orders of society within a larger cosmos of chaos. *The Education* is rife with his discoveries of discontinuity, disruption, revolutionary transformation, "new world orders." When he returns to the United States after the horrors of the Civil War, he finds a new order, one produced by "scientifically" organized means of production, new forces unleashed and seemingly controlled by the war effort,[10] new social requirements that make those of his generation and class outmoded and unfit—that is, new kinds of subjects resulting from the new order of war. Adams takes this to be a matter of global importance, for, from his perspective, Grant taught the rest of the world how to fight capitalist wars wherein logistics and production count for more as force than tactics, genius, or strategy. The Napoleonic wars of massed armies of the nation give way to wars driven by centralized state-systems making production efficient, massive, and exemplary. (We have seen the recent virtues of this system in the Gulf War; in this area the

United States continues to lead the world, having spent untold trillions of dollars to make it possible.)

Adams knows that finally politics is not an independent or determining force in relation to the power that drives the most productive aspects of an economy, of a society. Writing about northern Europe after his first visit to Russia, he notes one of the many examples of complete transformation in the social orders of politics, government, custom, landscape, architecture, etc., which take place whenever a new set of forces momentarily direct transnational transformation. Politics is an appendage of power:

> In 1858 the whole plain of northern Europe, as well as the Danube in the south, bore evident marks of being still the prehistoric highway between Asia and the ocean. The trade-route followed the old routes of invasion, and Cologne was a resting-place between Warsaw and Flanders. Throughout northern Germany, Russia was felt even more powerfully than France. In 1901 Russia had vanished, and not even France was felt; hardly England or America. Coal alone was felt,—its stamp alone pervaded the Rhine district and persisted to Picardy,—and the stamp was the same as that of Birmingham and Pittsburg. The Rhine produced the same power, and the power produced the same people,—the same mind,—the same impulse. . . . From Hamburg to Cherbourg on one shore of the ocean,—from Halifax to Norfolk on the other,—one great empire was ruled by one great emperor—Coal. Political and human jealousies might tear it apart or divide it, but the power and the empire were one. Unity had gained that ground. (*Education*, 1099)

What is interesting about this passage is its attention to a regime of economic production as formative of transnational societies. Adams is unique as an early American analyst of the transnational nature of capitalism and of the definitive power of collectively organized production within capital. Nation states are of consequence, since they can fight wars and attempt to direct production; but Adams' materialism does not allow him to take the state as foundational nor to take its politics as directive. While there can be war between coal interests, as, for example, we might say British and German coal fought in 1913, in the transformations of society and civilization, the dominance of coal as the name given to the most advanced form of production, the most developed form of power, is definitive and beyond direction.[11]

Adams is not a determinist, as one interpretation of these remarks might imply. Nor is he a voluntarist, a believer in free will. If we can imagine a theory of history in Democritus and other pre-platonic atomists, we might say that Adams is like them, that he sees history as anarchy, that is to say, as a succession of orders immersed in chaos, with no order ever more than transient and almost never knowable to any of its contemporaries. As a writer of history, Adams sets himself a peculiar task: can he develop formulae or other mechanisms to allow him to translate the forms and effects of force and energy in one social and productive regime into another. In other words, he asks if it is possible to understand history as a series of sequences, as a series of substitutions, and as a series of equivalencies in different forms. Adams tells us that as a "historian" he once attempted to imagine history as orders of every conceivable kind of sequence: "Satisfied that the sequence of men led to nothing and that the sequence of their society could lead no further, while the mere sequence of time was artificial, and the sequence of thought was chaos, he turned at last to the sequence of force." Adams' intellectual plans are always made in relation to political needs and intellectual tasks as they begin to come clear; as such, they are always belated and, as such, are equally always failed in advance and often never pursued. The sequence of force proved no exception; having determined to follow this strand through the Baconian moment of intelligence, he visits Paris: "And thus it happened that, after ten years' pursuit, he found himself lying in the Gallery of Machines at the Great Exposition of 1900, with his historical neck broken by the sudden irruption of force totally new" (*Education*, 1069). That is, he discovers radiation and X-rays, nuclear realities that once again frustrate the desire for order as sequence of natural selection or orderly transformation within and under uniform conditions, as a Darwinian might have put it. So Adams opens a new chapter in his education, transforming his project once again, attempting to see if he can "measure" the "common value" of all these nonsequential forces in terms of "their attraction on his own mind." His new effort will be to treat them "as convertible, reversible, interchangeable attractions on thought" (1069–70). This would be very unusual "history writing," indeed!

Adams takes up the project of a new physics wherein the object is to describe what at one time would have been called the penetration of the soul by matter, by atoms. Rather than adopting the positivist position that describing the phenomena provides adequate knowledge, he takes positivism as a fact of capitalism adequate only to a society without culture, unable precisely to access alternative forms of force that produce alternative social orders. Positivism expresses the society that cannot know, for example, the force of the Virgin, the existence of a culture, of a society produced as a set of complex relations of wholeness and difference different themselves in kind from those imagined and lived within capitalism, especially in America and northern Europe.

As a result of his increasing interests in ancient philosophy and in thermodynamics, Adams thinks through certain problems posed by capitalism. He understands, for example, that capitalism produces what those who stand within it call and experience as discontinuous history: with each substantial transformation in the mode and order of production made on the fundamental terrain of economy, civil society, and the state, a new order of political, economic, class, and intellectual relations is felt to come into being. In relatively short periods of time, such as that of the U.S. Civil War, entire generations' cultural capital—its skills, expectations, and subjectivities—are rendered out-of-date by and in a new order that repositions classes, sets the productions of new ones in process, and creates new subjects with new "skills" to deploy within that order.

Most important, intellectuals are also generally left behind; their earlier understandings of society, their earlier training in disciplines that belonged to earlier formations—these are all outmoded residue.[12] The young Adams, raised in the ways of the eighteenth century, skilled in its arts of diplomacy and law, geared to a print culture determined by outdated social and intellectual elites, suddenly confronts a world of mass production, government guidance of modes of production, mass journalism, the irrelevance of old social and intellectual elites—and at that moment—which is only one of many such moments in the text—Adams realizes that his education is wasted; it is malapropian; he has never been taught anything that carries over as true or useful from one fundamental formation to another. This insight requires a new effort at education, an effort that must be active, that is, involves an attempt to find new ways to adapt the older subject to new realities so that in new activities both new knowledge can be gained and new functions, new forms of life, can be produced that can fit intelligently with the new order. Adams is like Hegel in many regards, but perhaps most intently in rejecting alienation as a stance. Adams always says that he would have been happy to have been made use of if only anyone wanted him. Unlike Hegel, though, who could say in 1800 that he would decide in favor of a bold "'agreement with the age,'" Adams grew increasingly to know that "estrangement" was indeed a position within capitalism. While Hegel failed to understand Hölderlin's "estrangement" as more than personal, Adams understood that Hegel's alternative, to "feel at home" within capitalism, within America, was an objective impossibility for more than a few warholian minutes—even for those persons whose "subject-position" makes them intellectuals and workers organic to capitalism's success. Hence, I believe, Adams' fundamental insistence that after 1858 he had no choice but to travel, and to travel as the sort of person he had earlier scorned as "a tourist."

I cannot pursue all of the implications of the "tourist" in this text or in its companion, *Mont-Saint-Michel and Chartres,* in which Adams speaks of traveling in an automobile photographing with an early Browning. I mention it here to raise two important points: Adams increasingly understood that new forms of production and reproduction modified the entirety of society, that they need to be used and examined; and consequently, he also came to understand that each moment of civilization is marked by its own singular intelligence, that is, its own order emerging within the chaos of change and transformation.[13]

Testing the limits of various knowledge systems results in the discovery that no human intelligence guides or comprehends capitalism as it drives itself through rapid periods of societal transformation. Adams, we should recall, felt Marx was the one essential piece of reading for a nineteenth-century education; it was not the Marx of class and dialectic that interested Adams, but the materialism in Marx, the impulse that led him to a thesis on Democritus and Epicurus and away from the idealism of the Young Hegelians. In other words, the point of intersection between Marx and Adams is a materialist's interest in the pre-platonic atomists.

In *The Education,* Adams is an antihumanist. His analysis of capital results in no grand story of history transformed by agents called "classes," nor in any dialectical battle between abstractions such as necessity and freedom. (It would be equally wrong to see the differences between "The Virgin" and "The Dynamo" as conflict or struggle; they are merely names, if you will, for successive forms of intelligence, force, order, and consciousness.) He sees no prospect that humanity can "evolve" into the humanist ideal of free and informed agency. Indeed, he sees no reason to believe that capitalism alone is responsible for the existence of anonymous forces that sweep humans along. Capitalism comes into being, as it were, as a result of a transformation of forces, power, and form with no guiding agency, no directive human will, no sufficient intelligence to guide or understand it.[14] Yet, Adams shows that despite the relative insignificance of human intentionality in history, there are developed and developing forms of intelligence incarnate within certain moments of the structure when the leading productive forces that create the civilization organize themselves and produce a world. From within these shaped vortices, however, there can be no guiding, intentional, or comprehensive knowledge in the form of science or politics at the conscious disposal of individual or collective agents:[15]

> As an affair of pure education the point is worth notice from young men who are drawn into politics. The work of domestic progress is done by masses of mechanical power,—steam, electric, furnace or other,—which have to be controlled by a score or two of individuals who have shown the capacity to manage it. The work of internal government has become the task of controlling these men, who are socially as remote as heathen gods, alone worth knowing, but never known, who could tell nothing of political value if one skinned them alive. Most of them have nothing to tell, but are forces as dumb as their dynamos, absorbed in the development or economy of power. They are trustees for the public, and whenever society assumes the property, it must confer on them that title; but the power will remain as before, whoever manages it, and will then control society without appeal, as it controls its stokers and pit-men. Modern politics is, at bottom, a struggle not of men but of forces. Men become every year more and more creatures of force, massed about central power-houses. The conflict is no longer between the men, but between the motors that drive the men, and the men tend to succumb to their own motive forces.
>
> This is a moral that man strongly objects to admit, especially in medieval pursuits like politics and poetry. (*Education*, 1104–05)

Gramsci has it that intellectuals organic to a class have the task of bringing that class to self-consciousness. By contrast to such a dialectical understanding of history, Adams' reading of American capitalism shows it to require managers whose inability to articulate its realities, to speak its politics, are their most characteristic feature.[16] Adams reasons that neither political nor intellectual knowledge of the most advanced forms of production and how they produce civilizations is available from within the order of intelligence that creates that civilization. Insofar as the intellectual is politically conscious and attempts to produce articulate knowledge of the contemporary, that intellectual is irremediably belated, caught as it were on the limit between the old and new, the residual and emergent.[17] It becomes impossible then for the critic ever to cross that limit as the advanced productive forces compel civilization; the intellectual can at best foray within the limit, transgressing his own education, the knowledge of already existing disciplines, and the subjectivities of earlier formations.[18] The intellectual paradoxically joins capitalism in the disabling of past forms, by crossing against from within, but the intellectual's efforts are meant to prevent the transformation, the carrying across of older forms that might function as resources for the newest moves of capital. Marx, we remember, tells us that each generation builds on the work of the past, and quite precisely not as might be intended.

The intellectual is caught within an impossible situation. Within the vortex of capitalism and history, the historical intellectual can, no more than the scientist or financier, articulate the moment of singular intelligence that is the leading force of contemporary production. Having discovered the intellectual's fate as a transgressor, having learned the inescapable limits imposed on the historian are the same as those of the scientist—an inability to deal with the contemporary marked by Langley's ignorance of radiation—Adams' task becomes twofold: to move critically to disable the utility of current knowledge, to reveal it as ignorance, and, by disclosing the unbridgeable gaps between different singular orders of civilizing intelligence, to help us imagine and think differently within an order of the vortex.

Adams is not satisfied with weak perspectivism; being a twentieth-century American in the age of mechanical reproduction does not, in itself, fatally inhibit the intelligence in its efforts to work against what it does not know in order to study civilizations elsewhere in time and space. The constant contrast of knowledge claimed against the unknowable, of recent past knowledge against what was once known at other times, of present forgetfulness against past realities—all this makes it possible to limn difference, possibility, alterity, and to produce new knowledge not useful to the present. It can never make the intellectual contemporary with his time; as a tourist and materialist, the intellectual is not contemporary to his or her time at all. Contemporaneity is always with the past as it was coming to be known, but the chaos which overwhelms that knowable past order in the anarchy of transformation makes that knowledge a burden and obstacle which must be transgressed often in the act of discovering its inherent ignorance, its non-fit with the emerging and leading orders. In that the intellectual cannot rebuild the broken vessel of knowledge shattered by capital's movements Adams analyzes how the past acquires value for the present only insofar as the present can commodify it.

Standing in the face of radiation, of X-rays, a new and at that time incomprehensible form of vision and reproduction, Langley, Adams' guide to physics, becomes a figure, a trope for the entire project of *The Education:*

Langley could not help him. Indeed, Langley seemed to be worried by the same trouble, for he constantly repeated that the new forces were anarchical, and especially that he was not responsible for the new rays, that were little short of parricidal in their wicked spirit towards science. . . . Radium denied its God,— or, what was to Langley the same thing, denied the truths of his Science. The force was wholly new. . . . [T]he electric furnace had some scale of measurement, no doubt . . . but X-rays had played no part whatever in man's consciousness, and the atom itself had figured only as a fiction of thought. . . . [M]an had translated himself into a new universe which had no common scale of measurement with the old. He had entered a supersensual world, in which he could measure nothing except by chance collisions of movements imperceptible to his senses, perhaps even imperceptible to his instruments, but perceptible to each other, and so to some known ray at the end of the scale. Langley seemed prepared for anything, even for an indeterminable number of universes interfused,—physics stark mad in metaphysics. (*Education*, 1067–68)

There are many things worth noting in this passage. Two must be mentioned: the atomist notion, familiar to us from Lucretius, that atoms collide changing direction and force; and the metaphysical notion that there can be multiple interfused universes. The intellectual's task then remains to try to know what is by comparison with what was and, given the knowledge of comparison, to do a new science that in turn would have two aims: physics in the largest sense, that is, the atomistic metaphysics of interfused universes existing at once but never at the same time or same place; and the science of the forces transformed into the productive power of the present. This last task "was to follow the track of the energy; to find where it came from and where it went to; its complex source and shifting channels; its values, equivalents, conversions" (1075).

Adams' work analyzes why successfully established, indeed, nearly perfect systems necessarily must fail. Entropy requires it unless and until intelligence can be put in place so that systems constantly learn to modify themselves continually to maintain perfection. In his earlier writings, Adams argues that the Swiss émigré, Albert Gallatin, who became an American politician and secretary of treasury, that is, minister of finance, under Jefferson and Madison, was also the only successful American political intellectual. Gallatin knew how not to be restricted by the successes he managed. Unlike Jefferson, who could not overcome the perfected systems he developed to carry programs and forces to their completed end, Gallatin always revised, always mysteriously managed, like the artist John LaFarge, to see a matter from all facets, see around it and see it whole, not eccentrically, so that he was not caught within the perfections of past programs and desires.[19] (In this line of thinking, Adams has been followed by such diverse intellectuals as George Kennan, W. Edwards Deming,[20] and Thomas Pynchon.) Perfection is like "crystallization"; it depends upon cutting away, upon forgetting. His physics requires following the traces forces leave as atoms permeate the soul, as they mark humanity and society, on their movements, their swerves, their impacts through chaos—thereby creating anarchy.

The American economic and political systems appear as examples of perfection. Early in *The Education* perfection appears as England, the old imperial power, doomed by the inability of its system to learn, to overcome the great inertia of its perfection, to modify itself intelligently. It not only forgets the past, it takes itself as perfection for an end of time, an end of history. Such a story of decline, of inevitable failure based on the inadequacy of management and scientific knowledge to the forces that produce them—this story cannot be the story of America, for America is predicated mythically on its unique ability to supersede the fate of other nations, of other empires. (It is no accident that Gibbon's *Decline and Fall of the Roman Empire* was Adams' exemplary history.) In specific terms, Adams' thinking reveals America not to be a state: it is a government, but it is not the highest expression of the ethical ideal. Above all, it has no self-identity, it has no national continuity, it has no unified history, and it has no intelligence to guide it to the New Jerusalem it will attempt to impose on its own continent and the world. What it has is blind force and recurrent crises. The knowledge Adams produces in this analysis cannot reinforce the nation or capital because it cannot circulate within capital or within America. In one of many such comments, he remarks about the United States after the Civil War that it "was rotten with the senility of what was antiquated and the instability of what was improvised. . . . [T]he whole fabric required reconstruction as much as in 1789, for the Constitution had become as antiquated as the Confederation. Sooner or later a shock must come, the more dangerous the longer postponed" (*Education*, 947). This about the United States *after* the Civil War!

The United States could not be remade under the intelligent eyes of reformers; senility is not adjusted by reform. Crisis comes in the 1890s in the form of economic panic and depression, which financiers attempt to regulate through trusts and cartels. They fail. What transforms the entirety of the system is a grand transformation in economics and knowledge: radiation, photography, telephones, automobiles, and the sciences that arise around them. What had been the U.S. Constitution stands merely formally as government, which, like everything and everyone else, trails the new realities that are so powerful as to make irrelevant to their own development the legal forms of 1789.

Adams elsewhere traces the enormous, sometimes tragic but usually comic efforts to make the United States into a nation-state.[21] Along the way, he effectively places the talk of states and the forms of knowledge to which they belonged in an earlier contemporaneity, one that was already exceeded by the time the United States is normally thought to have made itself into a state, that is, in 1865. At that time, coal, railroads, and Americanism were overwhelming the structures, knowledges, subjects, and discourse of the unitary state, showing it too to be merely a singular form of intelligence within anarchy.

The intellectual's stance in relation to these discoveries is complex. It cannot itself be national; it cannot accept knowledge within disciplines as given, since it must be belated and, as such, working for powers other than the emergent within which it nonetheless belongs; it must search what is known for its mis-fit with whatever can be traced as leading material tendencies of the time. It must prevent capitalism from circulating equivalencies of value and knowledge within established systems of difference; it must harass their fungibility. They are the work of capital that obstruct the differential, comparative knowledge the materialist genealogist can try to unearth. It means as well having no regard to disciplinary limits, since transgression is the game and limits can only do the work of the immediate past, often at the expense of seeing other pasts, which interfuse with the present. It means leaving history for description, analysis, and theory so that whatever is produced cannot be capitalized by a present knowable at best at its limits, by its crudest and most offensive tendencies.

If this is what America revealed itself to be and if Americanism is still at work, even under different guises, perhaps the leading one of which is "globalization," then Adams should draw our attention toward both new orders of critique and new hopes for a world in which the old desire on the part of certain groups and nations to be expert leaders to the world will no longer be tolerated.

MARK BAUERLEIN

Henry James, William James, and the Metaphysics of American Thinking

In a well-known letter to his close friend Thomas Sergeant Perry (dated September 20, 1867), a young Henry James, already settled upon a literary career, turns what many consider the impoverished state of American culture into a surprising privilege for those growing up in it:

> We are Americans born—*il faut prendre son parti*. I look upon it as a great blessing and I think that to be an American, is an excellent preparation for culture. We have exquisite qualities as a race, and it seems to me that we are ahead of the European races in the fact that more than either of them we can deal freely with forms of civilization not our own, can choose and assimilate, and in short, aesthetically, etc., claim our property where we find it. To have no national stamp has hitherto been a regret and a drawback, but I think it not unlikely that American writers may yet indicate that a vast intellectual fusion and synthesis of various national tendencies of the world is the condition of more important achievements than any we have seen.[1]

This patriotic summation of American prospects explains James's constant expatriation: to realize one's Americanness, one must search out "forms of civilization *not our own*" and "fuse" and "synthesize" them into a vision of future "achievements." Rather than rebelling against the (European) past by casting it as some obsolete feudal mistake or preserving one's innocence or ignorance through some illusory commitment to nature, Americans must meet other cultures and their pasts and incorporate them, use them as an opportunity for growth. For what is "not our own" is merely the precondition of American expansion, the necessary otherness that Americans over-come in order to supersede (and yet justify) the past and transcend their present selves. Hence the Hegelian language of "fusion and synthesis," a language that does away with *simple* oppositions of nature and culture, past and future, East and West. Renouncing the Emersonian consignment of the past to oblivion, James characterizes his sojourn through Europe as the American Dream in reverse. Instead of sauntering off into the naked conti-nent and building a world elsewhere, he returns eastward, composing him-self into a conglomerate of foreign traditions, a sponge soaking up "vari-ous national tendencies of the world" and translating them into a new world understanding.

In both versions—we might call them the Adamic and the Jamesian—Americans "assimilate" and "claim . . . property" as "ours." However, in the former myth, Americans reclaim "original energy" and domesticate a wilderness, while in the latter they appropriate a national culture, not sim-ply by buying its artifacts and aristocrats, but fundamentally by applying to them a pre- or supra-national awareness. They will succeed so well, he pre-dicts, precisely because they have no culture of their own, "no national stamp," and so can "deal freely" with national differences, be uniquely receptive to the other's heritage and uninhibited by the propriety accompa-nying it. Their minds not limited by any filial perspective, Americans enjoy a rare structural privilege over those born into a nationalized time and place. While the Frenchman, Florentine, or Egyptian must regard national and ancestral borders as the condition of self-preservation, Americans treat all such geographical and historical differences with indifference, recogniz-ing the border as simply something to cross, to absorb. And this moment of overcoming is not just a political act of appropriation—it is the Ameri-can's epistemological act of self-recognition. Expansion is how they find themselves. They have "no national stamp," so they must stamp themselves "internationally."

For, apart from a vague attachment to abstractions such as "freedom" and "equality" and despite their hostility to anything un-American, Amer-icans (in James's interpretation) have no political or cultural commitments to America *per se,* that is, to America without its opposing other, for there is no pure America. Neither a nationality nor a history nor really a place, America is the *act* of confronting and overcoming Europe, of "fusion and synthesis," one that must presuppose a European thesis before it can come into its own. America is a dialectical process, not a natural identity, a strategy of assimilation out to realize itself by surpassing (but not blindly negating) its precursors. To James, *Adamic* America is simply a communal repression, an attempt to forget the very thing that identifies Americans as such: their difference from the Old World. The Adamic myth involves escaping such differences and confrontations entirely, doing so under the guise of a spurious recuperation of nature. In fact, notwithstanding those sublime descriptions of primal moments of seeing and being in Emerson, Whitman, *et al.*, Adamism stages simply a muddled impulse facing a natural vacancy, a subjective desire wanting to materialize its life in an atmosphere of historical depth and fine discriminations, but floundering on a blank objective surface.

This is the epistemological plight Americans endure if they insist on their exceptionalism, if they interpret their global difference as a rupture instead of as a relation. Severed from instead of defined against their past, Americans are culturally empty. James does refer a few lines further in his letter to Perry to "something of our own . . . our moral consciousness, our unprecedented spiritual lightness and vigor" (*Letters*, I, 77). But such features, though "exquisite qualities," are motives for action, not reflection. They neither compose an identity nor store up historical content. Rather, they are forces of acquisition, natural drives to know and to possess: "vigor" ceaselessly propels it, "lightness" commits it to no single project save projection. And "moral consciousness," simplifying it into easy justifications, enables Americans to move on to further growth without deliberating over the meaning or memory of past expansions.

This is what makes Americanization such an "excellent preparation for culture," what makes inessentiality an advantage, not a drawback (as long as Americans are properly adjusted to their dialectical condition). Because they realize themselves by progressive assimilations of the other, Americans form no *lasting* connections between personal experience and national institutions, between private interest and the body politic. They owe no allegiances to what they relinquish or what they "find," and so their flights and foundings can take the form of a clean break or an innocent discovery or a pure experience, one with no hermeneutical background or ideological intention to account for. With nothing of themselves personally at stake in past or present operations of culture and history, they retain their ingenuousness, their ignorance of any other motive but expansion. Always directed toward a future "synthesis," they remain relatively undetermined by any established history of what they wish to grow into. Even though this political dexterity sometimes assumes the form of a mythical pre-politics, a grounding in nature, it proves to have astonishing political force. Careless of evaluating their experiences by the yardstick of tradition, unconcerned with accommodating themselves to any genealogical demands, Americans can "choose and assimilate" with the dispatch and security of fearless children. And, to repeat, their actions stem from a mental condition, not a political decision (though the former has immediate political effects). The question is, how can Americans move from epistemology to action, from the mental "preparation for culture" to the process of "acculturation," without endangering—that is, historicizing—themselves?

To organize their arrogations innocently, Americans require only a congenial method, a practice as pure and "American" as their guileless, grasping sensibilities. If that method has an interest attached to it, and hence a content it must sustain, a direction it is predisposed to take, then it will compromise its wielder's neutrality and candor. If it has a limited application, then it will disappoint the limitless scope expected of an American vision. Also, as it engages mind with history or culture or nationality, a tenuous entry of mind into world, it threatens to commit mind to or ground mind in some historical moment—the very antithesis of Americanness. To avoid these pitfalls, Americans must develop a method of expanding comprehensions, one that will keep up with the dialectical restlessness of the American mind. Since Americans "find" themselves through actions of assimilation, the action itself must somehow coincide with them—mind and method must coalesce so that they come into being together in every moment of assimilation. If they do not, then although an other (be it a person or nation or artwork or event) may be assimilated, the means of assimilation itself remains other, a factitious technique, and every American's act of self-discovery by assimilation ultimately results in self-alienation. That is, if this essential action becomes reified into a technique, a perfunctory, repeatable abstraction, then the method becomes just as limiting and static as the particular historical-cultural content mind supposedly transcends *in* that act. Hence, American action must be a method simultaneous with mind, constantly in process, reflecting mind's self-revisions, "American" by virtue of its tendency toward no permanent national or political end.

Henry James provides us with a brief model of the American mind, a portrait of sensibility primed for global "achievements." His crisp formulation connects that mind to the question of method, forecasts method, international politics, and the American mind as the terms in which the future of Western civilization will be decided. But in his plots, that mind usually ends up as some kind of passive observer-victim whose American presumptiveness is treated ironically or tragically. One might say that his *American* characters fail to discover a workable method, one that would immerse them in other cultures yet preserve them as trans-cultural, free and active despite their circumstances. This is virtually the same criticism that William James leveled at Henry himself, or at his literary methods: that in his later novels he employed a "method of narration by interminable elaboration of suggestive reference," getting so caught up in depicting with brilliance and clarity a "high-toned social atmosphere" that his narratives lack any "great vigor and decisiveness in the action."[2] That is, according to William, when Henry applied his method, in this case, to turn-of-the-century London upper-crust society, he became lost in its minute discriminations, enervated by its semiotic subtleties. Method was seduced by subject matter, the American artist subsumed by his foreign material. The great American "synthesis" did not follow, and instead of transcending European culture, Henry found himself endlessly involved in enumerating its workings.

William eschews this kind of "abnormal" activity, as he described Henry's writing, preferring the "vigorous" thinking he describes and develops in his own writings. Though not as explicitly concerned with "American" issues as is his younger brother, William is virtually obsessed with the mental traits characterizing Henry's American *cogito:* prospection, assimilation, trans-historicity. He dedicates his researches to advancing philosophies that maintain mind's processual character, that keep mind from crystallizing into a mental substance or becoming grounded in a physical substance. In practical terms, one might say he seeks a psychic method ever ready to disengage from subject matter, a method satisfying Henry's sociocultural "fusion" but not becoming overly socialized or acculturated in one spot. For William, the most effective strategy for free mental action is, of course, pragmatism. Or rather, the pragmatic *method,* for pragmatism is an action, not a theory, a mode of thinking, not a philosophy—it "instrumentalizes" all intellectual concepts and abstractions: "Pragmatism unstiffens all our theories, limbers them up and sets each one at work." What makes pragmatism so effective is that it has no policies to represent, no ideas to espouse, no interests to promote except those of "satisfaction."[3] It promises to be as *trans*political as the American mind, inclined to submit any historical and political content to the latter's unrestricted, evolving assimilations. Bearing no content in itself, no predetermined answers or solutions, it maintains an ideological agility through time, a thoroughgoing openness to whatever future result may be in order. "It is a method only," James writes, a "program" that "stands for no particular results" and that "has no dogmas, and no doctrines save its method." A simple and simplifying activity, pragmatism's sole initial requirement is "an attitude of orientation": *"The attitude of looking away from first things, principles, 'categories,' supposed necessities; and of looking toward last things, fruits, consequences, facts"* (*Pragmatism*, 32).

One could treat this "attitude" as a moral adjustment in the way Americans philosophize. But while the ethical implications of pragmatism *per se* may, to James, confirm pragmatism's superiority to rationalism, idealism, monism, and so on, the success of any single implementation of its method rests not upon the community service it provides, but upon the mental satisfaction it yields to an individual. Just as an American's political "synthesis" rests upon a certain mental capacity (the absence of a national memory), so pragmatism's moral outlook needs psychological backing. Specifically, to James, the "cash-value" of any method or belief, pragmatism included, first and foremost lies in the extent to which it converts "inward trouble" to subjective ease. "Inward trouble" being caused by any "new experience" that "puts [old opinions] to a strain" (34), what is *"good in the way of belief"* is whatever "gratifies the individual's desire to assimilate the novel in his experiences to his beliefs in stock" (36). If mind can "admit the novelty" with "a minimum of disturbance," if it can "marr[y] old opinion to new fact so as ever to show a minimum of jolt, a maximum of continuity" (35), then life can continue in an unobstructed "stream of thought." What is "good" is whatever provides for epistemological relaxation, thought moving smoothly from one experience to the next. This is why James's descriptions of pragmatism at work usually portray it operating through minds, not on society or philosophy as a whole.[4] He relates ideas and beliefs, even those held by a community, to "individual desire" and "subjective reasons" and "temperament," implying that what is ethically "good" must first of all be epistemologically "good." So, before raising moral and political and national questions, James addresses the question of mental effectiveness (in other words, productive "American" thinking) by pursuing an accurate description of cognition and an accompanying outline for satisfaction. That is, while both brothers pose the question of "assimilative" thinking, Henry does so by drawing portraits of

Americans traversing and faltering over historical and political boundaries, William by scrupulously tracing a tortuous clinical excursion through the normal and aberrant workings of the mind from its rawest immediate experiences to its most abstract totalizing comprehensions. Like Henry's letters and essays on the American character, William's epistemological and psychological writings import more than a descriptive analysis of mind at work. They also bear a prescription for right thinking, for effective American mental growth, "American" having here not a historical sense but a pragmatic sense: the *act* of "assimilating" the foreign smoothly, of incorporating the other into a productive, evolving "world synthesis." For William, this drama of American success and failure really takes place not in Gilbert Osmond's villa or Adam Verver's American City, but rather in the psyche. The future of the American mind's growth, indeed, all the political and historical manifestations and outcomes of "American" prospection, rests upon how a mind perceives different colors, when it feels pain, what it thinks a thing is, whether it can endure mystery, how it apprehends its own death, and so on.

At first sight, it might seem that James's definition of pragmatic truth as whatever "ideas" help us *"get into satisfactory relations with other parts of our experience"* (*Pragmatism,* 34) invalidly joins two distinct subjective acts, that it confuses satisfaction and cognition. Common sense asserts that satisfaction is an aftereffect of cognition, strictly a concomitant of percepts and concepts (which properly remain uninfluenced by the designs of feeling). In that case, pragmatism vainly seeks to submit given sensations and rational ideas to subjective interests. But for James, cognition is always already a function of subjective interests, even at the brute level of sensation. In an early essay on "Spencer's Definition of Mind," he writes, "These interests are the real *a priori* element in cognition." Because many objects we encounter in sensation are sometimes "accented with pleasure [or] with pain," our "correspondences" are ordered as follows: "that the pleasant or interesting items are singled out, dwelt upon, developed into their farther connections, whilst the unpleasant or insipid ones are ignored or suppressed. The future of the Mind's development is thus mapped out in advance by the way in which the lines of pleasure and pain run. The interests precede the outer relations noticed."[5] This is not a willful, conscious pursuit of pleasure, but rather the preconscious standpoint that moves our thinking. A teleology of attention, it precedes mind's "notice." Mind "develops" *through* this unconscious arbitration of "pleasure and pain," and hence cannot assume any position beyond it from which to comprehend it. The only things we can consciously comprehend are those that the "interests" of pleasure and pain have prepared for us and compelled us to attend to, never the interests themselves. The only things we recognize as real, as true, are those that grasp us, that claim our observance: "The only objective criterion of reality is coerciveness" (*Essays*, 21).

Used skillfully, the pragmatic method converts this coercive attachment into a participatory affinity between mind and fact, a "satisfying relation" of ideas, for mind need not sit passively like a mirror registering sensations. If it adopts an inert, acquiescent attitude, it does so by choice, because it is *interested* in doing so (though this interest need not always be conscious). Coercion may smack of determinism, but because "[m]ental interests, hypotheses, postulates . . . help to *make* the truth which they declare, . . . there belongs to mind, from its birth upward, a spontaneity, a vote" (21). Mind's "judgments of the *should-be*, its ideals, cannot be peeled off from the body of the *cogitandum* as if they were excrescences," for cognition emerges as such only after it has passed through mind's pre-cognitive selective interest.

Mind's teleology, then, is to maintain "lines of pleasure" in the face of developing experiences, to ensure smooth transitions from one experience to the next. However, "satisfaction" does not spring from the "subjective stream" itself—only a consciousness can feel satisfaction. A *pure* stream of consciousness, a mind experiencing sensations, perceptions, and conceptions in continuous and indiscriminate succession has no coherence, makes no "selections," and hence does not constitute thinking: "without selective interest . . . the consciousness of every creature would be a gray chaotic indiscriminateness, impossible for us even to conceive." As he defines it, consciousness is a whole—not an addition of thoughts, but a totality of thinking, thoughts "all-belonging-together" (*Principles*, 381, 220). More than the sum of its parts, consciousness is an organization of Nature's "indistinguishable swarming *continuum*," a mobilization of interests so pervasive that even "simple sensations are results of discriminative attention" (274, 219). A sensuous "continuum" drifts aimlessly along in a "river of elementary feeling" (227), exercising its selective interest only at the passive level of physiology—for example, hearing only those sound waves ears *can* hear.

In other words, if such a continuum were to exist, mind would not, nor

would satisfaction ever occur. For mind to exist, for it to make discriminations, it must have something to discriminate against, some opposition,
resistance, impediment, or otherness to assimilate or overleap. Therefore, if
mind's teleology is to "stream-line" its pleasures, to determine its next experiences as fully co-extensive with its previous ones, then it aims in effect to
annihilate itself. If, James writes in "The Sentiment of Rationality," "any
unobstructed tendency to action discharges itself without the production of
much cogitative accompaniment, and any perfectly fluent course of thought
awakens but little feeling" ("Sentiment," 33), then the more we "gravitate
towards the attainment of such fluency," the more our consciousness disin-
tegrates. That is, consciousness is inversely proportional to "fluency" and
"unobstruction": "When enjoying plenary freedom to energize in the way
of motion or of thought, we are in a sort of anaesthetic state."

But this achieved anaesthesia never lasts long, for mind's self-directed
incognizance (an oxymoron) cannot sustain itself. Mind's tendency to "formulate rationally a tangled mass of fact," to sift all "mutually obstructed
elements" into "some new mode of formulation" that provides "mental
ease and freedom" inevitably stalls. It blocks itself, and not only for empirical reasons—say, the inexorable onset of a new "tangle"—but by reason
of an inherent contradiction in mind's method. Put simply, by postulating
an end, even an end that brings about its own end, mind immediately defers
that end. The postulated end here would be to stop mind's own postula-
tions, to achieve seamless continuity of experience, openness to the "river
of life." But as soon as mind proposes a *telos,* it lifts experience out of this
continuous present, weighs successive subjective moments against a desired
future. Giving itself a direction, mind must limit and guide the stream, and
in so doing it casts the majority of its experiences as distractions, resis-
tances, deviations, the very things necessitating mindfulness. Once mind
sights an end, it must manage its experiences accordingly, thereby becoming directed instead of drifting. No longer a simple "sentiment" basking in
"the sufficiency of the present moment," mind is now a linear projection,
inhabiting or rather anticipating a future ever about-to-be.

Hence, mind reaches an existential impasse. Even though its most fundamental interest is to become disinterested, entirely purposive-less, such a
goal is still a conclusion, and therefore obeys what might be called James's
"law of conclusion": *"For the important thing about a train of thought is
its conclusion. . . .* Usually this conclusion is a word or phrase or particular image, or practical attitude or resolve. . . . In either case it stands out

from the other segments of the stream by reason of the peculiar interest attaching to it. This interest *arrests* it, makes a sort of crisis of it when it comes, induces attention upon it and makes us treat it in a substantive way" (*Principles*, 251). To "treat [something] in a substantive way" is to substantiate it, to make it "stand out" and stand still *as* a "something" in some way opposed to mind but ready for mental consumption. A "peculiar interest attach[es] to it," making it an it, a discrete object, and setting off a psychological "crisis" which, as we have seen, makes mind mindful. Any "conclusion," even a conclusion of utter inconclusiveness, awakens mind, reverses mind's ostensible goal. Constituting mind and thing together as and in a suspenseful critical "arrest," interest "induces attention," "attention" being not simply a willful focus of concentration, but the very shape and shaping of experience. Even when mind "attends" to its opposite—"inattentiveness"—it objectifies the latter, cathects it, "treats" it as some *thing* to experience. So, mind (as mind) can never attain a *condition* of streamy disinterestedness. Although, James writes, "Thought is in Constant Change" and *"there is no proof that the same bodily sensation is ever got by us twice,"* experience does contain a fundamental repetition that belies *pure* "streaminess": *"What is got twice is the same* OBJECT" (*Principles*, 224–25). Because mind can only "attach" to it as object, thereby making the "stream" as a whole repeatable (a contradiction) and necessarily maintaining itself as a subject doing the experiencing, mind can never wholly join the current. It must always, to some extent, resist it.

In other words, in pursuing a perfect "substantiation" and, consequently, its own reduction, consciousness only ensures its survival. Mind applies a self-defeating strategy. The only way for it to work would be if, in setting up this pure stream of becoming as a desired state of being, mind reaches an absolute "conclusion," a site of ultimate discharge that, if not leading to mind's outright demise, does afford mind a calm nirvanic continuity of thinking. This instrument of utter satisfaction—James calls it a "metaphysical Datum"—would extend "men's thoughtless incurious acceptance of whatever happens to harmonize with their subjective ends" ("Sentiment," 34) to infinity, for now all experiences the subject would accommodate smoothly, "fluently," as simple influxes. The conditions of its existence abated, mind would emerge out of its final "arrest" immersed in immediate experience, achieving "perfectly unimpeded mental function," the equivalence, to James, of rationality (64). And, to repeat, *total* rationality, a *comprehensive* explanation of things, cancels itself out: "a unique datum which left nothing else outstanding would leave no play for further rational demand, and might thus be said to quench that demand or to be rational *in se*. No *otherness* being left to annoy the mind we would sit down at peace" (57).

This "unique datum" provides a uniform, blissful "peace" precisely because, in rationalizing absolutely, it leaves nothing else to rationalize, nothing "outstanding" to account for. It is the special truth, instrument, or object that converts all possible disruptive, upsetting encounters into familiar objects and assimilate-able experiences, thereby annulling its *raison d'être*. Under the "datum's" explanatory power, that condition of "annoyance"—"otherness"—the very anti-thing that compelled mindfulness, has given way. Now we may live without the worry every "jolt" causes us, the "inward troubles" that "demand" that we rationalize our existence. Life's moments become sufficient unto themselves, not rational in themselves but providing a sentiment of rationality for us, a feeling of relief and contentment that need not be explained or justified.

But mind (as mind) never reaches a final conclusion—such hope is untenable. First, it forecasts some ideal object that relieves absolutely, one "unique datum" resolving all past, present, and future data but not itself requiring any resolution. That is, while this object or truth facilitates mind's progressive assimilations, mind cannot and should not assimilate it. Second, and more important, this strategy assumes "annoyance" has an object, *"otherness,"* which supposedly is out there waiting to be assimilated. But *"otherness"* is not an object. Foreign objects may possess some "other" qualities, but *"otherness" per se,* radical otherness as such, is precisely that which stands over and against any object, that which haunts the outside of any objectification. It is not an analogous being, but the other of being, not simply non-being (which falls easily into the category of absent-being), but a bare other irreducible to categories of essence or existence and their contraries. Because ontological categories can only judge otherness as an other space or other time, not properly as space's or time's other, ontology can never name the other, never apprehend it as such. But then, neither can we borrow the language of epistemology and properly call otherness a noumenal idea, a "mere being of thought" (Kant), for it is the other of thought, not an other thought. It is the unthinkable, for we can only think what is either an object of possible experience or the subjective conditions of an object being experienced as such. Hence, we have no adequate means of asking the question, what is the being of otherness? Neither substance nor meaning nor intention, though our grammar compels us to articulate it so, "otherness" will not submit to an ontology of presence-absence or an epistemology of noumena-phenomena. "Between" any datum and "otherness" lies utter irrelativity.

This means that there is no way to think "otherness" smoothly (a more important problem to James than any ontological *aporia*). No philosophy of "otherness" is possible, is able to appropriate "otherness" and render it as object, for mind's methods inevitably hinder its appropriation of "otherness." Specifically, were "otherness" ever convertible into just another alternative datum, something mind could perceive and recognize, mind would have no "play" of rationality, no room for mind to work its attachments. That is, there would be no room for mind. Mind's task is to develop fluid relativities, to domesticate otherness by forecasting it as merely yet-to-be-assimilated "data." But a world made up entirely of objects, a world without radical otherness, would be already determined, fully cathected, fixed and complete—in a word, mindless. Experience would involve a simple addition of data to mind's inventory, an activity calling for little "attentiveness." With every experiential possibility already "substantiated" as a thing, mind's intentionality would be logically set, immutable—the only changes mind would experience would involve changes of sensuous content.

This satisfying elimination of "otherness" and connection with things may ostensibly be mind's *telos,* but mind itself may never occupy such a world, for "otherness" is mind's pre-condition, and every attempt to eradicate "otherness" *absolutely* only brings about the opposite of its own end. Although *"all* that is experienced is, strictly considered, *objective"* (*Principles,* 290), experience can only arise as such against a backdrop of the inexperience-able, the latter being an inescapable side-effect of any objectification. Indeed, "empirical" evidence itself shows that, while always pursuing "more universality and extensiveness" with every progressive philosophical "conception" ("Sentiment," 36), mind preserves that which prevents any absolute extension, any totalized experience: "it is an empirical fact that the mind is so wedded to the process of seeing an *other* beside every item of its experience, that when the notion of an absolute datum which is all is presented to it, it goes through its usual procedure and remains *pointing* at the void beyond, as if in that lay further matter for contemplation" (58). No datum can ever be absolute; every experience has a concomitant "beyond," a coincident not-experienced. Even the entirety of existence, the universe, has its other, the "void," the latter ever coercing but evading mind's attention. And no matter how much mind tries to "point" out the "void," to delimit it by deixis, otherness inevitably arises as the by-product of any delimitation. Whether mind's "wedded"-ness is a structural necessity or an empirical habit, an essential working of thought or merely thought's latent desire, it destines mind to endless negotiations with otherness. In other words, mind's tendencies compel it to treat the "void" as a "the," some thing to apply the definite article to, knowing that every such treatment is inadequate, that mind should try to constitute the "void" as a function, not a reality, to experience it as a "beyond"-effect, not a present object. The more we try to delineate it, the more we realize that "void" (or any "other" names) is a pseudonym, a noun deluding us into thinking that the void is simply another datum. But in truth, "there is no logical identity, no natural bridge between nonentity and this particular datum" (58).

The void is not another datum, for mind's "pointing" does not issue in an experience of a present object, but rather provides "further matter for contemplation." And "contemplation," though applied to some "matter," does not simply apprehend it, grasp it as object. "Contemplation" here signifies something closer to its etymological meaning: *con-* together + *templum,* a space marked out for divination. It differs from perception in that perception involves an integration of a present sensation and the similar past sensations it "revives" into a definite object, the whole activity being entirely empirical (see *Principles,* 722–27). "Contemplation," on the other hand, involves organizing a place where every perception becomes a metaphysical quest, entering a site in which the materiality of objects dissolves in the face of its "other" (be it the void, Being, God, and so on). Such a quest remains contemplative by *not* applying objectifying predicates to the other, by not letting otherness materialize into a mere negation of what is there, into a not-there or a not-now. A negation of objects shares the same structure as an instantiation of objects, but contemplation eschews such oppositions (and the hope they bear of the other eventually coming to presence, of the negation being negated). Instead, contemplation "minds" otherness and "data" in a tense, irreducible difference, where one is the radical alterity of the other. The antithesis of the natural attitude, "contemplation" takes the singularity of the thing as a result of forgetting this constitutive alterity, an outcome un-contemplative thinkers misinterpret as the base of all experience. It holds to its metaphysical awareness precisely by resisting the temptation to treat the object as all, or even as first.

However, this does not mean that "contemplation" merely reverses the empiricist tendency to objectify. Instead of turning around and positing the *beyond* as all, or as the locus of truth—a mystical assertion James would have rejected, despite his personal and professional investment in the viability of mystical experience—a contemplative mind preserves both the object and the beyond-other, regarding them not as discrete essences, but as functional differences, each one identifying the other. Or rather, because mind can think the other only as an identity, it maintains its contemplative standpoint by observing strictly the metaphysical difference that brings otherness to thought. That is, contemplation remains mindful of a differential effect that itself can never be substantiated. If mind were to do otherwise, to ignore this "fundamental" difference that outdoes identity categories, mind would think empirically only, meditating not an agon of object and other but a pairing of present-object and absent-object. Realizing that there is always "a possible Other than the actual" ("Sentiment," 59), that otherness is the opposite of actuality and vice versa, mind finds that every identification it makes, even of the most straightforward deictic kind, only throws mind back upon this object-other difference. And though mind might be able to articulate the object and the other, at least as concepts, the difference between them will not be identified, cannot even be thought except in the object-other terms "it" yields. Mind feels its effects, but can never point to it as "there." The most mind can *know* is that "there is a *plus ultra* beyond all we know, a womb of unimagined other possibility" (59).

But, does a metaphysical limit to cognition restrict the directions and uses of cognition? Does the fact that "the notions of a Nonentity . . . still haunt our imagination and prey upon the ultimate data of our system" (59) mean that our contemplations can never progress, that despair is our only legitimate feeling? Obviously, if mind purposes to appropriate "Nonentity" absolutely, to overcome the object-other limit so that there is no more beyond, then mind condemns itself to interminable dissatisfaction. But if mind recognizes "Nonentity" (without attempting to objectify it as a mere emptiness), then a startling adjustment may take place. That is, just because "Nonentity" never changes—change can be understood only in terms of metaphysical categories, precisely what radical otherness is beyond—does not mean that mind's relation to it and experience of it may never change. The Being (or Anti-Being) of "Nonentity" may be immutable (because it has no substance to mutate), but the *meaning* of this other can be other and better than previously thought. Specifically, James argues, it is a not so difficult step to convert "Nonentity" from being a paralyzing annoyance to a satisfying cognitive instrument, to accept it as other yet let it work. Indeed, "Nonentity" can even serve to liberate cognition, to grant it possibilities a mind repressing otherness can never experience. "If, for example, a man's ordinary mundane consciousness feels staggered at the improbability of an immaterial thinking-principle being the source of all things, Nonentity comes in and says, 'Contrasted with me, (that is, considered simply as *existent*) one principle is as probable as another'" (61). Belying its supposed nihilistic portents, "Nonentity" here performs the reverse of mental limitation: it lifts a common-sensical, object-oriented prohibition against believing in an "immaterial" First Cause and mocks the timid incredulity of a tranquil, "mundane" mind. Setting an existential limit to what "ordinary consciousness" entertains as true, the spectre of non-existence undermines the absoluteness of any contention and opens a space for a revision of things. While every datum appears complete and whole, Nonentity sits beside it and marks its incompletion, its dynamic position in a differential movement of being and non-being and otherness. Nonentity functions as an absolute exteriority essential to any interiority, any unconcealment, any thing being brought into a field of experience, but is itself never interiorized. A "parent of the philosophic craving" (59), this constitutive involvement that no available philosophical categories can subsume dislodges truth from the objects at hand and makes rationality a fluid propensity, not a binding agreement with those things. A ubiquitous alterity both "outside of" and "part of" the object, "Nonentity" shatters the simplicity of any given experience or reality, complicates the "raw immediacy" of "present data." With this "otherly" mediation presiding over experience yet remaining inaccessible to cognition, irreducible to experiential categories—for example, this "outside of"-"part of" structure is not equivalent to a transcendent-immanent one— the coerciveness of things and the plausibility of ideas become relative determinations, accessory facts no longer deciding mind's "conclusions."

Belief, then, becomes a matter of "probabilities," the latter determined pragmatically by the measure of fluidity a "principle" provides. Without this radical otherness, the differential occurrence dividing entity from nonentity, cognition would pursue a single destiny, or in fact would already be there. The universe would be totally immanent, the only things interfering with a total experience of the universe being empirical restrictions on *how much* can be thought at one time. That is, now everything *can* be experienced—it is just a matter of when and where mind gets around to doing so. Or rather, is *led* around to doing so, for with no more "beyond" to "point" to, mind would properly adhere to whatever object or idea is placed before it, would attach itself to the present and eliminate any further "play of rationality." With metaphysical limits to thinking lifted, with no "nonentity" de-stabilizing mind's grounding in a putative immediate experience, mind "fluid-ly" replicates the fluidity of phenomena, however dissatisfying that stream of objects might be. In such a world, that is to say, mind would not function as mind, would no longer pursue a satisfying destiny, but instead be carried along in a current of sensations. Mind would make no choices and draw no conclusions, for experience would involve a direct, obligatory correspondence of object and percept. To think, to carry out its essential function, mind must bear a degree of abstraction, a capacity to posit something besides what is given in sensation. But to achieve abstraction, and the freedom that goes with it, mind needs some *other* thing or agency or effect that limits the world at hand so that mind may withdraw from it. "Through" otherness, mind assumes a reflective distance toward the things it encounters, now recognizing the world as such, as an "as such" and not as an absolute. If existence were all, if it had no other (again, not simply non-existence but the other of existence), then mind could not even think it, could not even know it as a reality or concept. How could mind think existence, know what and how it is, unless mind knew what and how it is not, unless mind differentiated it, deprived it of universality? Otherness, therefore, is the precondition of any thing being thought, indeed, is the general basis for intelligibility. This other possibility is not just a way of thinking, not a particular tendency, say, of philosophic minds, nor is it an ethical choice or a historical contingency (although this is where ethics and history begin). Rather, otherness is an epistemological necessity, an essential part of thinking, one that we might ascribe agency, antecedence, or being to if our ascriptions (or any thinking of it) were not always already manifestations of some unthought relation to it.

Therefore, the assumption that a metaphysical limit to cognition inhibits cognition makes no sense, for this limit, this difference between knowable and unknowable, presence and absence, being and being's other (not just its opposite), is the "place" where thinking begins. So, the fact that the "idea of Nonentity can . . . neither be exorcised nor identified" ("Sentiment," 63) does not necessarily signify human inadequacy and cause ontological insecurity. Inadequacy and insecurity are, in fact, the result of attempting to "exorcise" otherness (the "boor's" method) or "identify" otherness (the *un-*

radical empiricist's method), of trying either to repress or to familiarize it. In ethical terms, mind feels impotent only when it fails to treat otherness as an instrument of freedom, when it interprets finitude as alienation, as the onset of annihilation. This despair is logically inconsistent, for how can the very constitution of human being, the emergence of human being "out of" or "through" radical alterity, at the same time be the destruction of that being? Only by forgetting the former fact does mind regard its life and death in purely objective terms, as empirical events entirely reducible to phenomenal categories. Though the "idea of Nonentity" does commit thinkers to a philosophy of "Empiricism"—mysticism, James implies, is a "subterfuge"— it is an empiricism that surmounts this forgetfulness and incorporates otherness into any experience of "brute Facts," thereby gainsaying the usual materialistic, deterministic interpretations that hinder mind's quest for comfort. More specifically, genuinely "empirical" minds abstain from "factualizing" otherness, but still admit it as a constitutive element in human being, one that registers in consciousness not as a fact but as an "emotion," a "mysteriousness" open to variations of mental adjustment.

To such minds, "Existence will be a brute Fact to which as a whole the emotion of ontologic wonder shall rightfully cleave, but remain eternally unsatisfied. This wonderfulness or mysteriousness will then be an essential attribute of the nature of things, and the exhibition and emphasizing of it will always continue to be an ingredient in the philosophic industry of the race" (63–64). Wonder and mystery, not truth or reality or revelation—that is the strange and utterly inconclusive end and spark of thinking, the answer to and inspiration of the essay's opening question, "Why philosophize?" More than a mere subjective accompaniment to certain experiences, "ontologic wonder" reaches out to embrace the "whole" of existence, indeed *is* the experience of existence as a "whole," as a thing miraculously different from non-existence. Hence, this "emotion" characterizes the most effective and comprehensive interpretive stances. While the idealist ignores "brute Fact" and the traditional empiricist impoverishes the "mysteriousness" of things, the Jamesian empiricist marvels at the universe, sees objects clearly and feels them profoundly, sensing at the same time a metaphysical counterpart, an other unseen, a pre-sentiment. The standard philosopher-scientist demands exhaustive explanations, a sharp delineation of objects and their properties, not a radical inquiry into ontic-ontological difference. His or her "theoretic rationality" covets simplicities, wants "the relief of identification"

(56), one *or* the other, entity *or* nonentity, not a tenuous apprehension of their concurrence and irresolution.

This interplay emerges as "wonderfulness" only after rationality is reconceived as a sentiment, after mind has ceased trying to exclude or appropriate or rationalize otherness and has instead begun to accept it. Forever concealed from systematizers and simplifiers, "wonder" is an affect of otherness withheld from substantiating gestures, of otherness maintained as other by a mind curious and open, risking a willful suspension of belief, grasping for bigger and better experiences yet fixating upon no single object. And even though "wonder" always touches upon some "thing" beyond the "there," the "emotion" still qualifies as empirical because it is not merely a derivative effect of experience, a secondary aesthetic response to a supposedly primary perception. "Cleaving" to all objects of thought, immanent everywhere, "wonder" is "an essential attribute of the nature of things"— "essence" here referring not to *ousia* but to whatever excites interest—and hence is always already part of an open mind's experience of things as such.[6]

So, contradicting the usual connotations of laxity and fuzziness and obscurity, the presence of wonder signifies an active, thoughtful intelligence, a mind neither trapped in "the *cul de sac* of contemplation" (64) nor rushing to master the world before it. The former error forsakes "contemplation's" proper task—to yield innovative action—and the latter disregards any novel happenings, for its mastery merely invokes established habits of thinking to produce the customary perceptions and assimilations. If mind has succumbed to James's epistemological analogue of conformity—"Most of us grow more and more enslaved to the stock conceptions with which we have once become familiar, and less and less capable of assimilating impressions in any but the old ways" (*Principles,* 754)—it can no longer feel wonder. Nor can it recognize a "fresh experience," for an "old way" of "assimilating" renders all events familiar. But "wonder" engages a novel event *and* raises the possibility of a new mode of assimilation: "The relation of the new to the old, before the assimilation is performed, is wonder" (754).

As pre-assimilative, wonder retains contact with that otherness inaccessible to ordinary cognition, that anti-ontological excess repressed with every apperception. Radical alterity enters its experience, but not in the manner of any philosophical negation (for example, moving from inside to outside, abandoning eternity for the here and now, or materializing noumenon as phenomenon). Hesitating at the threshhold of assimilation, before mind's conceptual determinations work, mind in wonder preserves old and new, familiar and unfamiliar, same and other as a pre-cognitive "relation," a dynamic mediation understood in such easy polarities as old and new only after assimilation's stabilizing activity. Wonder is the sensation of metaphysical difference, assimilation is the understanding of that difference, and the instance of wonder testifies to the inadequacy of that understanding, the inevitable rift radical difference traces between "itself" and its representation. (This is why wonder remains "eternally unsatisfied.")

But again, mind's cognitive shortcomings and resort to wonder do not paralyze it, for inadequacy is not a fallen, tragic, or nostalgic condition. A cognition may be adequate temporarily, if the concepts mind has developed prove compatible with the experiences it meets. But while experience changes, concepts do not—"Conceptions form the one class of entities that cannot under any circumstances change" (*Principles*, 442). So, mind's clinging to the idea of a permanently satisfying concept is not tragic, merely perverse. This conceptual rigidity rules out wonder, indeed, casts wonder as a dangerous immersion in the metaphysical flux, as a mental stream emulating the natural continuum that concepts aim to control, to endow with "sameness" (see *Principles*, 434–42).

To satisfy at the same time the exigencies of changing sensation and the need for mental coherence, mind requires this wondering flexibility more than it does a set group of concepts. With the "idea of Nonentity" hovering over each existential position, all concepts are rendered finite, context-specific, provisional no matter how much psychic investment they bear and despite their initial absolutist claims ("Every thought is absolute to us at the moment of conceiving it or acting upon it" ["Sentiment," 60]). No concept can exhaust the dynamic pull of otherness, and so as inertia invariably grows in conceptual thinking, the breach ever widens between mind's cognitive reserves and the experiences that outdistance them. Ontologic wonder cherishes this reduction, this relativizing of concepts, for it makes experience corrigible, exposes yesterday's conceptual inventions as today's dogma. More precisely, rather than being opposed to conceptuality per se, wonder is situated at the point of radical otherness' historical appearance, between an experience already conceptualized and an experience not yet conceptualized, perhaps not assimilatable by the current inventory of concepts. It is a method of compromise, an unfolding negotiation respecting conservative forces of mind yet admitting the progressive forces and disorienting effects of otherly encounters. As a "relation," a mindfulness of "nonentity" that limits every previous datum, it anticipates a new organization of experience, a revision of things, even a self-revision. This latter possibility prevents one from interpreting wonder as a forestructuring of the world, whereby the network of relations constituting things as such and in their specificity is reoriented, leading to a new world and to new experiences. Such an interpretation shelters wonder from its own transformative results, reserves it outside the general reorientation of thinking. But because wonder is an event of differentiation, not an object or concept, because it is a site of conceptual reinvention, not a mastering procedure or determined outcome (though any interpretation of it necessarily substantiates it), wonder can never solidify or recur.

Wonder itself changes, experiences difference differently each time. If it did not, it would become just as petrified and resistant as the concepts it mediates. If it were just a mental instrument, its mediating activity would settle into a repetitive pattern, a fixed application of schema or concepts, and mind would find itself in an untenable state, trying to sustain obsolete habits in the face of new experiences it can only interpret as disruptive and uncanny. But wonder never occurs in quite the same way, for even though mind can feel wonder over and over, wonder itself cannot be abstracted from the experiential flow, cannot be isolated or handled or instrumentalized. Being a "relation," not an identity, wonder is necessarily embedded in that flow, changing as the successive terms it relates change. More important, wonder originates in and properly adheres to radical alterity, to the experience of the limit of being. Hence any objectification of it implements the very categories of being wonder un-grounds. Since a particular experience can be wonderful once only—the second time already entails a loss of "mysteriousness"—its occasion manifests a mind's readiness to alter its thinking, to rechart its cognitive map. Neither shying away from nor trying to overcome otherness, wonder welcomes the latter's advent, converting uncanniness to exhilaration, disruption into re-creation. Mind then knows the (temporary) satisfaction of discovering new comprehensions, of bridging discordant states of mind, of lifting mind out of its commitment to a single concept, which is to say a single future (since concepts are "teleological instruments").

This radical new relationship is more than a simple juxtaposition of concepts. It has a transformative effect. While it is the case that "Not new sensations . . . but new conceptions, are the indispensable conditions of advance," the recognition and use of a conception as new rests on its coming about in a new relation: "the new truth affirms in every case a *relation* between the original subject of conception and some new subject conceived later on" *(Principles,* 439). This "between" must possess a dynamic, synthetic force, for concepts in themselves, maintained as discrete, paired passively, yield nothing but a reapplication and the same assimilation. However, "if two of them are thought at once, their *relation* may come to consciousness, and form matter for a third conception" (440).

Relation, therefore, is the place of progress, wonder the sign of its novelty, otherness the perpetuity of movement. What is unrelated is grounded, immobile, absolute: "The Absolute is what has not yet been transcended, criticized or made relative" ("Sentiment," 60). A mind pursuing absolutes simultaneously flees relation and otherness and advancement. Because it is always possible that "the notion of nonentity may blow in from the infinite and extinguish the theoretic rationality of a universal datum" (60), an absolutist mind embraces ever narrower conceptions and broader exclusions. But a mind seeking otherness yet suspecting "universal" conclusions passes through ever more liberal conceptions of being. Recognizing only difference as absolute—a contradictory formulation unless the idea of difference is differentiated from itself so that difference is not considered simply a "thing" between—mind is thrown into a different metaphysic, one no longer structured on the principle of identity and no longer compelling mind to think existence and otherness as an actual or potential unity. Welcoming otherness as an inspiration for growth, not a threat to stability, mind relinquishes the quest for absolute knowledge, thereby avoiding Hegel's mistake: that is, trying to eliminate all "conceivable outlying notions" so that "the whole of possible thought" may circulate within the "bounds" of an "adamantine unity" (59). To James, this "logical bridge" Hegel draws between "Nonentity and Being" functions as a repression, not a realization, a futile effort, since any attempt to assimilate nonentity to being solicits the very categories of being nonentity is exterior to (exteriority being one of them).

Of course, there are provisional others to familiarize or negate or become familiarized to—those processes are life. To these transformations James addresses the majority of his writings, often assuming the posture of scientist or positivist or clinical psychologist, arguing as if he has forgotten his metaphysical insight. However, that does not mean James believes he can ever settle the question of otherness, fix its meaning, or foresee its consequences. Even when his language affirms identities uncritically, James often inserts cautionary statements reiterating the conventionality of those identities. He remains mindful of the fact that incorporating *all* "outlying notions" into habitual thinking, familiarizing otherness absolutely and believing in the viability and justness of that *telos,* is to submit all other existences and lives to a single conception. This arrogance often passes for vision, for a universal understanding of things rightly transcending the limits of local knowledge. It wants to be unrelative, unrelated, but in so doing it precludes its own advancement. It consigns itself to isolation, minimizes its experiential possibilities. In constituting all others as finite, a "Hegelian" mind projects all its experiences as finite, fully contained by predetermined assimilations.

But, paradoxically, a mind knowing its own locality enjoys an expanding receptivity. Like a "Hegelian" mind, a Jamesian mind never actually obtains a unified prospect, a totally appropriated world. However, by forsaking the former's dream of complete immanence, by recognizing the infinite backdrop of alterity against which any locality emerges, the latter anticipates vaster, happier, farther and closer "beyonds," than does a mind hoping to consume the backdrop itself. Thought becomes a series of tenuous negotiations and amendments, a "constant play of furtherances and hindrances" (*Principles,* 286). Apprehending infinite otherness, mind becomes infinitely restless, captivated by that "'fringe' of unarticulated affinities" (250) trailing every present thing, transforming all local others into material to grow through, not recoil from or subdue.

Herein lies William James's radical constitution of thinking, his metaphysical solution to the geopolitical demands placed upon an acquisitive, desirous, inquiring modern consciousness. Whether William's meandering, detailed psychological and philosophical speculations actually or directly arise from or respond to or expound the "American" epistemological situation as described by Henry is a precarious historical question. But in any case, it is clear that Henry's program for "American global achievement" requires a radical innovation in consciousness, a fundamental mental adjustment that his characters often fail to achieve but which William's elucidations of this new thinking prophesy. He avoids the former's epistemological mistakes by reinterpreting and resituating otherness, by broaching otherness as a necessary, appropriate, yet un-objectifiable condition of momentous thinking. Deserving the predicate "American" precisely because it eschews any such limiting, ideologically sedimented terms as "American," this thinking thrives by being drawn to whatever reduces its thoughts to relativity. Any new experience, any wonder-producing otherness that "finite-izes" a concept previously held to be universal captivates James's American mind and, strangely enough, amplifies it. Though mind never wholly masters otherness, the latter's incessant "beyond-effect" still serves mind as an emancipating mechanism, sheltering mind from the fatal attraction Henry's characters suffer: outgrowing the provinciality of the American scene only to be submersed in just another locality. The American mind surpasses any conditional assimilation of otherness, any occasional appropriation of the new, for this happy achievement is temporalized as soon as radical otherness exercises its destabilizing pull. Mind finds itself rationalizing each new disturbance, feeling out new parameters of experience, in which old ones are retained as relative parts. This progress never ends, but it is the only attitude or orientation in which the (Jamesian) American mind finds its fulfillment.

HENRY SUSSMAN

At the Crossroads of the Nineteenth Century: "Benito Cereno" and the Sublime

Still swept up in the whirlwind that emanates in the nineteenth century, twentieth-century readers share the predicament of Benjamin's Angelus Novus,[1] even on the threshold of a millennial hyperspace in which the spatial barriers once separating social and cultural anomalies have been obliterated. The wind blowing in from the nineteenth century is a powerful one, not only in the land- and seascapes that Wordsworth, the Shelleys, and Melville described and that Friedrich, Blake, Courbet, and Turner painted, but in the pull, the constructive and destructive force, that its intellectual systems continue to exert. We turn to the void of a new millenium as a projective scene for our discourse, yet nineteenth-century systems stay on our minds; they yet furnish a template for our productive thinking.

No text illustrates the logical, social, and textual concerns occupying nineteenth-century thinkers more powerfully than Herman Melville's *Piazza Tale,* "Benito Cereno." The tale of an American sea captain's visits aboard a Spanish merchant ship that has already surrendered to a slave insurrection resides on the interstice, the very hinge, between Kantian sublimity and Hegelian dialectics. In the same story we are treated to a seemingly explicit illustration of the Hegelian dialectic between mastery and slavery and to a meditation on the awe experienced by an exemplary (ruling-class) subject contemplating naval logistics and a human quandary of sublime proportions. The dialectic of mastery and subjection or the sublime could themselves alone exhaust any single reading of this text. It is no doubt an act of extreme cheek on my part that I could, in a few pages, combine both analyses; yet I do so, even at the price of some loose ends, in order to suggest the power with which Melville intuited and inscribed within the framework of his fiction the epistemological investigations of his epoch.

It is perfectly fitting that a tale exploring slavery and incorporating the structuralist intellectual frameworks of a uniquely systematic age should be strikingly economical. "Benito Cereno" offers us in fact two stories for the price of one. It is a twice-told story; or rather, a story and the appearance of a story. It chronicles the initiation of one Captain Amasa Delano into the duplicates and duplication of irony and deception. With detachment the Hegelian omniscient narrator carries on while Delano falls into and rescues himself from naïveté, credulity, good faith, and the debilitating effects of rationality. Delano, whose Hispanic name echoes the French *de loin* and carries as well the nuance of wool (Sp. *lana*), the innocence of Christ-figures and martyrs is, always already and from the outset, a straw-man and a sop. (We will return to the possible significances of his name.) The play between Delano's antics, even when they include discoveries, and the narrator's detached vision and commentary describes already the parameters of a heavily ironized situation.

The narrative structure of "Benito Cereno" is ironic, while its situation and revelations are sublime. The history of irony runs concurrent to the play of dialectics and the disclosure of the sublime.[2] Without the presupposition of an inherently and unalterably divided subjectivity, there would be no place for the stories of irony and sublimity. These two seemingly diametrical reactions, the former a belittling and the latter a secularized awe, are rooted in the same epistemological settings and impasses.[3] Melville's tale confronts us powerfully with the ironies of Delano's utterly rational naïveté and of Babo's tendentious victory over his master and mastery in general; its setting and tone owe much to the expansiveness of sublime conditions, in nature and thought. Melville honors dialectical thinking in the stunning reversals between mastery and subjection, truth and fiction, and objectivity and subjectivity that the tale stages. Yet these acts of logical and structural subversion would come to naught if the setting did not communicate oceanic awe and global economy and conflict. Without the setting of sublimity, I am arguing, whether projected outward in vast seascapes or inward as stunning revelations, psychological *coups de foudre,* the drama of irony would come to small potatoes.

The setting of "Benito Cereno" thus combines the magnificence (sublimity) and devaluation (irony) that intertwine and supplant each other at the locus of the psychological and intellectual borderline. The sea in Melville is the locus of the borderline,[4] the place where exemplary subjects lose their rational bearings, experience the dissolution of measure, and enter the economies of artistic production or philosophical speculation. Contempt and awe are the terminal points of Melville's sea voyages. In between, characters experience their emptiness as fullness; they enter a systolic alternation between filling and emptying. The fiction of voyagistic movement segments the emptying of apparent findings into distinct episodes. In *Pierre*, the apex of Melville's domestic fiction, there is the possibility for only one move, from the constrained rural life to an even more claustrophobic Manhattan. The arrest of movement in this text leaves the protagonist in a situation of inescapable, arrested duplicity. The imprisoning landscape of oedipal triangles that Melville paints for this novel is more horrific, in a psychological sense, than the standard Melvillian sea-dangers. It could be argued that seascapes are so compelling throughout Melville's fictive career in part because their wider scope allows for a repetitive rhythm of interpretations and debunkings, of sublime expansions of uncertainty that break out from within the constraints of dialectical precision.

There are, then, in this tale, epistemological plots that coincide with the narrated events; rhetorical moves that both buttress and undermine the sequence of thoughts and happenings; social allegories that expand into commentaries on the possibilities of knowing. Captain Amasa Delano grows as an interpreter at the same time that he revises his "take" on an anomalous naval situation; yet it is not clear that he definitively augments his "self-consciousness" or his detachment from the social compromises (*e.g.,* slavery) of his age. The status of the "truth" seems to fortify itself as the events' narration progresses from an initial "take" to an informed explanation to a legal disposition. The sublime murkiness of first conditions in the tale has, however, *ab origine* undermined the possibility of dialectical increments in certainty. The slave trade is among the story's social "givens." The augmenting epistemological crisis that the text describes in spite of its progressive acts of clarification is indicative of the status of ethical certitude in a slavery-based economy.

Let's run through the tale as it was meant to be read in terms of the conventions of shorter fiction in the period when it was composed. That is to say, in our own first "take" on the story, let us (as Conrad would say) submit ourselves to its narrative sequence and to the train of developments in consciousness that is supposed to coincide with the narrative events.[5] But even here certain aspects of its hermeneutic and epistemological commentary make themselves materially known. Fully the first two-thirds of the novella concerns itself with the multifaceted (social, epistemological, moral) murkiness besetting a sea captain when he "steps aboard a boat."[6] The conditions defining the captain's "consciousness," knowledge, or existential state during this prepossessing prologue are characterized by the ambiguity of philosophical aporias in general and by Kantian antinomies in particular.[7] What gives this crucial initial segment any coherence it claims is Delano's attempts to interpret the status of Don Benito Cereno, captain of the renegade merchant ship. The anxiety that the disabled vessel causes Delano presents itself initially and superficially as an uncertainty regarding the power relations on board. Don Benito, the commanding officer, operates from a position of (possibly hypochondriacal) sickliness instead of from strength. His officers are largely out of the picture (or they are decorative corpses when we see them). As Delano's knowledge and consciousness emerge over the first two-thirds of the novella, he experiences a gnawing suspicion that Don Benito's underlings, slaves, particularly Babo, his personal servant, are more in control of the situation than he is.

The status of a ship under the control of its slaves *defines* for Melville the state of anxiety and horror in the mercantile world of Western Europe at the turn of the nineteenth century (this is the tale's temporal setting). "Normality" in this world consists of a set of (empirically located) paradoxes or antinomies gaining legitimacy from a control asserted by European powers whose societies are themselves structured by idealism. As it slowly and with considerable resistance dawns upon Delano that he has happened upon an utter dystopia, a setting in which all domestic European pretensions and hypocrisies have been declared null and void, the particularity of his (naval) situation expands itself into a general meditation, the intellectual conditions making the European civil order possible. It is no accident, then, at the end of this extended *précis* that Delano's departure from the phantom vessel, the *San Dominick,* triggers the crisis that unmasks the actual power relations prevailing on board. The conclusion of the story embraces, in quick succession, the revelation of the heretical power relations that have prevailed since the outset of the story, and the setting aright of this deviance by the authority of European judicial authority. Melville frames all but a few of the novella's "final words" within the seemingly objective format of a trial transcript. The authoritative status of a legal document promises to resolve the story's disquieting ambiguities. Yet the tale's ironies and half-awarenesses persist beyond this documentary ending, suggesting that mercantilism and slavery have shaken Western truth and knowledge to their innermost parts. The two-thirds of the narrative that Melville devotes to Delano's uncertainties, anxieties, and *crises de conscience* renders any restoration of the old order, any retreat into idealized eighteenth-century notions of authority, utterly hopeless.

"Benito Cereno" stages the Kantian allegory available to literary characters in post-Cartesian works of fiction; that is, the novella dramatizes the opening up of a dimension of sublimity (either in the "internal" or "external" represented worlds) to a character hitherto under the constraints and assurances of rationality. Economically, the opening up of the sublime, whether depicted as revelation, madness, rapture, or political insurrection in the present case, corresponds to a compensation, a Derridean supplement, to an aspect of poverty elsewhere in "existence." The sublime, as I explain elsewhere,[8] may be defined as the vestige of awe carried over into a secular religion in an age that has witnessed the severe qualification, if not the death of God. As figments of original genius, post-Cartesian literary characters lead us to a certain wonder and awe that they are privileged to unearth in compensation for the constraints that they are fated to endure.[9] These constraints include physical deformity (Hoffmann's René Cardillac and Poe's Hopfrog); unrequited, and then requited desire (Goethe's Werther and Faust); banal domesticity (Flaubert's Madame Bovary); personal isolation (Joseph K. in Kafka's *The Trial*); and "the subjective experience of emptiness" (Camus' Meursault). The expanded dimensionality of the sublime is a reward even where fatal. In a post-Cartesian episteme, this compensation, which is, in Heideggerian terms onto-theological even if not explicitly religious, is in turn passed on to the reader and cultivated society as a compensation for the constraints upon *their* hopes, desires, rages, and passions. The opening up of the sublime may kill, but then no one is going to escape the world alive anyway. These conditions for knowledge and existence were always already inscribed in the Cartesian dualism and division between soul and body. We associate Kant with the compensatory rapture of aesthetics because of the rigor and deliberation with which he elaborated the interplay between transcendent and empirical realms and because of his meticulous analyses of the beautiful and the sublime.

I can tell you already that Captain Amasa Delano, even though "Benito Cereno" ends with the ostensible clarification furnished by a legal document, is a close *confrère* and *semblable* to the characters mentioned immediately above and in many other literary sites in the confusion, derangement, and intensity that he experiences in trade for the closures surrounding his taking-off position. His "overall" experience corresponds to the Kantian allegory: empirical man desperately seeking revelation (secular, of course).

The tale is already primed for this allegory as it begins.[10] Delano enters a dimension of sublime expansion just after "He rose, dressed, and went on deck."

> The morning was one peculiar to that coast. Everything was mute and calm; everything gray. The sea, though undulated into long roods of swells, seemed fixed, and was sleeked at the surface like waved lead that has cooled and set in the smelter's mould. The sky seemed a gray surtout. Flights of troubled gray fowl, kith and kin with flights of troubled gray vapors among which they were mixed, skimmed low and fitfully over the waters, as swallows over meadows before storms. Shadows present, foreshadowing deeper shadows to come. (*PT*, 46)

There are many respects in which the seascape Captain Amasa Delano enters immediately upon the domestic task of dressing himself is uncanny, but none is more compelling than the stillness and monochromatic indifference that have befallen the fluid element of the sea, an imprisonment by rigidity if not by incarceration. Delano's starting position is an expanding sublimity of non-articulation. The perceptual and cognitive markers that would furnish orientation through differences (in color, tone, position) are absent. Delano has entered a slough of indifference and incertitude. Elements persist, but deprived of their elementary dynamic qualities. The most uncanny image (and we may begin to conceptualize the psychoanalytical uncanny as a sublimity projected "inward") is that of leaden waves or sea swells, of an aquatic medium frozen still. These waves are also men of pleasure, swells, whose amoral pleasure violates the sea's cruciform rigidity (roods). A distinctly gray sky dons a "gray surtout," foreshadowing an important comparison that will be made between the costumes of the sickly nobleman, the title character, and Babo, his poorly attired manservant.

The first scene of the story is already prepared for revelations, for disturbances of the encompassing torpor that will really matter. The narrator remarks upon a general aura of oddity prevailing upon ships at sea. They harbor a speculative element; seem an unreal setting for "costumes, gestures, and faces" every bit as unreal (50). The ship is a privileged locus for the bolts of lightning and enchantment that shake sea captains from their complacency and that inspire writers figured as curious, speculative subjects:

> Both house and ship, the one by its walls and blinds, the other by its high bulwarks like ramparts—hoard from view their interiors till the last moment: but in the case of the ship there is this addition; that the living spectacle it contains, upon its sudden and complete disclosure, has, in contrast with the blank ocean which zones it, something of the effect of enchantment. The ship seems unreal; these strange costumes, gestures, and faces, but a shadowy tableau just emerged from the deep, which must directly receive back what it gave. (50)

A ship is both a house and a naval vessel, satisfying both of Freud's major requirements for the uncanny. It is a temporary home or haven nonetheless pervaded by sublimity. The mood prevailing on board is unsettling, even if characterized as "enchantment." Captain Delano hovers between confidence, Melville's general term for remaining under the auspices of a functioning idealism, and premonitions of unchecked malevolence and death.[11] In the passage below, the narrator contrasts Delano's assurance with the imprisoning death of sarcophagi and with threats that pursue him with the silent intrusiveness of moss (a favored metaphor in Hawthorne).

> These natural sights somehow insensibly deepened his confidence and ease. At last he looked to see how his boat was getting on; but it was still pretty remote. . . .
>
> To change the scene, as well as to please himself with a leisurely observation of the coming boat, stepping over into the mizzen-chains, he clambered his way into the starboard quarter-gallery—one of those abandoned Venetian-looking water-balconies previously mentioned—retreats cut off from the deck. As his foot pressed the half-damp, half-dry sea-mosses matting the place, and a chance phantom cat's-paw—an islet of breeze, unheralded, unfollowed—as this ghostly cat's-paw came fanning his cheek; as his glance fell upon the row of small, round dead-lights—all closed like coppered eyes of the coffined—and the state-cabin door . . . now calked fast like a sarcophagus lid . . . and he bethought himself of the time, when that state-cabin and this state-balcony had heard the voices of the Spanish king's officers. . . .
>
> Trying to break one charm, he was but becharmed anew. Though upon the wide sea, he seemed in some far inland country; prisoner in some deserted

château, left to stare at empty grounds, and peer out at vague roads, where never wagon or wayfarer passed.

But these enchantments were a little disenchanted as his eye fell on the corroded main-chains. (*PT,* 73–74)

The *San Dominick* is a former ship of state fallen into disrepair. Once a showcase (or show vessel) of national power and grandiosity, in its reduced condition it awakens in the American sea captain an aimless undulation between ongoing ideals and hypochondria, the latter in Melville's widest sense as the loss of confidence, the inability of (Western) idealism to repair breeches in positivity and positivism. Amasa Delano, an exemplary Kantian subject, enters a rhythm of falling in and out of charms and enchantments. The strangeness of the *San Dominick* fundamentally undermines his confidence, but then, lost in his thoughts, his equilibrium is, as if by magic, restored. His entry into a renegade vessel offers the compensations of sublime experience; but it poses the threat undergone by all Romantic heroes that sublimity cannot be cast aside when its rigors prove too demanding.

In light of this scene setting, it cannot come as too much of a surprise that Delano's chief interlocutor and object of interest, title-character Benito Cereno, is a veritable personification of sublime attributes. Don Benito Cereno is beset by the multifaceted but vague malaise that forms, for contemporary object-relations theorists, the presenting complaint for the narcissistic disturbances. His twitchiness also corresponds to late-nineteenth-century characterizations of neurasthenia.[12] The apparent absences in his consciousness, insofar as they can be inferred from behaviors, are of vast and sublime proportions. An aura of "cloudy languor" (*PT,* 52) hovers about the title character, a description not without significance in terms of the novella's initial atmospheric conditions:

Still, Captain Delano was not without the idea, that had Benito Cereno been a man of greater energy, misrule would hardly have come to the present pass. But the debility, constitutional or induced by hardships, was too obvious to be overlooked. . . . His mind appeared unstrung, if not still more seriously affected. Shut up in these oaken walls, chained to one dull round of command, whose unconditionality cloyed him, like some hypochondriac abbot he moved slowly about, at times suddenly pausing, starting, or staring, biting his lip, biting his finger-nail, flushing, paling, twitching his beard, with other symptoms of an absent or moody mind. This distempered spirit was lodged, as before hinted, in as distempered a frame. . . . His voice was that of one with lungs half gone— hoarsely suppressed, a husky whisper. No wonder that . . . his private servant apprehensively followed him. Sometimes the negro gave his master his arm, or took his handkerchief out of his pocket for him . . . less a servant than a devoted companion. (52)

As in a painting by Caspar David Friedrich (*e.g., Morning in the Riesengebirge,* 1810–1811), the Romantic subject, the subject of Kantian sublimity, hovers at the precipice of an immense abyss that is, in many senses, too much for him.[13] The vacuity of the void without is mirrored in absences within—of composure, awareness, self-possession. Don Benito's voice is an emanation from the other world, not the expression of a particular subject rooted in a specific context, Heidegger's *Welt.*[14] His variegated hypochondriacal debility bespeaks terror at some aspect of the Transcendental, the Lacanian Real,[15] that has manifested itself to him. Within the framework of Melville's extended tale, Captain Amasa Delano serves as a medium of transmission by means of which this encounter with the inconceivable reaches *us,* the reading and thinking public.

So much for the Kantian framework to Melville's novella (Derrida would call it Kant's "frame").[16] Among Melville's splendid achievements in "Benito Cereno" is its encompassing, through literary dramatization, the major achievements of nineteenth-century systematic thought. Our bearings place us in a Hegelian world particularly when we confront the tendentious dimensions of "Benito Cereno." The story situates us on the fronts of multiple wars, whether between races, social classes, spheres of national influence (the Spanish, American, and Senegalese), modes of subjectivity (free individuality or slavery) or metaphysical attitudes ("confidence" as opposed to hypochondria). The compulsion with which antagonistic statuses supplant each other in "Benito Cereno" affirms the necessity of something like Hegelian dialectics during the epoch whose thinking it described and qualified.

The allegory of domination or control in the novella is a complicated one. The story's unsettling quality is not exhausted by the thought that, on one occasion or another, resistant and even imaginative and manipulative slaves were able to usurp control of a ship. More than control of one sea-vessel has been shaken when Don Benito, on the verge of Delano's departure, quakingly informs him, late in the story, that he is *not* free to disembark from his own ship and enter a free American vessel. At this moment, a quintessential social mask, the basis for public "false self," is cast aside.[17] A whole social system has been shaken to the roots, a system in which hypochondria is not merely the foible of certain neurotics, but in which it comprises the enabling legislation for a society founded on repression and exploitation. In "Benito Cereno" slavery is the most compelling instance of the repression keeping the ruling class in place, at the cost of a few displaced symptoms here and there for its members; but it is not the only architectural support to this system. While the novella is replete with illustrations of the "master/slave dialectic," no more graphic than in Babo's shaving his master, the full extent of its Hegelian infrastructure accounts for the repression keeping all hierarchical social orders "afloat," for the dissimulation that structures civil interactions, for the price that under classes pay, most often willingly, for preserving the peace in civil societies.

Melville brings to bear the dissimulation at the basis of the civil order upon the narrative performance of "Benito Cereno." At pivotal moments he effects a marvelous coordination between the thematic exploration of social violence and a performative acting out of narrative duplicity. With Conradian tact he infuses descriptive passages with rhetorical complexity and polemical import. The initial sketch of the *San Dominick* serves in this regard as a fine example.

> Whether the ship had a figure-head, or only a plain beak, was not quite certain, owing to canvas wrapped around that part, either to protect it while undergoing a refurbishing, or else decently to hide its decay. Rudely painted or chalked, as in a sailor freak, along the forward side of a sort of pedestal below the canvas, was the sentence, *"Seguid vuestro jefe,"* (follow your leader); while upon the tarnished headboards, near by, appeared, in stately capitals, once gilt, the ship's name, "SAN DOMINICK," each letter streakingly corroded with tricklings of copper-spike rust; while, like mourning weeds, dark festoons of sea-grass slimily swept to and fro over the name, with every hearse-like roll of the hull. (*PT,* 49)

With a disingenuousness at the full reach of irony, the narrative introjects "Benito Cereno's" vertiginous meditation on power and authority into the innocuous description of the ship's prow: at the outset, the narrative asks whether there is a figurehead on board or not. The ship's disrepair is a pretext for posing the tale's ultimate questions while the reader, with Delano as an intermediary, hovers between blindness and insight into its hidden laws and as yet inarticulate story. The tale makes Lacanian subjects of its protagonist and readers.[18] In the beginning, they are too unschooled in the semiology of subjection and resistance to make sense of the telltale signs. As in *The Confidence-Man,* this text begins with a motto, in whose evolving meaning the fate of the characters and the trajectory of reading is contained: "follow your leader," a simple command made exasperatingly difficult in a post-Cartesian world in which an identifiable Judeo-Christian deity is in retreat, monarchical authority is under siege, and in a colonial setting where the chain of command—whether emanating in Spain or the United States—has been hopelessly attenuated and weakened. A sequence of plant images runs through the story—vegetables that insinuate themselves in loci of physical stress and strategic importance; for example, in the above passage, the sea-grass obscuring the ship's identity. The entire text may be read as a commentary on how exasperatingly difficult it has become, in such a world, to follow the simple command, "Seguid vuestro jefe." Compliance is arbitrary and intolerable (in a situation of competing multiple jurisdictions, who can take credit, exactly, for being "your leader"?); yet non-compliance brings about the horror that Captain Amasa Delano (and in a later tale, the Marlowe of "Heart of Darkness") transmits to the reading public and civil polity.

It is in such a situation of dialectical fluidity that Melville gives us a glance at the basic master-slave diad as it can be pictorially represented at the historical moment of his awareness. The icon of an erect white man accompanied by a lesser black man at his side, a black man of the stature of a domesticated dog, has a certain integrity of its own in Melville's writing. (It is invoked, for example, to describe the operator known as "Black Guinea" in *The Confidence-Man*.)

> The Spanish captain, a gentlemanly, reserved-looking, and rather young man to a stranger's eye, dressed with singular richness, but bearing plain traces of recent sleepless cares and disquietudes, stood passively by, leaning against the main-mast, at one moment casting a dreary, spiritless look upon his excited people, at the next an unhappy glance toward his visitor. By his side stood a black of small stature, in whose rude face, as occasionally, like a shepherd's dog, he mutely turned it up into the Spaniard's, sorrow and affection were equally blended. (*PT,* 51)

Here is a vignette of the relation in which the dominant white man and his black servant stand. This is again the sickly white man, whose dyspepsia is an essential element in the system of dissimulations making the slavery-based civil order possible. The white man's vulnerability and need are fundamental pretexts in the perpetuation of this order; otherwise, why would slaves be necessary? By his side stands, or rather kneels, the black bondsman. The black owes his place in this system to the white man's need; yet his placement in it has been forced; his fidelity to the system is, by all premises of reason, divided.

The arbitrariness of the system bringing master together with slave lends the interaction between these classes a certain aura of unreality. There is a pronounced theatrical quality to Don Benito's staged interactions with Babo. The immediate context for this is, of course, the "horror" of usurped authority that both parties have an interest in hiding. Yet since the slave-system has implications for reaches of the civil order from which it is hidden (as German concentration camps affected civilian life in the cities from which *they* were separated), Don Benito and Babo's staged affirmations of brotherly love comment as well on civility in general during the epoch of mercantile slavery.

In the passage immediately below, Delano joins Don Benito in a professed admiration for the camaraderie and bonhomie of slavery. At the same time that Delano serves as a detached American observer to the situation, in certain respects he also functions as Benito Cereno's double in the story (both, for example, have linguistically Hispanic names). While Benito Cereno undergoes a trajectory of mental absences and recoveries, the American sea captain enters his own rhythm of anxieties and relaxations. Delano is the privileged internal audience in the story to the civil theater of slavery, the domestic drama of mutual compliance upon which its institutional continuity depends:

> Once more the faintness returned—his mind roved—but, recovering, he resumed:
>
> "But it is Babo here to whom, under God, I owe not only my own preservation, but likewise to him, chiefly, the merit is due, of pacifying his more ignorant brethren, when at intervals tempted to murmurings."
>
> "Ah, master," sighed the black, bowing his face, "don't speak of me; Babo is nothing; what Babo has done was but duty."
>
> "Faithful fellow!" cried Captain Delano. "Don Benito, I envy you such a friend; slave I cannot call him."
>
> As master and man stood before him, the black upholding the white, Captain Delano could not but bethink him of the beauty of that relationship which could present such a spectacle of fidelity on the one hand and confidence on the other. The scene was heightened by the contrast in dress. . . . Excepting when his occasional nervous contortions brought about disarray, there was a certain precision in his attire, curiously at variance with the unsightly disorder around; especially in the belittered Ghetto, forward of the main-mast, wholly occupied by the blacks. (57)

This brief interlude, which invokes specifically the Hegelian dialectic of the master and the slave, transpires between the extremities of "fidelity on the one hand and confidence on the other," that is, between feigned compliance and complicity at one extreme and the idealism that powers the progress made by (Western) societies and communities. Yet the public profession of need and appreciation by the master and fidelity by the slave is, precisely, a theater piece: it is described as a "scene." The feigned collaboration between master and bondsman in this scene is reminiscent of the forced amiability between Frank Goodman and Charley Noble late in *The Confidence-Man*. Deep in the bowels of this stage setting reside the blacks, in their "Ghetto."

The masquerade of slavery-based civility and urbanity draws upon a preexisting ideology for its legitimation and engenders a revised ideology of its own. While it is not ideology that rounds up slaves and shackles them in ships (historians estimate that fifteen percent of the individuals captured for slavery died in transit alone), ideology played a decisive role in making commercial practices palatable to the domestic population. In *The Confidence-Man* Melville demonstrates some attentiveness to rationalizations for Indian hunting disseminated on the home front. In this sense, the attitudes that Hegel betrays toward Africa and Africans in *The Philosophy of History* serve as an ideological backdrop to the events and conditions that Delano (and we) are left to interpret. Hegel's role in furnishing an ideological pretext in the endeavor of slavery is as duplicitous as Delano's in the story. Hegel *both* elaborates a schema for world history and progress in which Africa plays at most a supporting role *and* elaborates the formal and structural mechanisms in which power relations (whether between masters and slaves or syntheses and antitheses) are tenuous at best. On the one hand, Hegel consummates the tradition of Western thinking that rewards fidelity to idealism in its theological, scientific, and ontological dimensions.[19] Within this historical framework, the cultures of Egypt, Persia, and India are appropriable because they *anticipate* the ideological fidelity that powers both monotheistic religion and rigorous scientific method. On the other hand, this designation of an *interior* to the homeland faithful to Western idealism relegates the societies not meeting its specifications to the conceptual equivalent of a netherworld. Within the scenario of history as the History of the progressive unfolding of the Idea, the place of Africa is not a very esteemed one. "Africa proper, as far as History goes back, has remained—for all purposes of connection with the rest of the World—shut up; it is the Gold-land compressed within itself—the land of childhood, which lying beyond the day of self-conscious history, is enveloped in the dark mantle of Night" (*PH,* 91), writes Hegel in *The Philosophy of History* (1830–1831).[20]

Hegel consigns Africa to a history of eternal childhood, in which its single positive value is as a treasury of natural resources. Its imprisonment, and by implication, the enslavement of its peoples, is always already predetermined, by virtue of its irreversible withdrawal from the progressive realization of the Idea through the dynamics of self-reflexivity. In effect, argues Hegel, excision from the map of World Culture is just desserts for cultures rejecting the multifaceted gift constituted by progressive, self-originated idealism. Hegel not only places Africa at the margins of the map of World Culture: he accounts for the fate of its peoples:

> The peculiarly African character is difficult to comprehend, for the very reason that in reference to it, we must quite give up the principle which necessarily accompanies our ideas, the category of Universality. In Negro life the characteristic point is the fact that consciousness has not yet attained to the realization of any substantial objective existence. . . . The Negro, as already observed, exhibits the natural man in his completely wild and untamed state. We must lay aside all thought of reverence and morality—all what we call feeling—if we would rightly comprehend him. There is nothing harmonious with humanity to be found in this type of character. (*PH,* 93)

Even allowing for the fact of the increasing schematic bent of Hegel's later writing, there is a remarkable dissonance between the categorical dismissal of Africa and Africans in the above passage and the dialectical complexity that challenges such generalizations, upon which Melville draws in his fictive meditation upon slavery. So horrified is Hegel by a presumed total absence of idealism in African culture that he would place African peoples beyond the pale of humanity. "Benito Cereno" stands astride the same extremities as the Hegelian discourse: on the one hand placing blanket dismissals in the narrative discourse; on the other entertaining the dialectical subtlety constituting the downfall of authority aboard the *San Dominick* and the puncturing of the American sea captain's *confidence.*

So too for the narrator of "Benito Cereno" is the African a child of nature, so ignorant as to bear the caste of the untouchable with relentless and natural good humor; a natural handmaiden or manservant.

> There is something in the negro which, in a most particular way, fits him for avocations about one's person. Most negroes are natural valets and hair-

dressers; taking to the comb and brush congenially as to the castinets, and flourishing them apparently with almost equal satisfaction. There is, too, a smooth tact about them in this employment, with a marvelous, noiseless, gliding briskness, not ungraceful in its way, singularly pleasing to behold, and still more so to be the manipulated subject of. And above all is the great gift of good-humor. Not the mere grin or laugh is here meant. Those were unsuitable. But a certain easy cheerfulness, harmonious in every glance and gesture; as though God had set the whole negro to some pleasant tune.

When to this is added the docility arising from the unaspiring contentment of a limited mind, and that susceptibility of bland attachment sometimes inhering in indisputable inferiors, one readily perceives why those hypochondriacs, Johnson and Byron—it may be something like the hypochondriac, Benito Cereno—took to their hearts, almost to the exclusion of the entire white race, their serving men, the negroes, Barber and Fletcher. . . .

Among other things, he was amused with an odd instance of the African love of bright colors and fine shows, in the black's informally taking from the flag-locker a great piece of bunting of all hues, and lavishly tucking it under his master's chin for an apron. (*PT,* 83–84)

In preparation for a shaving scene in which the full dynamics of the Hegelian master-slave interaction emerge, a bevy of clichés concerning Africans emerges: natural docility and humor, love of music and bright colors; endless generosity in the face of abuse and exploitation.

Melville's fictive exegesis of the institution and dynamics of slavery is divided between its domestic and mercantile/military theaters. Slavery engenders, on the home front, the hypocritical civility enabling (so-constituted) business to go on and confidence, public idealism, to maintain itself. Out in the "field" (the field of the emerging social sciences as well as that of the slave trade), explicit relations of dominance and power still prevail. In the rendition of the story that Hegelian thinking makes possible, the cosmopolitan hypocrisy of slavery reaches a climax in the scene where Babo shaves Benito Cereno, a moment when the narrative does not omit to register the title character's extreme anxiety. When the mask protecting this mutual hypocrisy is penetrated, that is, when Babo and cohorts restrict Don Benito disembarking from his own ship, the time has arrived for the (Western) power underlying the masquerade of slavery to assert itself. Let us remain cognizant of how little (Western) power it takes, even for an outnumbered Delano and a depleted Spanish crew, to subdue the resistant slaves:

Setting down his basin, the negro searched among the razors, as for the sharpest, and having found it, gave it an additional edge by expertly strapping it on the firm, smooth, oily skin of his open palm; he then made a gesture as if to begin, but midway stood suspended for an instant, one hand elevating the razor, the other professionally dabbing among the bubbling suds on the Spaniard's lank neck. Not unaffected by the close sight of the gleaming steel, Don Benito nervously shuddered; his usual ghastliness was heightened by the lather, which lather, again, was intensified in hue by the contrasting sootiness of the negro's body. Altogether the scene was somewhat peculiar, at least to Captain Delano, nor, as he saw the two thus postured, could he resist the vagary, that in the black he saw a headsman, and in the white a man at the block. . . .

Again Don Benito faintly shuddered.

"You must not shake so, master. See, Don Amasa, master always shakes when I shave him. And yet master knows I never yet have drawn blood, though it's true, if master will shake so, I may some of these times. Now master," he continued. "And now, Don Amasa, please go on with your talk about the gale, and all that; master can hear, and, between times, master can answer." (84–85)

In this passage, the subtleties of a masterful literary meditation upon a situation and the institutions making it possible become evident. There is a wonderful counterpoint between the razor suspended in midair, suspended between its servile and aggressive potentials, and Don Benito's congenital (and well-founded) *Angst*. The gravity of the situation punctures the soft playfulness of the soap bubbles. Babo's soothing words have the same effect as the bubbles: they mark at the same time that they soften a severe, even deadly conflict. Babo has never drawn blood, he attests, but that could change at any moment. Henceforth, Delano has to consider quite seriously the possibility that "master and man, for some unknown purpose, were acting out, both in word and deed . . . some juggling play before him" (87).

The dramatic climax of the novella may be described as an unmasking of the uneasy social contract prevailing on board (a microcosm of slavery-based economies) coinciding with a sudden semiological clarification. The cat is let out of the bag as far as power relations are concerned when Benito Cereno blurts out, "This plotting pirate means murder!" (98), precipitating the scuffle that leads to Babo's demise. Yet a number of other meanings receive clarification at this revelatory moment as well. Indeed, one of Captain Delano's major roles as an exemplary speculative and Kantian subject has been his encounter with gestures and other signs of dubious and possibly malevolent signification. Among these I would have to catalogue the inscription "Seguid vuestro jefe" (49, 99, 117); the "imperfect gesture" made by a Spanish sailor as he advanced toward the balcony (74, 79, 110); and above all, the uncanny percussive chorus of the oakum pickers, presumably in the act of cleaning their hatchets (50, 59, 79–80, 96).

It is precisely where the exemplary speculative subjects of Romanticism become exegetes of sign-systems that the seeds of Modernism, with its Saussurian insistence on the priority of signs over any significations they may "contain," are planted. It is the achievement of Romantic theory to place the subject on two parallel but divergent paths: toward speculation, carrying the classical accoutrements of subjective metaphysics; and in the midst of a play of signs, a rigorous aesthetics, from which this baggage has been jettisoned. The modernist works that we remember for their distinctive style took their cue from this second pathway that Romanticism cleared.

The dramatic climax of the story coincides with a renunciation of "all but the last appearance of courtesy" on the imprisoned Spanish sea captain's part (94). The dropping of pretenses constitutes a consummation for the novella's Hegelian allegory:

> Glancing down at his feet, Captain Delano saw the freed hand of the servant aiming with a second dagger—a small one, before concealed in his wool—with this he was snakishly writhing up from the boat's bottom, at the heart of his master, his countenance lividly vindictive, expressing the centred purpose of his soul; while the Spaniard, half-choked, was vainly shrinking away, with husky words, incoherent to all but the Portuguese.
>
> That moment, across the long-benighted mind of Captain Delano, a flash of revelation swept, illuminating, in unanticipated clearness, his host's whole mysterious demeanor, with every enigmatic event of the day, as well as the entire past voyage of the *San Dominick*. He smote Babo's hand down, but his own heart smote him harder. With infinite pity he withdrew his hold from Don Benito. Not Captain Delano, but Don Benito, the black, had intended to stab. (99)

The final sentence in this graphic description leaves the direct objects of its actions as well as its intended victim unclear. It may be that the black had really intended to stab Don Benito; but a singular syntax demonstrates that the black as well as the American could well have succumbed to a hateful wound. It takes no more than a slap from a white man's hand to quell a slave uprising. At the moment when relations of power become clear, an entire aesthetic configuration of signs and symbols falls into place. Indeed mystification, within the framework of this novella, is a function of a deliberate obscurantism regarding conditions of authority and power. This is Melville very much in synch with a certain polemic in Marx.[21]

Yet for the story to achieve its dramatic force, its horror (whether one of usurped power or impenetrable signs) must be depicted in terms intelligible to the hegemonic class.

> Both the black's hands were held, as, glancing up towards the *San Dominick*, Captain Delano, now with the scales dropped from his eyes, saw the negroes, not in misrule, not in tumult, not as if frantically concerned for Don Benito, but with mask torn away, flourishing hatchets and knives, in ferocious piratical revolt. Like delirious black dervishes, the six Ashantees danced on the poop. Prevented by their foes from springing into the water, the Spanish boys were hurrying up to the topmost spars, while such of the few Spanish sailors, not already in the sea, less alert, were descried, helplessly mixed in, on deck, with the blacks. (*PT,* 99)

For *us,* reading in 1995, in the wake of Saussure and Kafka and Joyce and Stein and Barthes and Derrida and Riddel, a crisis in signification may be an adequate and ultimate horror for this novella. But Melville, writing at a certain time and for a specific readership, chose to paint the story's threat as a dance of crazed dervishes, with the winsome colonial boys in retreat. Yet the orientalist stage props do not obscure the fact that Melville has set his chief surrogate, Captain Amasa Delano, out on the treacherous double path on which the post-Cartesian subject negotiates the delirium of aesthetics while s/he bears the baggage of existence and metaphysics. The novella's Hegelian framework could *both* generate categories and generalizations so crude as to be laughable *and* account for the subtle dynamics of shifts in power, logic, and intellectual discrimination applying to the oppressed as well as the oppressors.

There is no more telling indication of the novella's semiological crisis, the manner in which it anticipates modernist aesthetics, than the play within its system of naming. I have already noted how the Hispanic surnames of Cereno and Delano mirror each other. Melville demonstrates in this text that irony does not rely upon a theatrics of subterfuge and debunking; the act of naming is complicated enough to open powerful registers of irony.

Like Hawthorne, Melville draws upon plays of naming as a significant fictive resource. He draws our attention to this fact, just as, in a wider sense, through Delano he makes us aware of suspicious conditions aboard the *San Dominick. Naming* can participate in a certain complicity just as individual agents do. Melville does not allow us to pass over the ironic potential in Don Benito's name in total ignorance:

That strange ceremoniousness, too, at other times evinced, seemed not unchar-
acteristic of one playing a part above his real level. Benito Cereno—Don Benito
Cereno—a sounding name. One, too, at that period, not unknown, in the sur-
name, to supercargoes and sea captains trading along the Spanish Main, as
belonging to one of the most enterprising and extensive mercantile families in
all those provinces; several members of it having titles; a sort of Castilian Roth-
schild, with a noble brother, or cousin, in every great trading town of South
America. (64)

Not unlike the Joycean notion of "soundsense,"[22] Benito Cereno is pos-
sessed of "a sounding name." The narrative here gives us leave to read sense
into sound, specifically, to register the "serenity" infused into Don Benito's
name even if it is not orthographically evident. Within the sphere of
romance languages, then, the name Benito Cereno translates into something
like "the good, serene one." Given that the title character is too beleaguered
to be serene and too debilitated to be good, this appellation is nothing if not
an ironic one.

Yet it is into the American counterpart's name that Melville compresses,
in the sense of the Freudian *Mischwort* or condensation, the greatest complexity and irony.[23]

"What I, Amasa Delano—Jack of the Beach, as they called me when a lad—
I, Amasa; the same that, duck-satchel in hand, used to paddle along the water-
side to the school-house made from the old hulk—I, little Jack of the Beach, that
used to go berrying with cousin Nat and the rest; I to be murdered here at the
ends of the earth, on board a haunted pirate-ship by a horrible Spaniard? Too
nonsensical to think of! Who would murder Amasa Delano?" (*PT,* 77)

Ironically, the brief swatch of text giving us the greatest insight into
Delano's name is the only moment in the novella even approaching autobiographical reminiscence. At this single point in the narrative we are afforded a glimpse of the sailor as a young man. There was a "touch of the
artist" about Amasa who, as a child, already encompassed a fictive double.
Underlying the adult speculative navigator resides the artist as a young man.
This point is brought home irrefutably by the brief exclamation, "I—
Amasa." A bit of play with this strange name—disjointing it—produces the
phrase, "I am as a," the very basis for the hypothetical individual, the person who lives in the possibilities of art rather than through the empirical
facts. Amasa is also "a massa," a Master. To be hypothetical about slavery,
to see it but not to see it at the same time; not to be engaged in it as either

the Master or the Slave, and therefore to be free to be indecisive about it—this is precisely the position of mastery on the home front. It is in this sense, as well as in others, that Amasa is also "a massa."

The name Amasa Delano links, then, the play of the possible to the detachment of seeing *de loin*, from far away. Captain Delano is disquieted by the conditions and events he observes not only because of the double messages in the empirical data, but also because he, quintessentially, in name, is a hypothetical subject, a creature whose possibility defines his margin or range. This is the position, in modern-day psychoanalytical theory, of the "as if" personality, the subject whose narcissism predicates an endless deferral of self-definition.[24] Politically as well as fictively, Delano functions at most as a hypothesis.

The novella fatefully links two sea captains, one Spanish, the other North American. One cannot fulfill the good serenity in his name; the other realizes only too fully a hypothetical approach to some concrete problems: slavery, the exploitation implicit in mercantile economics. The story transpires between an impossible goodness and a detached hypothesis, two counterversions of idealism severed from the tangible conditions it otherwise might have amplified and reformed.

In at least two powerful senses, then, Melville's novella issues from the very crossroads of the nineteenth century. It serves as a fictive interface between predominant Kantian and Hegelian scenarios for intellection, interpretation, and subjectivity. And in its tendentious dimension, the minute attention it devotes to conditions of power and authority, it combines the speculative awareness of romantic literature and theory with the realistic depiction of social conditions that will become one characteristic feature of nineteenth-century European and U.S. fiction. "Benito Cereno" manages to place the Kantian scenario of the penetration of everyday, empirical constraints by the sublime, the aesthetic facet of the Transcendental, in contact with an exquisite Hegelian sensitivity to the reversals implicit in every situation of power, whether physical, logical, or political. The fictive investigation of slavery and its domestic ramifications that Melville undertakes in this novella is rigorous and far reaching. *Fidelity* is a charged term in the Melvillian lexicon. Melville's fidelity to his investigation enables "Benito Cereno" to chart a course *between* the metaphysics of romantic fiction and the social realism of, among others, Balzac, Crane, and Zola. (Needless to say, for the sake of its own comprehensibility, there is a powerful metaphysical element to nineteenth-century social realism.)

"Benito Cereno" may be described as the *between* that illuminates what falls on both sides of its wake. It arises *between* nineteenth-century speculative models, races, spheres of colonial influence, modes of economy (slavery and abolition), epochs of literary production, and theoretical bearings (metaphysics and language-oriented aesthetics). This *between* is an impasse at the same time that it is a fulcrum with access to enormous power. There is no way out of it. At most, any way out of it is a ruse, a dissimulation again harkening back to the epoch of irony, which persists from Plato to the postmodern indifference that disqualifies it by dissolving its constitutive differences between levels of knowledge.

Melville himself must resort to ruse in feigning a way out of "Benito Cereno's" imprisoning (if not enslaving) system of intermediary locations. And his strategem, in keeping with his epistemological moment, corresponds to a "flight into art," giving aesthetics the final word, ascribing the ultimate indeterminacy to the freedoms and rights pertaining to the aesthetic enterprise. Do note that this way out is itself conditioned by features of education, social class, and the intended audience.

Into the network of his novella, Melville has incorporated representations of slavery, colonialism, oppression, and duplicity, images still remarkably powerful today. But his recourse, in closing off his fictive system, is to remind his readership that the text is a narrative, comprised of narratives by its characters. Explicit fictionality is both the pretext and the horizon for this literary work.

Early enough in the novella when he can still entertain doubts about the bizarre collation of facts confronting him, Delano can muse on the status of Benito Cereno's narrative.

> He recalled the Spaniard's manner while telling his story. There was a gloomy hesitancy and subterfuge about it. It was just the manner of one making up his tale for evil purposes, as he goes. But if that story was not true, what was the truth? That the ship had unlawfully come into the Spaniard's possession? But in many of its details . . . Don Benito's story had been corroborated not only by the wailing ejaculations of the indiscriminate multitude, white and black, but likewise—what seemed impossible to be counterfeit—by the very expression and play of every human feature, which Captain Delano saw. If Don Benito's story was, throughout, an invention, then every soul on board, down to the youngest

negress, was his carefully drilled recruit in the plot; an incredible inference. And yet, if there was a ground for mistrusting his veracity, that inference was a legitimate one. (*PT*, 68–69)

In this passage, Captain Delano weighs the advantages and costs of believing a story. To accept Don Benito's account of the unusual conditions on board is to swallow, on the side, some implausible attestations; but the alternative to this possibility amounts to not only a dimissal of certain explanations but a renunciation of civility itself. It would be uncivil, beyond the norms of domesticity, to reject, in the absence of incontrovertible evidence, the representations of a fellow officer and gentleman. Credulity is a civic virtue; this is the hinge linking the making and reading of fiction to the dynamics of public life. *Not* to accept Don Benito's account is to posit that "every soul on board, down to the youngest negress [the pecking order of statuses is telling here] was his carefully drilled recruit in the plot: an incredible inference" (69). Civic duty and fiction, then, demand diametrically opposed ideals. Critical awareness *demands* the skepticism constituting, in terms of interpersonal equanimity, bad faith.

"Benito Cereno" ends in the form of a transcript of a legal proceeding. Both the deliberation itself and its certified record should resolve the crises in knowledge and social conscience that the related events have initiated. It is possible for written documents to arrive at a more authentic draft of events and conditions than has previously been available; yet the form of the document, the choice of *genre* alone, does not silence the questions to which the web of social conditions and responses has given rise. In *The Confidence-Man* and elsewhere, Melville attests to the centrality of credulity as a civic value. At the end of "Benito Cereno" he offers his readership a legal transcript as a means of definitively establishing the facts, as a pretext for shelving any persistent doubts. Yet at the same time that he holds out to his readers this formal device for achieving resolution, he couches the tale's ending in a rhetoric of endless reversal.

Melville concludes "Benito Cereno" in the *form* of legalistic determination but in the *language* of interminable fictionality. He thus pits his literary medium *against* the forms or genres of certifiable knowledge. Rhetoric and form are at each other's throats as this extended tale brings itself to an end, perhaps explaining the indeterminacy that must serve as the text's excuse for an ending. Neither fiction nor "objective reportage" are exempt from censure and suspicion in this terminal battle of discursive modes. A legal transcript may bear witness to a slave uprising otherwise hidden from public view, but its exaggerated pretense to authority may impose closure on questions whose urgency derives precisely from a fictive presentation. Fictionality, on the other hand, may bring questions of sustained moral indeterminacy to public attention; yet the aestheticization of violence and repression may, as Melville indicates, domesticate and legitimize these phenomena. Melville would appeal to overt fictionality and objective reportage in attempting to bring his tale to some satisfying conclusion, yet the compromises at play both in fictional allegory and in purportedly objective report aggravate the hermeneutic and moral indeterminacies.

It is in this context that the narrative, in reaching for its ending, adapts a rhetoric of deliberate fictionality at the same time that it would presume to limit the play of fiction through the assumption of non-fictive (*e.g.*, legalistic) discursive forms. "Hitherto the nature of this narrative, besides rendering the intricacies in the beginning unavoidable, has more or less required that many things, instead of being set down in the order of occurrence, should be retrospectively, or irregularly given; this last is the case with the following passages, which will conclude the account" (114).

Indeed, it is only with a sense of utter dissatisfaction that one can approach, or even speak of any *resolution* to "Benito Cereno." The resolution of the plot consists in a hopeless standoff; this standoff may constitute the consummation, the final *Aufhebung,* of any comment the novella can render upon its age. It is possible to formulate the impasse that emerges from our final glimpses of Don Benito Cereno and Babo, the intractible slave, in several ways. We can think of Don Benito, the personification of European idealism, relegated to silence by the subversive agent who seduces and overturns him. Yet we are never afforded the possibility of viewing the insurrection from the perspective of those who initiated it. Babo is in effect elided from the legal transcript, disenfranchised from uttering an account of the events as they impacted upon the slave cargo. If silence reigns at the end of the novella, the silence of an endlessly repeated and hopeless argument, this is in part the silence reigning in a Western metaphysics long-primed for ghosts and marginal, threatening blackness, in part the silence of the disenfranchised.

There was no more conversation that day.
But if the Spaniard's melancholy sometimes ended in muteness upon topics like the above, there were others upon which he never spoke at all; on which,

indeed, all his old reserves were piled. Pass over the worst, and, only to eluci-date, let an item or two of these be cited. The dress, so precise and costly, worn by him on the day whose events have been narrated, had not willingly been put on. And that silver-mounted sword, apparent symbol of despotic command, was not, indeed, a sword, but the ghost of one. The scabbard, artificially stiffened, was empty. (116)

It is best if we depart from this interpretation of Melville's story—as a critical commentary on its age deploying both the major speculative systems and aesthetic liberties available to it—with the final substantial image that the author offers us. Don Benito and Babo—relegated to counterversions of definitive silence, exile from the discourse of social negotiation—complete their trajectories locked in a petrified gaze. Melville has afforded us access to this very gaze, upon a set of intractable human conditions. Even in death, Babo's decapitated head gazes upon a society that has accorded him a pur-gatorial status. Given the skew of the powerful social forces and counter-forces perpetuating an untenable status quo, his mute and vacuous stare, with its attentiveness beyond death, may constitute the most radical response available to him as a figment of the literary artifact.

As for the black—whose brain, not body, had schemed and led the revolt, with the plot—his slight frame, inadequate to that which it held, had at once yielded to the superior muscular strength of his captor, in the boat. Seeing all was over, he uttered no sound, and could not be forced to. His aspect seemed to say, since I cannot do deeds, I will not speak words. . . .

Some months after, dragged to the gibbet at the tail of a mule, the black met his voiceless end. The body was burned to ashes; but for many days, the head, that hive of sublety, fixed on a pole in the Plaza, met, unabashed, the gazes of the whites; and across the Plaza looked toward St. Bartholomew's church, in whose vaults slept then, as now, the recovered bones of Aranda: and across the Rimac bridge looked towards the monastery, on Mount Agonia without; where, three months after being dismissed by the court, Benito Cereno, borne on the bier, did, indeed, follow his leader. (116–17)

EDGAR A. DRYDEN

Mute Monuments and Doggerel Epitaphs: Melville's Shattered Sequels

Like all youths, Pierre had conned his novel-lessons; had read more novels than most persons of his years; but their false, inverted attempts at systematizing eternally unsystemizable elements; their audacious, intermeddling impotency, in trying to unravel, and spread out, and classify, the more thin than gossamer threads which make up the complex web of life; these things over Pierre had no power now. . . . By infallible presentiment he saw, that not always doth life's beginning gloom conclude in gladness; that wedding-bells peal not ever in the last scene of life's fifth act; that while the countless tribes of common novels laboriously spin vails of mystery, only to complacently clear them up at last; and while the countless tribe of common dramas do but repeat the same; yet the profounder emanations of the human mind, intended to illustrate all that can be humanly known of human life; these never unravel their own intricacies, and have no proper endings; but in imperfect, unanticipated, and disappointing sequels (as mutilated stumps), hurry to abrupt intermergings with the eternal tides of time and fate.[1]

The symmetry of form attainable in pure fiction cannot so readily be achieved in a narration essentially having less to do with fable than with fact. Truth uncompromisingly told will always have its ragged edges; hence the conclusion of such a narration is apt to be less finished than an architectural finial.

How it fared with the Handsome Sailor during the year of the Great Mutiny has been faithfully given. But though properly the story ends with his life, something in the way of sequel will not be amiss. Three brief chapters will suffice. (*Billy Budd*, 128)

Herman Melville, like his young hero in *Pierre,* is troubled by the problems raised by those complicated boundary lines that mark the limits between the literary text and that which lies beyond its borders. From *Moby-Dick* on, the primary theoretical difficulty inherent in his writing involves the question of the "whatness" of literature, and that issue is directly related to the question of literary form, for "form" is the term traditionally used to designate the borderlines of literature. "In literature," Paul de Man writes, "the concept of form is, before anything else, a definitional necessity. No literary metadiscourse would ever be conceivable in its absence. . . . This does not mean, however, that the concept of form is itself susceptible of definition."[2] For Melville, as for de Man, the concept is theoretically central to any attempt to ascribe epistemological authority to aesthetic experience. As "Hawthorne and His Mosses" makes clear, Melville, at this point in his career, sees the boundary between literature and philosophy, between the poetic and epistemological, as a fluid and negotiable one. "For by philosophers," he writes, "Shakespeare is not adored as the great man of tragedy and comedy.—'Off with his head! so much for Buckingham!' this sort of rant, interlined by another hand, brings down the house,—those mistaken souls, who dream of Shakespeare as a mere man of Richard-the-Third humps, and Macbeth daggers. But it is those deep faraway things in him; those occasional flashings-forth of the intuitive Truth in him; those short, quick probings at the very axis of reality;—these are the things that make Shakespeare, Shakespeare" (*PT,* 244). This emphasis on the hermeneutical aspect of literature and on the related activities of an "eagle-eyed reader" would seem to have the effect of undermining any attempt to establish a poetics of literary form, for it undoes the notions of self-sufficiency and self-referentiality that identify the literary as such (251).

In the epigraph from *Pierre* the focus is on an essential difference between two kinds of texts. The first remains true to the traditional notion of narrative, which consists of a complication and an unraveling or denouement. These are works that to the novel's newly disenchanted hero seemed to be filled with "speculative lies," for they attempt to systematize "eternally unsystematizable elements," "to unravel, spread out, and classify the more thin than gossamer threads which make up the complex web of life." The pleasures of closure, of untying and resolving, those that come with the triumph of form over content and produce the secure sense of the aesthetic unity of the whole are at once seductive and inauthentic. But the "profounder emanations of the human mind" offer no such mystifications, for they have no "proper endings" but are always followed by "imperfect, unanticipated, and disappointing sequels," hence can never be said to be unequivocally finished. The "sequel" as a continuation or extension of the narrative explodes its borders and destroys the myth of its self-sufficiency, for it suggests that the narrative proper does not suffice. It follows what ought properly to close itself, undermines the proper as such, and in that sense is the sign of a contamination of literary language by other forms of discourse. At the point the narrative is supposed to end, there appears something else, something that enables the narrative but which is not present in its represented or articulated meaning. Not even death offers the possibility of a definitive ending, for there either remains some chance survivor to continue the story by providing the dead with voices and names or, as in the case of Poe's "Manuscript Found in a Bottle," an intrusive account or explanation of the survival of the text. Or to put the point as John Irwin does, "the very mechanics of written narration . . . excludes the written narrative from any access to the absolute."[3]

In *Moby-Dick* one of Ahab's unnamed oarsmen, hurled from the boat during the final encounter with the white whale, remains "afloat and swimming" *"on the margin of the ensuing scene"* and reappears in the Epilogue as Ishmael, *"another orphan"* who has "'escaped alone to tell thee'" (*Moby-Dick*, 569, 573). *"The drama's done. Why then here does any one step forth?—Because one did survive the wreck"* (573). However, the Epilogue is not presented as proper ending or exemplary conclusion, the end point toward which the story has been moving and which will provide a retrospective unity for the whole. Rather, as Ishmael suggests in the "Castaway" chapter, it stands outside the narrative proper and is an imperfect or mutilated supplement to it. "The thing [Pip's abandonment] is common in that fishery; and in the sequel of the narrative, it will then be seen what like abandonment befell myself" (414). This proleptic mention of the Epilogue in the body of the text is a formal anticipation of that which will violate the symmetry of form, an inscription within the narrative of that which will mark an exit from it. For the sequel succeeds or follows the narrative proper in the form of residue or flotsam. Without a proper place or name, the orphaned Ishmael survives as one of those "queer castaway creatures found tossing about the open sea on planks, bits of wreck, oars, whale-boats, canoes, blown-off Japanese junks, and what not," and it is he who will tell the tale of death and destruction and speak the terrible truth of his own abandonment (230–31). And that story, as is traditionally the case with first-person narratives, is presented as a form of recollection—"now that I recall all the circumstances, I think I can see a little into the springs and motives which being cunningly presented to me under various disguises, induced me to set about performing the part I did"; but it is a recollection that, like Pip's transforming experience, is also a prophecy (7). "It was but some few days after encountering the Frenchman, that a most significant event befell the most insignificant of the Pequod's crew; an event most lamentable; and which ended in providing the sometimes madly merry and predestinated craft with a living and ever accompanying prophecy of whatever shattered sequel might prove her own" (411).

This passage, the first paragraph of "The Castaway," anticipates that chapter's final one (cited above) where Ishmael associates Pip's abandonment with his own. Pip's experience here seems anticipatory or prefigurative—its end provides a living prophecy—but that is a quality that it gains retrospectively when read in the light of the novel's "shattered sequel." The act of anticipating and the act of remembering seem entangled in such a way that it is impossible to distinguish one from the other. From the perspective of the Epilogue, "The Castaway," like the Cowper poem that it echoes, is an extended epitaph which, like the memorial tablets in the Whaleman's Chapel, seems to "refuse resurrections to the beings who have placelessly perished without a grave" (36). But the Epilogue, as a sequel to the narrative, deprives that narrative of the architectural or monumental quality that a story that properly ends with life would have and puts into question the traditional view of first-person narrative as a "discourse of self-restoration."[4] For while Ishmael's narrative strategy seems to allow him figuratively to experience his own death by anticipation (*cf.* "The Hyena") and to write the epitaph that, in Wordsworth's words, will assure that "some part of our nature is imperishable," the "shattered sequel" that improperly ends his account makes it clear that he can only represent death as something that happened to someone else in the past.[5] As Paul de Man has said, "it is always possible to anticipate one's own epitaph . . . but never possible to be both the one who wrote it and the one who reads it in the proper setting, that is, confronting one's grave as an event of the past.[6] The sleight of hand that permits Ishmael the feeling that he "survive[s] [himself]" by writing his will—"my death and burial were locked up in my chest. I looked round me tranquilly and contentedly, like a quiet ghost with a clean conscience sitting inside the bars of a snug family vault" (*Moby-Dick*, 228)—is a trick of rhetorical substitution that leaves one's trace in writing, a process that is analogous to the one described by the *Pequod's* carpenter when he is asked to convert Queequeg's coffin into a life buoy.

> Are all my pains to go for nothing with that coffin? And now I'm ordered to make a life-buoy of it. It's like turning an old coat; going to bring the flesh on the other side now. I don't like this cobbling sort of business—I don't like it at all; it's undignified; it's not my place. Let tinkers' brats do tinkerings; we are their betters. I like to take in hand none but clean, virgin, fair-and-square mathematical jobs, something that regularly begins at the beginning, and is at the middle when midway, and comes to an end at the conclusion; not a cobbler's job, that's at an end in the middle, and at the beginning at the end. (525)

To convert a coffin into a life buoy is to take a "dreaded symbol of grim death" and to transform it into an "expressive sign of the help and hope of the most endangered life," to perform an act that crosses and confuses borderlines in a way that suggests Ishmael's strategy in "The Castaway" (528). Pip's abandonment at once results in the death of his conscious self (signified by the disappearance of the personal pronoun, "I")—"'base little Pip, he died a coward'" (480) and offers a living prophecy or prefiguration of the "shattered sequel" that takes the form of Ishmael's Epilogue. But it is only from the perspective of this sequel that Pip's experience achieves its significance. It is Ishmael's later awareness of the sense in which his abandonment repeats Pip's that imaginatively reconstitutes Pip's experience long after Pip's death. And just as Pip's experiences in the "middle of . . . a heartless immensity" result in the substitution of a third-person subject for a first-person subject, Ishmael's exposure to that same "awful lonesomeness" (414) leads him to put Pip and an unnamed oarsman in the place of "I." This is to say that Ishmael's narrative like the carpenter's art is a "cobbling sort of business," that is at the end in the middle, and at the beginning at the end, apparently at once coffin and life buoy. On the one hand, Ishmael, orphan and castaway, like the *Pequod's* blacksmith, seems a man with a "career" for which "death [is] the only desirable sequel" (486). But death is mute and signless, the absolute end, and Ishmael's Epilogue, like Queequeg's transformed coffin, is an emblem of the space beyond death that is literature. Ahab "voicelessly" vanishes, and the rest of the crew soon follow as the "smallest chip of the Pequod" is carried out of sight and covered by the "great shroud of the sea" (572). But the silence that marks the drama's end is broken by the voice of the lone survivor, who will tell the story of those who are now dead, a process emblematized by Queequeg's coffin life buoy, covered with the same "hieroglyphic marks" that on his body had seemed destined "to moulder away with the living parchment whereon they were inscribed" (481). As it rises from the center of the vortex to serve as a life buoy for Ishamel as well as a written record of his bosom friend, we are reminded that Ishmael will return to write the book in which Queequeg is resurrected in the form of a written character. But we are reminded too that the book, like the coffin life buoy, will be the product of a "cobbling sort of business" and will not possess the quiet dignity and formal purity of an epitaph or a monument. Such a dignity and purity are suggested by the final lines of the narrative proper: "Now small fowls flew screaming over the yet yawning gulf; a sullen white surf beat against its steep sides; then all collapsed, and the great shroud of the sea rolled on as it rolled five thousand years ago" (572). The quiet seriousness of these lines suggests that the entire novel, like the six-inch chapter that is the "stoneless grave of Bulkington," is a monument that provides the dead with a final resting-place and stands in its self-sufficient symmetry as an example of perfect closure (106). But the sense of repose is disturbed by Ishmael's resurrected and resurrecting voice, which offers a sequel to the narrative and provides the logic for and forecasts its writing.

The tension here between the impulse to close and the felt need "to tell" is an enabling one and suggests that Melville has found a way to integrate a poetics and a hermeneutics of literature. *"The drama's done. Why then here does any one step forth?—Because one did survive the wreck"* (573). And this survivor is the voice of the text, that personifying figure that unfreezes pure inscription and resuscitates the natural breath of language. However, as the troubling eccentricities of *Pierre* suggest, the creative tensions of *Moby-Dick* are not easily sustained. "The End" of that later novel offers an illuminating contrast to *Moby-Dick*'s Epilogue, for it makes us aware of the extent to which Ishmael's voice is a figure that disguises a muteness. Here the eponymous hero, his own "vile book" unfinished, and having "extinguished his house in slaughtering the only unoutlawed human being by the name of Glendinning," sits alone in his dungeon and speculates on the meaning of his shattered life (*Pierre,* 348, 360).

> "Here, then, is the untimely, timely end;—Life's last chapter well stitched into the middle! Nor book, nor author of the book, hath any sequel, though each hath its own last lettering!—It is ambiguous still. . . . I long and long to die, to be rid of this dishonored cheek. *Hung by the neck till thou be dead.*—Not if I

forestall you, though!—Oh now to live is death, and now to die is life; now, to my soul, were a sword my midwife!" (360)

Pierre's language here echoes that of the *Pequod*'s carpenter as he works to transform a sign of death into an instrument of life, like turning an old coat he says, thereby bringing the flesh to the other side or stitching the middle into the end. But here there is no coffin life buoy; *Pierre* has no sequel and hence it ends voicelessly, "dumb as death" in the realm of the dead letter (115). Lucy shrinks up "like a scroll, and noiselessly [falls] at the feet of Pierre"; Delly is left a "lone dumb thing," wringing her "speechless hands"; Pierre dies silently, as his hands make one "speechless clasp"; and the final words of the novel come ambiguously from the stone walls of the prison (360, 361, 362). "'All's o'er, and ye know him not!' came gasping from the wall; and from the fingers of Isabel dropped an empty vial—as if it had been a run-out sand-glass—and shivered upon the floor; and her whole form sloped sideways, and she fell upon Pierre's heart, and her long hair ran over him, and arbored him in ebon vines" (362).

Here as in *Moby-Dick* the "curtain . . . falls upon a corpse" (197), but in this case there is no "great shroud of the sea" to provide a decent burial and no resurrected "I" with the power of naming and speaking. Of course we know only the assumed name of *Moby-Dick*'s storyteller, but it is one richly allusive and suggestive. By the end of *Pierre*, however, the hero's family name has been extirpated and his given name reduced to its literal meaning, as his corpse is figuratively transformed into a silent, stony ruin, "arbored . . . in ebon vines." This is a transformation that at once acknowledges and ironizes the Wordsworthian epitaphic gesture that gives "to the language of the senseless stone a voice enforced and endeared by the benignity of that nature with which it was in unison."[7] And in so doing it completes a system of figuration that is announced at the beginning of the novel and developed throughout, a system that consists of a chain of analogies linking together the acts of inscribing and interring and associating them with the vain attempts to represent the unrepresentable, name the unnamable, and conceptualize the inconceivable. Controlling the system is the figure of voice, a conception that confers upon absent, deceased, or voiceless entities the power of speech. For Melville, Wordsworth's famous conceit of the "speaking face of earth and heaven" is a "dark similitude" that is "sweet in the orator's mouth, [but] bitter in the thinker's belly" (*Pierre*, 42).[8] For in his world nature and heaven are mute and featureless.

In that wet and misty eve the scattered, shivering pasture elms seemed standing in a world inhospitable, yet rooted by inscrutable sense of duty to their place. Beyond, the lake lay in one sheet of blankness and of dumbness, unstirred by breeze or breath; fast bound there it lay, with not enough life to reflect the smallest shrub or twig. Yet in that lake was seen the duplicate, stirless sky above. Only in sunshine did that lake catch gay, green images; and these but displaced the imaged muteness of the unfeatured heavens. (109)

Here is a world where the human being is precisely not at home, a motionless, faceless, voiceless realm where an "unstirred lake" reflects a "stirless sky." Nature does not mirror the human face or echo the human voice but duplicates as it reflects the "muteness of the unfeatured heavens." It is through this mute and faceless world that Pierre wanders as he prepares himself to hear the "story of the face," that "face that must shortly meet his own" (37, 111). And Isabel's face is precisely a speaking face, a "fearful gospel" that will refigure as it disfigures Pierre's world (43). This emphasis on spoken language is important, for Melville is aware of the extent to which both face and voice are products of language's "talismanic" power. Since the "vast halls of Silent Truth" are inhabited by the "Wonderful Mutes" and "Silence is the only Voice of our God," speech becomes a fiction that masks a silence (244, 204). "That profound Silence, that only Voice of our God, which I before spoke of; from that divine thing without a name, those imposter philosophers pretend somehow to have got an answer; which is as absurd, as though they should say they had got water out of stone; for how can a man get a Voice out of Silence?" (208). *Pierre* exposes the "talismanic secret" whereby the fiction of divine speech is maintained. By linking together the "sculptured woes" of Memnon, Moses' account of his conversations with God on Mount Sinai, the Gospels' representation of Christ's "first wise words . . . in his first speech to men," and Pierre's abortive attempts to "gospelize the world anew," the novel systematically dispells the spell of voice that seeks to maintain itself by effacing the difference between the human and the natural (91, 273).

The natural as such always appears in the form of "horrible and inscrutable inhumanities," imaged in the form of the "dark-dripping rocks, and mysterious mouths of wolfish caves" that surround Pierre's ancestral home (122, 343). Among the "enormous rocky masses" is a "demonic freak of nature," a huge mass of rock, an "American Enceladus, wrought by the vigorous hand of Nature's self" (345, 346). This "sphinx-like shape" appears in the text in the form of a "remarkable dream or vision" that

Pierre experiences during a "state of semi-unconsciousness," a dream that seems a "horrible foretaste of death itself" (345, 342).

> Such was the wild scenery, which now to Pierre, in his strange vision, displaced the four blank walls, the desk, and camp-bed, and domineered upon his trance. . . .
>
> "Enceladus! it is Enceladus!"—Pierre cried out in his sleep. That moment the phantom faced him; and Pierre saw Enceladus no more; but on the Titan's armless trunk, his own duplicate face and features magnifiedly gleamed upon him with prophetic discomfiture and woe. . . .
>
> Nor did Pierre's random knowledge of the ancient fables fail still further to elucidate the vision which so strangely had supplied a tongue to muteness. But that elucidation was most repulsively fateful and foreboding; possibly because Pierre . . . did not flog this rock as Moses his, and force even aridity itself to quench his painful thirst. (346)

Pierre's remarkable dream is a displacement that is initiated when the "actual artificial objects around him slid from him, and were replaced by a baseless yet most imposing spectacle of natural scenery" (342). And this initial displacement is followed by another, for the rock in its "untouched natural state" is just its senseless self (345). Self-contained, fixed, anchored to its place, it does not stand in the place of anything else. But in Pierre's vision it ceases to be itself by becoming a sign for something that is absent. And that sign itself takes the form of an interpretive response to the dreamer's paralyzing anxiety concerning his authorial and familial crises. By inscribing a name and face on a senseless stone, giving sight to blind eyes and a "tongue to muteness," the vision illustrates the talismanic act that brings fictions into the world by turning things into what they are not. But that act is a double-edged one. Melville implies that when the writer inscribes himself on nature and makes it into an emblem, he creates a sign that prefigures his own death. Hence when Pierre sees his own "face and features" on the stone, we and he are made to understand that he will take on its same mute fixity.

The logic of this complicated process is rooted in the important role that stones play in Melville's imagination. "We read a good deal about stones in Scriptures," he writes. "Monuments & stumps of the memorials are set up of stones; men are stoned to death; the figurative seed falls in stony places; and no wonder that stones should so largely figure in the Bible. Judea is one accumulation of stones—Stony mountains & stony plains; stony torrents & stony roads; stony walls & stony fields, stony houses & stony tombs; stony eyes & stony hearts" (*Journals,* 90). These stones neither hear nor speak, and yet in the Bible they are systematically represented as doing so. Indeed, according to Moses, God "[*He*] *is* the Rock" (Deuteronomy 32:4) and from its silence Moses' song flows: "Give ear, O ye heavens, and I will speak; and hear O earth, the words of my mouth. My doctrine shall drop as the rain, my speech shall distil as the dew, as the small rain upon the tender herb, and as the showers upon the grass" (Deuteronomy 32:1–2). For Melville these drops are the "last dews of death" (*Pierre,* 344). For like the water that gushes from Moses' arid, "stubborn rock," the "soul-melting stream of tenderness and loving-kindness" that flows from the "divine mount" that is the site of Christ's first speech to man, the tears that trickle from the "stone cheeks of the walls" of Pierre's prison cell, and the "stream of the narrative" itself that flows from the "majestic mountain, Greylock," "dedicatee" of the novel, the dew, is a figure that at once conceals and reveals a silence (346, 207, 360, 244). That is to say that the persuasion that the text has a voice is the product of the same force of figuration that gives name and voice to "that profound silence . . . that divine thing without a name" (208). *Pierre,* then, as its title suggests, presents itself as a text with the rigidity and muteness of a statue or monument, self-sufficient and self-enclosed, a kind of "Mute Massiveness" (134).

Dead characters, in short, tell no tales, but for Melville as for Wordsworth they do have an insistently assertive way of reminding us of our own mortality.[9] Consider, for example, the story of "Bartleby," an attempt by its narrator to provide the homeless, "silent man" with a decent burial and final resting-place by writing a "few passages in [his] life" (*PT,* 44, 13). But this "Story of Wall Street" at once accomplishes the desire to "mason up [Bartleby's] remains in the wall" and enacts a substitution in which Bartleby stands in the place of the "elderly" narrator and anticipates his death in a reflective mode (38, 13). Because Bartleby "was one of those beings of whom nothing is ascertainable, except from the original sources," the narrator's relation to him is a specular one, and this specular structure is disturbed only by the story's disappointing sequel: "What my own astonished eyes saw of Bartleby, *that* is all I know of him, except, indeed, one vague report which will appear in the sequel" (13). The story, in other words, as a generation of critics has seen, is at once biographical and autobiographical: "Ere introducing the scrivener, as he first appeared to me, it is fit I make some mention of myself, my *employés,* my business, my chambers, and general surroundings; because some such description is indispensible to an adequate understanding of the chief character about to be presented" (13). The chief character is, of course, the specular pair formed by the "unambitious" lawyer and his eccentric clerk, and the alignment between the two, which begins with the "advent" of "a motionless young man" at the lawyer's "office threshold," ends with the narrator's contemplating Bartleby's dead body, the "head touching the cold stones" of the wall of the Tombs (15, 19, 44). The epitaphic gesture suggested here is accentuated in the version of this scene that appears on the only known surviving leaf of an earlier version of the story.

> Some few days after my last recorded visit, I again obtained/admission to the Tombs, & went through the yard in quest of Bartleby,/but without finding him. "I saw him standing by the wall there some few hours ago," said a turnkey/ maybe he's gone to his cell.
> So saying he led the way a few steps, & pointed out the direction/of the cell.
> It was [a *canceled*] clean, well lighted & scrupulously whitewashed. The/head-stone was standing up against the wall, & stretched on a blanket at its base, his head touching the cold marble, & his feet upon the threshold/lay the wasted form of Bartleby. (574)

In the final version the headstone is replaced by the stone wall, the "Egyptian . . . masonry" that makes the Tombs seem the "heart of the eternal pyramids" (44), those "monument[s]-of-life-in-death . . . monument[s]-of-death-in-life," as Derrida calls them.[10] But as Melville's substitution of wall for headstone makes clear, the Tombs is an improper, figurative name for the "more properly" (though still figuratively) designated "Halls of Justice" (*PT,* 42), and hence cannot, like the family crypt, consecrate the "disappearance of life by attesting to the perseverance of life."[11] Here there is nothing to shelter life from death, for here is no sign for death but the scandal of the literal corpse, the "shell of the flown bird," as Wordsworth, borrowing from an "ancient Philosopher," puts it.[12]

> Strangely huddled at the base of the wall, his knees drawn up, and lying on his side, his head touching the cold stones, I saw the wasted Bartleby. But nothing stirred. I paused; then went close up to him; stooped over, and saw that his dim eyes were open; otherwise he seemed profoundly sleeping. Something prompted me to touch him. I felt his hand, when a tingling shiver ran up my arm and down my spine to my feet.
> The round face of the grub-man peered upon me now. "His dinner is ready. Won't he dine to-day, either? Or does he live without dining?"
> "Lives without dining," said I, and closed the eyes.

"Eh!—He's asleep, ain't he?"
"With kings and counsellors," murmured I. (44–45)

This passage, which marks the end of Bartleby's life and story properly speaking, is quite clearly epitaphic, though with an ironic edge that distinguishes it from the more traditional Wordsworthian model. The shiver that the corpse sends through the living body as the "I" closes the lifeless "eyes" confirms the text's specular structure as the narrator is brought face to face with his own mortality. His "pause," in short, is not the pleasurable one that halts Wordsworth's traveler who either "from weariness or in compliance with the invitation 'Pause traveller!' so often found upon the monuments" stops to ponder the "lively and affecting analog[y] of life as a journey"; and his final words are neither a "pious admonition to the living" nor a "humble expression of Christian confidence in immortality," for the phrase "With kings and counsellors" is taken from Job's anguished lament on having been born (Job 3:11–15).[13] Nevertheless, these benedictory words do offer a form of closure and totalization by conforming to the generic laws of the epitaph. For the effect is to still the reader into a contemplative meditation with the implied assertion that he or she will be in turn dead and read.

But while the narrator's benediction concludes his account of what his "own astonished eyes saw of Bartleby," he adds by way of sequel "one little item of rumor, which came to my ear a few months after the scrivener's decease," a "vague report . . . not . . . without a certain strange suggestive interest" (*PT,* 13, 45).

> The report was this: that Bartleby had been a subordinate clerk in the Dead Letter Office at Washington, from which he had been suddenly removed by a change in the administration. When I think over this rumor, hardly can I express the emotions which seize me. Dead letters! does it not sound like dead men? Conceive a man by nature and misfortune prone to a pallid hopelessness, can any business seem more fitted to heighten it than that of continually handling these dead letters, and assorting them for the flames? For by the cart-load they are annually burned. Sometimes from out the folded paper the pale clerk takes a ring:—the finger it was meant for, perhaps, moulders in the grave; a bank-note sent in swiftest charity:—he whom it would relieve, nor eats nor hungers any more; pardon for those who died despairing; hope for those who died unhoping; good tidings for those who died stifled by unrelieved calamities. On errands of life, these letters speed to death.
>
> Ah Bartleby! Ah humanity! (45)

One effect of this "vague report" is to violate the generic laws of the epitaph even as the sequel does the story's symmetry of form. As Paul de Man has shown, a "latent threat . . . inhabits prosopopeia, namely that by making the death [*sic*] speak, the symmetrical structure of the trope implies, by the same token, that the living are struck dumb, frozen in their own death. The surmise of the 'Pause Traveller!' thus acquires a sinister connotation that is not only the prefiguration of one's own mortality but our actual entry into the frozen world of the dead."[14] Such an insight underlies "Bartleby's" disruptive sequel. For the letters here are "dead" not merely because they are separated from the living voices that they seek to [re]present. These are letters to the dead, not of the dead to the living, and as such they destabilize the characteristic gesture of epitaphic inscriptions, for there is no one to read them. The voice of the sequel is neither that of the "tender fiction" that represents the deceased as "speaking from his own tombstone" or that of the survivors who "loved him and lament his loss."[15] It is the voice of rumor, heard but not read, and it has a curious effect on the listening narrator. "Dead letters! does it not sound like dead men?" The answer is yes, I suggest, only in the sense that death has no sound; it is voiceless. Or to put the point another way, the very idea of voice is entangled with a concept of understanding that depends on the model of an exchange between an author and a reader, a model that is unable to maintain its stability in the face of the "vague report" of the reader's death, for beyond that is only silence.

Consider, for example, Melville's remarkable description in "The Encantadas" of the death of the husband and brother of Hunilla, the Cholla widow.

> Before Hunilla's eyes they sank. The real woe of this event passed before her sight as some sham tragedy on the stage. She was seated on a rude bower among the withered thickets, crowning a lofty cliff, a little back from the beach. The thickets were so disposed, that in looking upon the sea at large she peered out from among the branches as from the lattice of a high balcony. But upon the day we speak of here, the better to watch the adventure of those two hearts she loved, Hunilla had withdrawn the branches to one side, and held them so. They formed an oval frame, through which the bluely boundless sea rolled like a painted one. And there, the invisible painter painted to her view the wave-tossed and disjointed raft, its once level logs slantedly upheaved, as raking masts, and the four struggling arms undistinguishable among them; and then all subsided into smooth-flowing creamy waters, slowly drifting the splintered

wreck; while first and last, no sound of any sort was heard. Death in a silent picture; a dream of the eye; such vanishing shapes as the mirage shows. (*PT,* 154)

In this remarkable passage the real appears as figure, perception as a form of representation. The present, that which is maintained in front of Hunilla's eyes, is already represented. The simple acts of selecting a seat and withdrawing some branches transform the natural into the artificial. She experiences the death of her loved ones as if they were painted figures in a Salvator Rosa sea piece, or a work such as *The Slave Ship* or *The Raft of the Medusa.* Melville's point seems to be that words and images tease and frustrate the imagination by imposing a structure on the self and world, so that not even our response to death is natural in the sense of being an underived and spontaneous reaction. It appears as picture, dream, or mirage, and its truth or reality is rendered only in Hunilla's mute response. She "gazed and gazed, nor raised a finger or a wail. But as good to sit thus dumb, in stupor staring on that dumb show" (154).

Some further implications of Hunilla's "nameless misery" (155) are suggested when we notice that the passage cited above echoes Wordsworth's memorial description in *The Excursion* of a "gentle Dalesman," a deaf-mute whose "living ear" hears nothing.

> When stormy winds
> Were working the broad bosom of the lake
> Into a thousand, thousand sparkling waves,
> Rocking the trees, or driving cloud on cloud
> Along the sharp edge of yon lofty crags,
> The agitated scene before his eye
> Was silent as a picture.[16]

Wordsworth goes on to describe the solace that the Dalesman takes in books, "ready comrades" (l. 440) whose "familiar voice,/Even to old age, with unabated charm/Beguiled his leisure hours" (ll. 442–44); and after his death this voice is replaced by that of the "monumental Stone" that "preserves/His name, and unambitiously relates/How long, and by what kindly outward aids,/And in what pure contentedness of mind,/The sad privation was by him endured" (ll. 472–76). The Dalesman's deprivation is partially compensated for by means of books, which have a voice that he can hear. But the nature of that voice is suggested by Wordsworth's focus on their role as "ready comrades" for a deaf-mute. As Cynthia Chase puts the point, "books do not have a voice themselves; they provide a substitute 'voice,' once they have been personified (as 'ready comrades,' in the phrase of *The Excursion*)."[17] And if the voice of the books that beguile the deaf-mute is figurative and fictive, that of the monumental stone that "unambitiously relates" his "sad privation" is doubly so, for in speaking to the readers as books spoke to the deaf-mute, it offers them in their muteness "death in a silent picture."

What then, I might ask in concluding, is at stake in Melville's borrowing from Wordsworth? Does he, for example, like Wordsworth and Keats, who turn to Milton when their own voices are threatened, or like the Dalesman himself, seek a compensatory voice in the "ready comrades" of books?[18] My discussion, I would hope, suggests that the answer is no. Melville's negative way leads him to confront directly the fiction of the claim for restoration in the face of death, a claim that he sees as implicit in the nature of the literary as such. Hence quotation and allusion in his work, like the shattered sequels that violate its symmetry of form, function not to preserve but to tear out of context and to destroy.[19] Both allusions and sequels function as fragments that finally dislocate and unwork the text in which they are embedded or to which they are attached. At one point in his career, Melville, like the German Romantics, dreamed of making the fragmented sequel into a "'form without form,'" that is to say, without the artificial element of form, thereby joining literature and philosophy.[20] But he quickly sees that the shattered supplement merely confirms the deprivation that the literary monument proclaims. Although Melville could have known only the first of Wordsworth's three "Essays upon Epitaphs," he faces directly a truth about literary language that Wordsworth articulates only as a fearful possibility in the last of the three essays.[21]

> Words are too awful an instrument for good and evil to be trifled with: they hold above all other external powers a dominion over thoughts. If words be not (recurring to a metaphor before used) an incarnation of the thought but only a clothing for it, then surely will they prove an ill gift; such a one as those poisoned vestments, read of in the stories of superstitious times, which had the power to consume and to alienate from his right mind the victim who put them on. Language if it do not uphold, and feed, and leave in quiet, like the power of gravitation or the air we breath, is a counter-spirit, unremitingly and noiselessly at work to derange, to subvert, to lay waste, to vitiate, and dissolve. (*Prose Works*, 84–85)

The tunic of Nessus to which Wordsworth refers here is a nice figure for the force in literary language that Melville's disruptive sequels acknowledge. For it points to the way an apparently restorative power may result instead in a worse deprivation, the loss of sense and life.[22] As *The Confidence-Man* makes clear, literary language does work "unremittingly" and "noiselessly" to "subvert" and "lay waste." Consider for example the scene of reading that centers the final chapter of the novel, one of several occasions when other texts are read in a way to suggest possibilities of reading the larger narrative that contains them. As the Confidence-Man, in his final incarnation as the worldly Cosmopolitan, enters the Fidele's Gentleman's Cabin, which is illuminated by a Solar Lamp on the shade of which are images of a horned altar and a robed man with a halo, he finds there "beneath his lone lamp, which lighted his book on the table," a "clean, comely old man, his head snowy as the marble, and a countenance like that which imagination ascribes to good Simeon, when, having at last beheld the Master of Faith, he blessed him and departed in peace." The book, of course, is the Bible, and the Cosmopolitan, "marking the old man, and how he was occupied," maneuvers to get the book of "good news" into his own hands (*Confidence-Man*, 241).

> After reading for some minutes, until his expression merged from attentiveness into seriousness, and from that into a kind of pain, the cosmopolitan slowly laid down the book, and turning to the old man, who thus far had been watching him with benign curiosity, said: "Can you, my aged friend, resolve me a doubt— a disturbing doubt. . . . I am one who thinks well of man. I love man. I have confidence in man. But what was told me not a half-hour since? I was told that I would find it written—"Believe not his many words—an enemy speaketh sweetly with his lips"—and also I was told that I would find a good deal more to the same effect, and all in this book. . . .
>
> "Why," moved, "you don't mean to say, that what you repeated is really down there? Man and boy, I have read the good book this seventy years, and don't remember seeing anything like that. Let me see it," rising earnestly, and going round to him.
>
> "There it is; and there—and there"—turning over the leaves, and pointing to the sentences one by one; "there—all down in the 'Wisdom of Jesus, the Son of Sirach.'"
>
> "Ah!" cried the old man, brightening up, "now I know. Look," turning the leaves forward and back, till all the Old Testament lay flat on one side, and all the New Testament flat on the other, while in his fingers he supported vertically the portion between, "look, sir, all this to the right is certain truth, and all

this to the left is certain truth, but all I hold in my hand here is apocrypha."

"Apocrypha?"

"Yes; and there's the word in black and white," pointing to it. "And what says the word? It says as much as 'not warranted'; for what do college men say of anything of that sort? They say it is apocryphal. The word itself, I've heard from the pulpit, implies something of uncertain credit. So if your disturbance be raised from aught in this apocrypha," again taking up the pages, "in that case, think no more of it, for it's apocrypha."

"What's that about the Apocalpyse?" here, for a third time, came from the berth. (242–43)

Like the language of the novel itself, that of the Bible works to deceive, confuse, and destabilize. With the canonical and uncanonical parts "bound up together" so as to blur the distinction between apocrypha (conceal) and Apocalypse (reveal), the Bible illustrates the sinister slipperiness of language (243). For like the various coats of the Confidence-Man, the "word in black and white" does not so much represent as disguise. Hence one cannot, for example, "exactly see how Shakespeare meant the words he puts in Polonius' mouth." Some say "that he had no express intention at all, but in effect opens [people's] eyes and corrupts their morals in one operation" (171). And this corrupting power is that of language itself, for although literary characters exist only in the "powerful imagination which [evokes] them, they are nevertheless "living creature[s] . . . though only a poet was [their] maker." And it may be that in their "paper-and-ink investiture" they can act "more effectively upon mankind than [they] would in a flesh-and-blood one" (172). And their acts are as alienating garments rather than "the air we breath," decreative and disfiguring.

It is this decreative power that leads Melville in his final novel apocalyptically and ironically to mark the end of things with an equivocal mention of a sequel that does not follow. "The next moment, the waning light expired, and with it the waning flames of the horned altar, and the waning halo round the robed man's brow; while in the darkness which ensued, the cosmopolitan kindly led the old man away. Something further may follow of this Masquerade" (251).

MICHAEL BEEHLER

"Riddle the Inevitable": Levinas, Eliot, and the Critical Moment of Ethics

[To] riddle the inevitable
With playing cards, fiddle with pentagrams
Or barbituric acids, or dissect
The recurrent image into pre-conscious terrors—
To explore the womb, or tomb, or dreams; all these are usual
Pastimes and drugs, and features of the press.
                        —T. S. Eliot, *Four Quartets*

If there is to be American literature, it will have already come to itself too late. Its fate will be to have always remembered itself as having been, from the beginning, post- or postmodern or even, in a certain manner of speaking, ethical: a witness to the inevitability of an excessive and incalculable precedence.

Such is the profound assertion that moves through much of Joseph Riddel's work and that he forcefully summarizes in his provocative essay, "Decentering the Image: The 'Project' of 'American' Poetics?" Opening with an analysis of the oxymoronic character of the concept American literature, Riddel continues his argument by risking a definition. "'American literature,'" he suggests, "is a search which repeatedly suspends the dream of literature, the dream of totalization, of poetic closure."[1] Olson, Williams, and Pound are poets whose works, as Riddel reads them here, radically suspend this reductive dream in the name of a writing that opens the future by "open[ing] up once more the possibility of generative repetition" ("Decentering," 327). Opposing them, in Riddel's outline of American literature's constitutive postmodernity, is T. S. Eliot, who consistently plays the fall guy, the conservative representative of a dead-ended theological, moralistic, and philosophical tradition that closes the future by looking nostalgically toward the past. If American literature suspends the dream of totalization, Eliot, for Riddel, is un-American, or at least pseudo-American, in his misguided desire to redeem the dream.

In "Decentering the Image," Riddel reads Eliot's mythical method as a key moment in the poet's "nostalgia for the center" and his advocacy of what Riddel calls the "metaphysical view of history and textuality" ("Decentering," 347). Retreating from the chaos of modern history, Riddel's Eliot, taking his cue from Yeats and Joyce, seeks the security of a structural ground his work can imitate, a "timeless fiction . . . [that] not only lends authority to the signs or images appropriated from it, but [that] signifies the general form of mastery or totalization" (347). Temporal mastery becomes possible through this strategy of textual incorporation, which finally confirms art as the "'timeless' repetition of the Same" and understands repetition itself not as a generative opening to the otherness of the future, but as the recollection of every future into the past and the "incorporation" of every other into the Same. Thus "Eliot" becomes for Riddel another name for closure, mastery, and totalization: the proper name of a corpus that stands as the modernist incarnation of a kind of poetic Hegelianism longing for the "gathering or regathering of the many into One" (346). Where Williams, Olson, and Pound are, to varying degrees and in different ways, "anarchic" for Riddel, Eliot turns out to be simply and nostalgically "archeo-logical," the repressive other to the projective, postmodern character of American poetry and poetics (358).

Riddel's Eliot thus bears a striking resemblance to Eliot's Prufrock, whose dream of the closure and completeness of knowledge—"For I have known them all already, known them all"—projects a future that can be nothing other than an archeo-logical relic that recalls and repeats the Same. Prufrock's synchronizing vision gives *no chance* to the future as *other,* or to what must come *as the unexpected* from the future: no chance, that is, to the future *as* future, as the unanticipatable coming of the other. His vision repeats what Emmanuel Levinas has shown to be the fundamental feature of the Western philosophical tradition, which for Levinas "culminat[es] in the philosophy of Hegel" and is characterized by a Prufrockian "panoramic vision of the real," which philosophy takes to be the whole of "the truth."[2] For Levinas, the history of Western philosophy is the story of the "insurmountable allergy" that has directed its thinking. "From its infancy," he argues, "Western philosophy . . . has been struck with a horror of the other that remains other," and, by strategically identifying being and knowing, it has sought to mollify its horror by incorporating the other as an element of its own knowledge, such that in its "disclosure of the other . . . the other, in manifesting itself as a being, loses its alterity" ("Trace," 346). Thus philosophy for Levinas has repeatedly sought the *"reduction of the other to the same,"* and its continual "refutation of transcendence" has vehemently renounced the absolute otherness—the alterity—of the other (*OB,* 169). As a consequence of this refutation, philosophy has viewed its corpus as the discursive incarnation of every other and therefore has insistently remained "indifferent to the other and to others, refusing every movement without return": every movement, that is, that it has not already anticipated as incarnatable in its own body. "Action recuperated in advance in the light that should guide it"—this is, for Levinas, "perhaps the very definition of philosophy" in, we might say, its most Prufrockian tradition ("Trace," 347). In the pervasive glow of this light and its guiding knowledge—just as in the totalizing vision of a Prufrock—no other takes (its) place *as* other, and no future escapes philosophy's anticipatory recuperation, its explanation or riddling of every other, for every future is already recollected by and every other already incorporated *in advance* into the whole that constitutes philosophy's timeless body.

But it is not only philosophy that, like the totalizing poetics Riddel attributes to Eliot (a reductive riddling I will later question), "sees no problems with this incorporation" ("Decentering," 347), for as Levinas points out in "Reality and Its Shadow," it is the "fate" of art to reenact just this kind of reductive, Prufrockian incarnation. For him, art "is the very event of obscuring, a descent of the night, an invasion of the shadow" that lets go of the reality of time and erects, in its place, the totalizing image and the self-sufficient "statue": "Every artwork is in the end a statue—a stoppage of time" (*LR,* 132, 137). Art neutralizes the "living relationship" we have with "a real object"—a relationship Levinas here characterizes as a kind of rhythm, a "primary conceiving through action"—by incorporating it into a static corpus or image (132). In so doing, it effects a "disincarnation of reality by the image" and produces the *"meanwhile,"* the "eternal duration of the interval" enclosed in itself and shut off from any future (132, 134, 141). For Levinas, the temporality of the "living relationship" that constitutes "reality" is thus disincarnated when art incorporates it into the body of an image that then appears as the self-sufficient incarnation of eternal duration or timeless presence. It is therefore the fate of art to foreclose temporality rather than to open it, for by means of the image it immobilizes time in an "instant that endures without a future." Prufrock reenacts this Levinasian instant and the life-denying fate of an art that "does not have the quality of the living instant which is open to the salvation of becoming, in which it can end and be surpassed" (138, 141). The *meanwhile* of art's images obscures the "instant" whose living quality is *at once* its finitude and its exposure to an unincorporable and unincarnatable future that surpasses, transcends, and lives on beyond that finitude. Thus art, for Levinas, is afflicted by the same allergy that infects the Western philosophical tradition—namely, the "horror of the other that remains other"—and for him the foundations of art's "irresponsibility" can be found in its fatal refutation of transcendence and of the "living instant" whose taking place is never a matter of an incarnation as a being-present-in-a-body. In this manner, then, art in Levinas is the general case of Riddel's "dream of literature": the Prufrockian dream (or nightmare) of closure and totalization in the eternity of the timeless *meanwhile*. The exemplary figure, for Levinas, of complete and other-denying self-sufficiency, art commands nothing but silence: "Do not speak," art says to its appreciators, "do not reflect, admire in silence and in peace—such are the counsels of wisdom satisfied before the beautiful" (141). It is a sign of inhuman irresponsibility that "all the arts, even those based on sound," create the total "silence" and immobility of the lifeless statue. But, he goes on to argue, "all this is true for art separated from the criticism that integrates the inhuman work of the artist into the human world." There is a project for criticism, a project to open art's timeless, silent *meanwhile*, its totalizing "world that is entirely *here* and self-sufficient," with the mobilizing life of speech. "The immobile statue," Levinas writes, "has to be put in movement and made to speak" (147, 142). He points toward what he calls the "necessity of critique," the "need to enter into a relation with someone," and to its critical moment: "the moment when finally a man who speaks replaces the inexpressible sadness of echoes" (147, 148). Opposed to art's eternal *meanwhile* and to its lifeless incarnation of temporality, this instant of critical speech witnesses to an unincarnatable "living relationship" that exceeds every embodying image, a relationship in which the "real presence of the other is important." Unlike the sadness of echoes, the language of criticism "wrenches experience out of the aesthetic self-sufficiency of presence, the *here* where it has quietly been lying," and "brings the image in which art revels back to the fully real being," which, for Levinas, is the "direct social link between persons who speak" (149).

To speak the language of criticism is thus to speak again the "living word" that art disincarnates into silence and to be exposed to the real sociality in which "I am simultaneously a subject and an object," a sociality "realized in concrete terms" by "my voice." Therefore "to speak is to interrupt my existence as a subject and a master" and to be taken out of the dream of total presence and self-sufficiency: "The subject who speaks does not situate the world in relation to himself, nor situate himself purely and simply at the heart of his own spectacle, like an artist. Instead he is situated in relation to the Other (*Autre*)." In bringing back to the self-sufficient visions of art the critical moment of speaking, criticism awakens us to what is for Levinas the "first fact of existence," which is "neither being in-itself (*en soi*) nor being for-itself (*pour soi*) but being *for the other* (*pour l'autre*)" (149). The transcendence of words is therefore not to be found in some eternal message they convey or a-historical truth they embody, but in the fundamental ethical relationship—the being-for-the-other—that exceeds and overtakes any message or semantic incarnation as such. Criticism for Levinas enables the hearing of *this* transcendence as the surprising interruption of philosophy and art by a relation that repeatedly suspends their dream, "the dream of totalization, of poetic closure," which Joseph Riddel has also described as "the dream of literature" ("Decentering," 323). Thus criticism is, we might say—perhaps in the way Riddel himself has also instructed us—the writing of the excess, or of the *post*—that lives on beyond the totalizing incarnations of philosophy and literature. As such, it would, for Levinas and, as I will suggest, for Eliot as well, be profoundly ethical.

In his analysis of Edgar Poe and "Poeisme," Riddel again positions Eliot as the stodgy traditionalist purveying the dream of closure and totalization, and lamenting its loss. "The 'Crypt' of Edgar Poe gets under way with Riddel's review of Eliot's "From Poe to Valéry" and with his account of Eliot's "waspish remarks on the 'crisis' produced by 'poesie pure'" ("Crypt," 118). Here, Riddel sets Eliot against Williams on the Poe question and asserts that, for Eliot, Poe "had the mind of a 'pre-pubescent adolescent'"; whereas for Williams, Poe became a postmodern precursor and the "forger of a 'new' language" Eliot finds repellent. In particular, Riddel focuses in on Eliot's attack on Poe as representative of an "'amoral' modernism" culminating in the "'intellectual narcissism'" of Valéry (118, 119). As Riddel reads Eliot reading Poe, this "moral deficiency" has its roots in Poe's theories of language and its aborted fruition in the "symbolist quest for a 'purity' in which the word is refined of its worldliness, both its referentiality and its materiality" (120, 118). From Poe to Valéry there stretches, for Riddel's Eliot, a line tracing the "impasse of a language turned from the world upon itself" and upon the "machinery of its own operations," and a "poetics which dissolves the traditional 'ground' of a 'real' world" (120, 118, 120). Riddel finds Eliot anxiously predicting that this poetic line is a dead end because it promises nothing other than a "literature of moral exhaustion, of purely surface play" in which the word, as the groundless reflection of itself in its own broken mirror, threatens "to exhaust itself in pale fire" (120, 118).

Faced with the abandonment "of referentiality and at least the illusion of representation," and with a certain modernism in which "an abyss has opened up between word and world, and hence in the *word itself,*" Eliot, for Riddel, sees no future in Poe's "new" language, rejects its mad immaturity, and blames modern literature's impasse of narcissism on this poe-tic aberration (118, 120). The implication, for Riddel, is that Eliot fears the loss of the representational "ground" and the dissolution of the concept of "theme" or "subject matter" that, in a more traditional, metaphysical, and pre(post)modern a-Poe-tics, might have been thought to organize, underwrite, and, by that underwriting, restrict the power and play of literary words (118). His "moral" critique of Poe and Valéry, therefore, would be the sign of this anxiety and of the traditionalist's desperate need to resist words' play—to resist, that is, the poe-tic "scene of writing" in which, according to Riddel, there is "only a play of signifiers" with no incarnated "signified" (136, 137)—by holding fast to the notion of words' transcendent, referential ground or theme. In Riddel's argument, Eliot appears again as the embodiment of the totalizing Western philosophical and artistic tradition critiqued by Levinas, a tradition that dreams of closure and the refinement of an open, living temporality into the eternal presence of the timeless *meanwhile.* Indeed, Riddel's T. S. Eliot becomes the purveyor of this inhuman art.

But Eliot's resistance to Poe is not exhausted by its caricature as a belligerently conservative nostalgia. Like Eliot before him, Levinas also finds Poe to be exemplary of "something inhuman and monstrous" in art but, as I have suggested above, that inhuman something is not, as it appears to be in Riddel's appropriation of Eliot, the loss of some eternal ground or timeless fiction in the scene of writing, but rather the cancellation of time and the constitution of the eternal *in that very scene:* in, that is to say, the *meanwhile* that art produces (*LR,* 141). Poe appears at a critical moment in "Reality and Its Shadow," a moment when Levinas briefly turns from the "limited problem of art" to focus upon death and dying. Prior to evoking the name of Poe, he suggests that humanity provides itself with art as a strategic way of coping with the "uncertainty of time's continuation," and thus that the appearance of art marks the "insecurity of a being which has the presentiment of fate . . . in death." By producing the "petrification of the instant in the heart of duration," by giving humanity a "constituted duration," art, for Levinas, sublates death and removes from it the "power to interrupt": "To situate [death] in time is precisely to go beyond it, to already find oneself on the other side of the abyss, to have it behind oneself." Sealing itself off from a death that could come to it from a future that exceeds its reductive anticipations, art produces the timelessness of the *meanwhile* in the "eternal duration of the interval" (140, 141). It is in this sense that art cannot die, that it has already put (its) death behind itself by successfully situating it or incorporating it into itself in such a fashion that death loses any interruptive power. Just as there is no exposure to the future in the meanwhile of art, so also there is no exposure to death. In both cases, art closes itself off from the alterity of time.

This non-exposure to the interruptive power of death *as the other that is to come from the future* constitutes, for Levinas, the "inhuman and monstrous" exemplified in "certain tales by Edgar Allen Poe." In these tales, characters are eternally *dying* in the instant that "cannot pass," the instant in which "the future as a promise of a new present . . . is refused." In the closed self-sufficiency of this instant, the real presence of the other is missing, and the interruption of the eternal presence of dying is disallowed. Here, dying is not a disruptive difference marked by the surprising advent of death, but an infinite repetition of the eternally present, of the *Same itself.* One is left, therefore, "in the interval, forever an interval." The anxiety of Poe's characters is thus "like a fear of being buried alive," of being entombed in the "empty interval" that "can never end" because it can never be surprised or overtaken by any other (141, 140). It is, Levinas argues, "as though death were never dead enough," as though the *meanwhile* of dying—which, in Levinas' larger argument, is produced by the reductive images of art—cannot itself die, and is therefore "impotent to force the future" (141, 138). Thus in his characters' interminable dying, Poe, for Levinas, figures the fate of an inhuman art (or philosophy) closed to temporality and to the other: closed, that is, to the other *as* temporality and death. Art's refusal of the future produces the *meanwhile* without end, the totalized, eternal duration that seals itself off from any transcendent excess or interrupting other. Its strategic success results, for Levinas and for his characterization of Poe, in the monstrous fate of *dying,* and in the inhumanity of the self-sufficient, "empty interval" entombed in itself.

In "From Poe to Valéry," Eliot focuses his attention on the similarly inhuman entombment produced by a poetics of extreme self-consciousness beginning, as he has it, with Poe and reaching its limit with Valéry's "introspective observation of himself engaged in writing."[3] What Eliot is anxious to resist in this ideology of self-reflection, and in its poetics of consciousness and language in- and for-itself, is neither the destruction of the illusion of referentiality nor the loss of some timeless ground. That is to say, his critique of this poetics is not based in the conservative nostalgia that figures so prominently in Riddel's dismissals of Eliot. Rather, his concern is that the intellectual narcissism of a Valéry is, like the totalizing vision of Prufrock, not only a dead end for poetry, but an inhuman trap entombing thought in a closed vault in which it can hear only the "inexpressible sadness of echoes" (*LR,* 148). Eliot's fear for poetry, then, is surprisingly like the fear Levinas finds in Poe's characters, the fear of *dying:* the fear, that is, of being buried alive in the empty interval of a totalizing self-consciousness sealed off from time and from the interruptions of any other. In the circularity of what Eliot sees as Valéry's self-reflective poetics, the experience of an other whose excessive alterity *cannot be interiorized as an object of speculative thought* is neutralized in an inhuman, narcissistic fantasy of self-sufficiency. Thus the very critical position Riddel attributes to Eliot—the dead-ended metaphysical dream of totalization and closure—is in fact the position Eliot himself criticizes in Valéry and in his precursor, Poe. Through these multiple appropriations, Eliot's Poe begins to look surprisingly like Riddel's Eliot.

Eliot points out that one of the key notions Valéry gets from Poe is that "the composition should be as conscious and deliberate as possible, that the poet should observe himself in the act of composition," and he finds in Valéry, whom he calls the "most self-conscious of all poets," the extreme limit of an anticipatory theorizing guiding and directing the production of poetry (*TCC,* 40, 39). Valéry, according to Eliot, "writes consciously according to [his] theory" (39): he writes "very consciously and deliberately indeed . . . observing himself write" and focusing, as he himself puts it, on "'the very act of thought and its manipulation'" (41, 40). This "introspective critical activity" ties the writing of poetry to a theoretical knowledge and intentionality that precedes it and to a methodological calculation that accounts *in advance* for the poetry that comes out of it and returns to it (41). The power of this intellectual narcissism is thus like the power of the Hegelian dream of totalization Levinas finds in the Western philosophical tradition, since its focus on its own *"processes"*—on what it is *for itself;* that is, on its being-for-itself—repeats philosophy's allergic refutation of transcendence (40). It is the power of a vision that presumes to see everything, and to see everything as incorporated—and incorporable—into its own self-identity: to see every other returning to itself and its own interiority. But although his poems constitute the limit case of this speculative and "introspective critical activity," Valéry's best writing, Eliot is careful to suggest, is "perhaps not wholly under the guidance of theory" (39). Later, I will return to this critical "perhaps."

It is Poe's "Philosophy of Composition," though, that supplies Valéry, as Eliot sees it, with "a method and an occupation": with *the* speculative philosophical method of self-reflection and introspection, in which the writing subject becomes an object for itself, and thus with the occupation of "observing himself write" (41). Eliot takes this essay seriously, as he assumes Valéry has done, even though he admits that it "has not been taken so seriously as it deserves," because it has never been clear if Poe "in analysing his poem was practising either a hoax, or a piece of self-deception" (33). In a critical moment for his argument, Eliot simply *decides* this indeterminacy, dismissing it as insignificant—"It does not matter" (41)—in order to calculate what he sees as the essay's real importance: the relation between Poe's critical work, which comes after "The Raven" but purports to recollect its past—that is, to present again, in the present, the methodological law of its construction, the poem's true self-identity—and the poem itself. It is this relationship that Valéry, according to Eliot, carries "to the limit" (41). In a speculative circularity that only closes on itself, Poe's essay demonstrates for Eliot the reductive desire of a self-reflective critical activity that returns the poem to the law that fathers it and that the poem's writing simply incarnates. In tracing this Ulysses-like return of the Same to itself, Poe models a triumphantly totalizing intentionality that, not unlike the mad speaker of the poem itself, hears only its own echoes returning to itself. The essay, "in setting down the way in which [Poe] wanted to think that he had written ["The Raven"]" (33), shows the law promising itself to itself and the self-fulfillment of that law in the poem, in which, Poe asserts, what he intended to say, he did say—and nothing other. It thereby short-circuits what Levinas has called the "living word" of criticism by guaranteeing that the poem bears no signature other than that of "Poe" (*LR,* 148). The process of self-conscious introspection thus *confirms,* through recollection, the self-sufficiency of an anticipatory intentionality that guides the writing of the poem. Eliot's concern here is that, in the extreme to which Valéry takes this process, the introspective critical activity "begins to destroy" the poetry by sealing it off in a self-reflective echo-chamber—in the *meanwhile*—in which, to recall Levinas' definition of philosophy in general, there is only "action recuperated in advance in the light that should guide it" and the refusal of "every movement without return" ("Trace," 347).

A similar sealing-off seems, for Eliot, to be the result of the quest for *la poesie pure,* a quest rooted in Poe's emphasis on words as pure sound and in his scorn for or "irresponsibility" toward sense (*TCC,* 32). In focusing on the "incantatory element" of Poe's poetry, Eliot criticizes the dream of timeless self-sufficiency conjured up by "'the magic of [his] verse.'" This magic enchants us with an "immediacy" that is "unchanging" and "undeveloping": its spells, like the disincarnating effects of the image, neutralize time into the shadow of an eternal present. Seeking to divorce the word from the human reality of sense and meaning—the living relationships in which the life of the word *is* its exposure to an other—and thereby to dream the totalizing dream of a self-sufficient purity incarnated in verbal sound, Poe's incantations repeat the irresponsibility Levinas attributes to art in general. They produce, as Levinas might say, "an instant that endures without a future," and it is this futurelessness, this impotence to force the future (*LR,* 138), that constitutes, for Eliot, their inhuman irresponsibility. There is no future in the "unchanging immediacy" of Poe's incantatory *meanwhile*: in, that is, his particular kind of verbal "'magic'" that synchronizes all time into an eternal present (*TCC,* 31). There is only an uninterrupted repetition of the Same, or an interminable *dying.*

Thus it is that one does not re-read Poe: one remembers having read him in "the memory of an enjoyment which he may for a moment recapture" (30). This memory is recollective, recuperative, circling back to a past moment of enjoyment in order to incorporate it into the present. Like Prufrock's memory, it gathers time into the unchanging immediacy of an eternal present: here, Poe past is Poe present and, presumably, will be Poe future. And yet the Poe that "*somehow* [my emphasis] stick[s] in the memory" of Eliot forces a different thinking of memory, one that is not recuperative—and, perhaps, not even enjoyable—for this Poe cannot be thought of as inhabiting a past "moment" subject to a present incorporation or to the "recapture" of a voluntary memory (29, 30). Indeed, Eliot opens the essay with the question of capture, and of who has captured and is capturing whom. This question is covered over by his later dismissal of the "Philosophy of Composition's" bewildering indeterminacy, but it returns here with this disruptive memory of Poe, or with this memory of Poe as a disruptively incalculable excess in Eliot's own essay. Riddel stops his quotation from Eliot's first paragraph too soon, for immediately after Eliot nominates Edward Lear as the only poet "whose style appears to have been formed by a study of Poe," he hesitates. In a strategic move that mimics Eliot's own calculating caricature of "The Philosophy of Composition," Riddel himself is silent on this hesitation, which nevertheless highlights the problematic relationship Eliot finds himself in with respect to Poe, a relationship riddled neither by recollection nor by the criticism of his poetic method. Edward Lear was influenced by Poe: of that Eliot appears certain. "And yet," he goes on, "one cannot be sure that one's own writing has *not* been influenced by Poe" (27).

Who, then, signs "From Poe to Valéry"? Poe *sticks* in the memory, involuntarily haunts it, in such a way that his memory disrupts the self-identity and self-sufficiency of Eliot's "own" writing. When Eliot remembers Poe, he recalls "a wanderer with no fixed abode" (29), not only with respect to the physical location of Europe and America but also with respect to *memory* itself. For Eliot's memory of Poe does not mark the successful interiorization of the other into the identity of the self-reflective rememberer, but rather demonstrates an *aborted interiorization* that is the obverse of the intellectual narcissism Valéry takes from Poe. To remember Poe is, for Eliot, to remember an excess *that has never given itself to calculation* and that memory can never gather into itself. It is to remember what the dream of a recollective memory or the narcissistic fantasy of a total self-consciousness tries to forget: the non-interiorizable other to which identity finds itself ineluctably exposed. This exposure haunts the intellectual narcissist whose dream of self-sufficiency or *non-exposure* Eliot critiques as amoral and inhuman. Eliot's own essay (but, as he points out, he can never be certain that it is simply his "own") is itself the site of this haunting in which his voice is delivered over to an other whose coming he cannot finally calculate or anticipate, but only experience as an aporetic memory, or as the memory of an aporia: the memory of that which does not give itself to self-reflective memory, consciousness, or identity, and thus the experience of memory not as recollective totalization, but as the repetition of a non-interiorizable an-archy. The "introspective critical activity . . . carried to the limit by Valéry" succumbs to the narcissistic fantasy of interiorization except, "perhaps," where Valéry's poetry is "not under the guidance of theory": where, like Eliot's own essay, it bears the trace of a certain incalculable excess in memory or anticipation (41). The role performed by the name of "Poe" in Eliot's essay leads us to think the finitude of memory, a finitude that, as Derrida puts it, can be experienced only "through the trace of the other in us, the other's irreducible precedence." In contradiction to the reductive intellectual narcissism Eliot criticizes in Poe's own work, "Poe," in "From Poe to Valéry," becomes Eliot's name for this irreducible and excessive precedence evoking a *"nonsubjectivizable* law of thought beyond interiorization."[4]

Thus unlike the *poesie pure* he deplores, Eliot here finds himself situated in a relationship with an other—"Poe"—for whom he cannot account, an other that precedes him and that, in ways that are not certain, calculable, or recollectable, has left his mark or trace, *from the beginning,* on the inside of Eliot's style and voice. Eliot is exposed to Poe, pre-inscribed by him, and it is his evocation of this ineluctable pre-impression—this "structure of the relation to the other"—that enables Eliot to think the limits of what he sees as Poe's own intellectual narcissism and to light up an eclipse "in the movement of interiorization."[5] For what Eliot's essay suggests is that self-reflection always arrives too late to *know* the other, to represent or interiorize the other as a theme incarnatable in writing's body. One only experiences the call of a certain precedence, of an excessive, unthematizable influence or pre-impression that interrupts the dream of presence, and therefore the narcissistic fantasy of totalization, mastery, and self-sufficiency. Eliot's uncertainty is the acknowledgment of an indefinite and incalculable debt, and his essay begins not in a free intentionality but in responsibility and *as a response* to the others ineluctable precedence. It begins not in the recollection of a past present, but in the impossible memory of an immemorial past, of a precedence always too early to be represented as occurring—or having occurred—in some recollectable present. The "structure of the relation to the other" sketched by Eliot's uncertain exposure to Poe highlights the inevitable temporalization or dia-chrony of this relation and the non-synchronizable delay or lapse—the irreducible post- or *coming after*—that, as the failure of interiorization, nevertheless preserves the alterity of the other. This exposure, covered over by the incarnating thematizations of speculative philosophy and by the *meanwhile* of art, is like the failed mourning Derrida describes in "Mnemosyne," in which *"success fails. . . .* And, inversely, the *failure succeeds:* an aborted interiorization [that] is at the same time a respect for the other as other."[6]

The dia-chronic structure of this relation, and the inevitable failure of a synchronizing interiorization that seeks the reduction of the other to the Same, is outlined by the Third Priest in *Murder in the Cathedral.* Opening within the tomb of Western philosophy, in the eternal interval of art's *meanwhile,* in Prufrock's totalizing ego or Poe's unchanging immediacy, is the "critical moment," the irreducibly dia-chronic moment of aborted interiorization that, as the trace of the passage of the other *as* other, acknowledges a certain transcendence:

> What day is the day that we know that we hope for
>   or fear for?
> Every day is the day we should fear from or hope from.
>   One moment
> Weighs like another. Only in retrospection, selection,
> We say, that was the day. The critical moment
> That is always now, and here.
>
>   (MC, 57)

Although the Priest's observation that "One moment/Weighs like another" might suggest the reductiveness of philosophy's insurmountable allergy to the other *as* other, his subsequent comments point toward the irreducible *delay*—the nonsynchronizable dia-chrony—that stamps any "now, and here" with a dividing trace, or with the trace of an irreducible division. For if it is "*Only* [my emphasis] in retrospection, selection,/We say, that was the day" then we can never say, in the present, that *this* is the day: we can only ever say that this present day is not day simply in- and for-itself, is not *the* day incarnate, and thus that "the day"—the self-identical day, the day present to itself—is not now present, but has already *passed* or withdrawn into the past. The present, then, marks the trace of this passage of presence—of the present—into a past that cannot be re-presented or made present (except as that which has always already passed) in the "now, and here." But this non-recuperative "retrospection" also suggests that there is *no rememberable past when this division was not the case:* no "now, and here" without the pre-inscription of a lapse or delay; no thinkable present without the trace of an immemorial past or an irreducible precedence.

Thus the philosophical calculations of retrospection and selection are not only the explanatory and reductive incarnations of this precedence in a discursive body. They do not, that is, *only* riddle, and thereby neutralize, the other's inevitably disturbing precedence. Rather—additionally or *supplementally*—these calculations ineluctably repeat the trace and its "differential 'stamp,'" to quote Derrida quoting de Man: the mark or signature . . . [the] patent or trademark that 'time prints on our sensations.'"[7] The "critical moment" for Eliot, then, is not exhausted by the intellectual narcissism that reduces the others alterity to thought, although such calculation and reduction must, inevitably, take place in it. Excessively—and as *another* inevitability, as the irrecusable inevitability of the other's signature—the critical moment also witnesses to an "essential 'having-taken-place'" and to an irreducible dia-chrony that opens the reductive narcissisms of philosophy and art by provoking the "thinking of the very possibility of what still remains unthinkable or unthought."[8] As the taking place of this double inevitability (it must inevitably riddle the unriddlable other, which therefore it must inevitably not riddle), the critical moment in Eliot evokes the structure of the relation to the other: remembering memory's failure, recalling the ineluctable delay and dia-chrony that aborts recollection, it announces in itself the precedent trace of the other. Inevitably and irrecusably, it alludes to itself as post-.

This annunciation of the post- in the critical moment is for Eliot radically fundamental, and resonates with what Levinas calls the "fundamental experience which objective experience itself presupposes": namely, "the experience of the Other" that constitutes "experience *par excellence*."[9] Its inevitability is marked by its pre-voluntary occurring: by, that is, its always already having taken place. Like breathing, we might say. In what is perhaps a fortuitous metaphor, Eliot himself makes this connection, at the beginning of his most influential essay—"Tradition and the Individual Talent"—where he writes, "we might remind ourselves that criticism is as inevitable as breathing" (*SE*, 13). There is a dia-chronic rhythm to the "critical moment" and to the language of criticism, a "diachronic temporality, outside, beyond or above, the time recuperable by reminiscence, in which consciousness abides and converses, and in which being and entities show themselves in experience" (*OB*, 85). The inevitability of this dia-chrony—*witnessed to* by the breathing of criticism—"wrenches experience out of its aesthetic self-sufficiency" and solicits an "ego awakened from its imperialist dream, its transcendental imperialism" or, we might say, with Eliot, from its intellectual narcissism (*LR*, 148; *OB*, 164). For the breathing that is fundamental to the ego is also the ego's witness to a pre-voluntary exposure: "the breathing by which entities seem to affirm themselves triumphantly in their vital space would be a consummation, a coring out of my substantiality" that signifies the precedence of my "opening to the other." For Levinas, in breathing "I already open myself to my subjection to the whole of the invisible other," and thus breathing is "transcendence in the form of opening up." Before ego, before intentionality, before the *dying* of narcissism and the *meanwhile* of art, there *has been* the irrecusable precedence of breathing: there inevitably *has been* being-as-exposure, being for- the- other. Before criticism *says anything,* it testifies to this inevitability and to the "pneuma of the psyche . . . the identity of a body exposed to the other, becoming 'for the other' . . . the diachrony of the one for the other" (*OB*, 181, 69). Criticism witnesses to this exposure: it is, as Eliot puts it, "as inevitable as breathing," and it is of this first fact of existence that the critical moment reminds us.

If American literature, to hear again the words of Joseph Riddel, is a "search which repeatedly suspends the dream of literature, the dream of totalization, of poetic closure," then it must not be a search that addresses itself only to knowledge and to the love of knowledge ("Decentering," 323). It must not, that is, be a matter only of philosophical calculation, of philosophy "itself," but must disturb philosophy by evoking the experience of the fundamental precedence of the other's nonencompassable alterity, the experience to which philosophy is incurably allergic. I have argued that this is a function of criticism in Levinas and in Eliot: to awaken thinking from the dream of totalization implicit in the intellectual narcissism and the "idealization of self-reflexivity," as Riddel puts it ("Anomalies," 81), of a certain modern philosophy and art by opening in them the question of ethics. In both Eliot and Levinas, this interruptive question emerges in the evocation of what is, for them, the fundamental human experience of alterity and transcendence—the experience of being situated "in a relation with something which for ever remains other, with the Other as absence and mystery"—and in the rediscovery of this relation "in the very intimacy of the 'I'" (*LR*, 165). Despite the calculating caricatures of Eliot by unsympathetic readers, he like Levinas repudiates modern humanism because it is *too much* a repetition of the same, *too much* another philosophical refutation of transcendence in the name of a technological know-how or positive knowledge, *too much* a modern idealization of self-reflexivity. This is the sense of his "Second Thoughts About Humanism," and the basis of his critique of Norman Foerster and Irving Babbitt. These second thoughts spin out of Foerster's comment that "'the essential reality of experience is ethical'" (*SE*, 485). Although Eliot agrees with this observation, he goes on to distinguish between what humanists mean by the experience of the ethical and what *he* means by this experience: "For the person with a definite religious faith, such a statement has one meaning; for the positivistic humanist, who repudiates religion, it must have another" (485). He argues that the "positivistic tendencies" of Humanism "are alarming" because they reduce the experience of the essentially ethical reality of existence to a question of positive knowledge, thereby collapsing to insignificance the disturbing experience of alterity. For Eliot, Humanism is another instance of Western philosophy's complacent rejection of transcendence: another expression of its totalizing desire to "encompass every other in the same";[10] or, as he puts it in "The Dry Salvages," another in the series of philosophy's "usual/Pastimes and drugs" designed to perpetuate the dream of closure—to "riddle the inevitable," and thereby to neutralize the experience of alterity (*CPP*, 136, 135).

But ethics, for Eliot's person of "religious faith," is neither a matter of positive knowledge, nor of the institution of a set of general prescriptions governing in advance our relations to others. Rather, it emerges in the experience of the other *as* other, in this first fact of the subject's exposure to an other that precedes it and that it does not determine, an other that "bears alterity as an essence" (*LR*, 50). This is the "inevitable" "itself," the experience that does not give itself to the "riddled" solution of positive knowledge or self-reflective consciousness, but that awakens the thinking of an an-archic ethics, an ethics without essence. It is, in short, the experience of transcendence—of a remainder that exceeds the riddled calculations of a reductive humanism—that Eliot associates with a Greek conception of *logos*. As he writes in a footnote to his discussion of Foerster, "Mr. Foerster's reason seems to me to differ from any Greek equivalent (*logos*) by being exclusively human; whereas to the Greek there was something inexplicable about *logos* so that it was a participation of man in the divine" (*SE*, 485). This Greek *logos*, as opposed to Humanistic reason, is not "exclusively human," but rather intrudes upon the totalizing self-completeness and self-sufficiency of the human as an "inexplicable" surplus human con-sciousness can never finally internalize as an object of its own comprehen-sion, but to which it cannot be indifferent. This irreducible excess *in* the human evokes, for Eliot, the essential non-self-sufficiency and incomplete-ness *of* the human, and thus it is the trace of the relationality—the inevitable and precedent being-for-another that *remains* other—that evokes the ethi-cal reality of human experience.

Finally, it is the experience of the inevitable—of the *ethical relation*—that makes us late, that opens a *post*-modernity gesturing toward a human-ism beyond or before philosophy's totalitarian designs, a humanism beyond or before the Humanism of a modernity that, for Levinas, "has to be denounced . . . because it is not sufficiently human": because, that is, it repeats the understanding of humanity only "on the basis of transcenden-tal subjectivity" or, as Eliot might put it, only on the basis of the "meta-physical theory of the substantial unity of the soul" (*LR*, 117; *OB*, 139; *SE*, 19). For such a postmodern humanism, "the other is the end; I am a hostage, a responsibility and a substitution supporting the world in the pas-sivity of assignation [or the "passivity of exposure"] . . . which is undeclin-able" (*OB*, 139).

When Eliot writes, in one of his more scandalous critical assertions, that "Literary criticism should be completed by criticism from a definite ethical and theological standpoint" (*SE*, 388), his revisionary demand is not for another criticism based in a traditional, positivistic ethical philosophy, or in the modern, Prufrockian narcissism of speculative knowledge, but rather for a criticism, like that described by Levinas, that solicits in the critical moment the disturbing call of the other and that enables the "voice of this Calling" (*CPP*, 145) to be heard as an irrecusable inevitability: as a surprise that overtakes all critical totalizations, and that thereby supplements—disruptively—the modernism of art and philosophy with the *post-* of ethics.

MARGOT NORRIS

The Trace of the Trenches: Recovering Modernism's World War I

"Today the Somme is a peaceful but sullen place," Paul Fussell writes in *The Great War and Modern Memory*. "When the sun is low in the afternoon, on the gradual slopes of the low hills you see the traces of the zig-zag trenches." His book itself is, of course, one of those traces of the trenches, a "compassionately" inflected account, as Elaine Scarry has called it, that in its study of "trench poetry" both recreates a major discourse of World War I and concedes that its historical referent, "the trench experience," was itself already textualized. Indeed, if the book had a subtitle, it would be something like "An Inquiry into the Curious Literariness of Real Life." Not only the trench poetry but the competing poetic discourses of modernism and avant-garde writing too preempted and preceded the Great War. "You will be astonished to find how like art is to war, I mean 'modernist' art," Wyndham Lewis writes in *Blasting and Bombardiering*, and Gertrude Stein makes a similar point—that the art was the war's historical referent and not the other way around—when she describes it as a cubist painting: "Really the composition of this war, 1914–1918, was not the composition of all previous wars, the composition was not a composition in which there was one man in the center surrounded by a lot of other men but a composition that had neither a beginning nor an end, a composition of which one corner was as important as another corner, in fact the composition of cubism."[1]

Lewis reiterates this argument throughout *Blasting and Bombardiering*.

135

Asked if the fighting was hell, he replied "it was Goya, it was Delacroix—all scooped out and very El Greco. But hell, no" (*BB*, 180). The war was preceded by its simulacra not only as art, but as language. Even the "proper names" that might have overcome its formlessness and become its historical sign (Verdun, Ypres, Passchendaele, the Somme) fail to cohere as battles (Fussell says later historiography calls them battles to imply that they had a rational causality [*GW*, 9]) and, according to a modernistic logic, prescripted the events that transpired there. Lewis (who painted a picture called *The Plan of War* six months before its outbreak) writes of Passchendaele: "The very name, with its suggestion of splashiness and of passion at once, was subtly appropriate. This nonsense could not have come to full flower at any other place but at Passchendaele. It was pre-ordained" (*BB*, 160). This prior textualization contributed to the strange phenomenon of a "Great War" that was present to itself chiefly as a misleading sign, misleading because none of its multiple discourses, themselves in considerable dispute, were able to totalize either its experience or its significance. T. S. Eliot wrote in 1929, "perhaps the most significant thing about the War is its insignificance."[2]

This aesthetic and poetic *en*scription of the war—both before and after the event—raises the question of whether the significant insignificance that Eliot identifies as its outcome is not produced by what Marianne De Koven calls the suppression of the historical referent in modern writing.[3] If that referent is identified with the mass dead of World War I—"Nearly 60,000 of these men were to become casualties on the first day of the Somme offensive in 1916"—then the early effects of a kind of Baudrillardian hyperreality produced by the self-reflexive World War I discourses can also be examined as an ideological problem in modernism's construction, or lack of construction, of World War I.[4] The elegant figurations of the modernists—such as Pound's powerful synecdoche in Canto IV ("Troy but a heap of smoking boundary stones"), which tropes the destructiveness of the war as the atomic power of rhetoric itself, capable of reducing the world to a burning stone—so dramatically inverts the ground of the reference (rhetoric as figure of war, or war as figure of rhetoric) that the question of the poem's Nietzschean amnesia can begin to be interrogated as an ideological violence.[5] Canto IV, written in 1918 and 1919, either "forgets" or pointedly (using Troy to point) disregards the recent closure of World War I, and the elision of the dead bodies in the self-reflexive figure and poem can be inserted into Elaine Scarry's argument about the role of disavowal in the phenomenology of war itself. The ten million war dead of 1918 are the historical referent of the war without having themselves a referent. This gives them the referential instability that allows them to serve what Scarry oxymoronically describes as "their fiction-generating and reality-conferring function." Dead bodies make the issues and outcomes of war real because "the human body, the original site of the real," serves a semiological function as a code of the real.[6] This endows the bodies of the war dead with the power to transfer the signification of reality onto the abstractions that have been the issues of war. The unreality and insignificance of the Great War may thus be implicated in modernism's disavowal of mass warfare's material and affective reference. The dead, whose sign is needed to make war's issues real, must always be simultaneously there yet disavowed, in order to serve the purely symbolic function (to signify reality) that conceals their lack of instrumental function (to effect control over territory). This lack has never been more glaringly obvious than in this war in which territorial gains and losses were sometimes nearly zero over the course of a year's unimaginable carnage. Modernism's self-reflexive pre-scription of the war as (energetic) formalism may thus have colluded in shaping a phenomenology of the Great War, a model of its perception, in which the dead fail to serve a referential function. By placing the mass dead's irrational and illogical production under erasure, the literature of World War I may have contributed to making their reproduction in World War II unstoppable. I am not suggesting that modernism produced World War II but rather that it failed in its formalistic aestheticization of World War I to imprint literary history with a prophylactic trace of the mass dead.

Modernism's suppression of the war dead, which was repeated in its suppression of trench poetry, provides a particularly useful example of the imbrication of its aesthetic and ideological agendas. Since the mass is the enemy of form, the mass killing of the Great War confronted the modernists with an aesthetic unintelligibility that they nonetheless coded politically as "the crowd" or "anarchy." The modernist resistance to "the mass" and "the masses" thus has simultaneous formal and historical roots. Modernism's response to the challenge of mass warfare and mass death was to narrativize the nineteenth-century discourses of population control and quality—Malthusian arithmetic and Darwinian competition, Nietzsche's herd and Arnold's mass culture—as mandates to aesthetic formalism and artistic connoisseurship. William Chace differentiates Pound's changed sensibility toward the war ("The poet who had once luxuriated in the prospect of violence now rages against war") from Fabian pacifism ("socialists caught up by doctrines of 'mass-men'").[7] The war destroyed artists and their art and reproduced mass culture in the voluminous production of its dead. Modernism responds by replacing representation with performance, both in textual strategy and in institutional practice. Its formal prolepsis of the war—the violent disjunctions, illogical parataxes, mutilated figurations, and "series . . . of explosive fragments"—give war a rhetorical performance prior to representation.[8] Its displacement, extrusion, and silencing of the trench poetry that clearly aspired to become poetry *as* historical referent, poetry as defense against the lethal intertexts of the very classicism (Owen's attack on Horace in "The old Lie: Dulce et decorum est") that served as modernism's premier episteme, constitutes its institutional gesture.

Yeats's dramatic expulsion of the trench poets from the canon, when in 1936 he excluded them from *The Oxford Book of Modern Verse* on the ground that "passive suffering is not a theme for poetry," demonstrates the heteroglossia of the war's poetic discourses, that the field of art itself marked a contested terrain of disputed phrases, in Lyotard's sense.[9] But Yeats's gesture also emphasized the doubling of the war's textualization: war poetry shapes other war poetry. As the war's pre-text, poetry served an apologetical function both in Wilfred Owen's "Dulce et Decorum Est" and Stephen Crane's classical intertexts: Horace spurs the soldiers of World War I as surely as *The Iliad* spurs the Civil War troops in *The Red Badge of Courage*. Texts of war replicate themselves in future texts of war. As texts for mass education—Fussell notes that copies of *The Oxford Book of English Verse* were carried into battle like Bibles (*GW*, 157)—anthologies like *The Oxford Book of Modern Verse* that Yeats edited could have enfolded the disputed poetic discourses of World War I, whose disjointed forms and aims would have dramatized their inability to provide the Great War with even imaginary unities. Yeats's gesture in exiling trench poetry from the canon removed the most eloquent articulation of the Great War's mass violence from the intertextual spiral that might have (in 1936) pre-scripted the mass violence of World War II. As a result, the poetry of the Great War skipped a generation, as it were, leaving little trace of itself on the literature of World War II. When it resurfaced rather dramatically in *Apocalypse Now*, popular culture's most significant address to Vietnam, it reappeared in its most oblique, aestheticized, and canonical version as High Modernism.

Yeats's motives—he once characterized Wilfred Owen's poetry as "unworthy of the poets' corner of a country newspaper" and "all blood, dirt and sucked sugar-stick"—are best inferred from the dialogical interplay of his own Great War poem, "An Irish Airman Foresees His Death," with both trench poetry and other modernist poetry.[10] Yeats's poem expels the vortex as much as the trenches, deleting the airplane and other advanced technology along with the mass slaughter on the ground. The gesture of Yeats's poem is to abolish the war in the interest of saving poetry from the proletarian masses in the trenches that Owen likens to the Midland collieries ("dark pits/Of war") peopled by blind troglodytes ("Bent double, like old beggars under sacks,/Knock-kneed, coughing like old hags").[11] Yeats replaces the "passive suffering" of the trench soldier with the epiphanic vision of the seraphic warrior, who is purified into an unbearable lightness of being through a total ideological divestiture of the war. The war marks the poem with vapor trails of emptied determinants: political ("No likely end could bring them loss/Or leave them happier than before"), patriotic ("Those that I fight I do not hate,/Those that I guard I do not love"), moral ("Nor law, nor duty bade me fight"), and polemical ("Nor public men, nor cheering crowds"). What remains from the affective erasures that produce perfect equanimity ("I balanced all, brought all to mind") is the autotelos of a pure Nietzschean will-to-power, "A lonely impulse of delight," that doubles as the poem's empyrean of form: pure symmetry, simplicity, and equipoise.[12] Yeats abstracts the Georgian impulse that made much war poetry a pastoral outpost (see Fussell's chapter on "Arcadian Recourses") of a war troped widely as an industrial slum whose fighting was a species of urban violence—a "shindy," Woolf's Septimus Smith calls it. In "An Irish Airman Foresees his Death," Yeats translates the complex political referent, Lady Gregory's son dying in the service of his colonial master, into the formal stasis of a poem as pure peace. The poem's gestures—enacting Major Gregory's death in the practice of his self-erasure, his lines' chiasmic self-cancellations ("The years to come seemed waste of breath/A waste of breath the years behind")—reproduce, by discursively killing him into a poetic peace, the perverse illogicality of war as a practice of massive slaughter in the service of peace-production.

Yeats's tacit interplay with trench poetry is one among several dialectical disputes in the poetic performance of the Great War. While Yeats enacted romantic impulses without their form, Wyndham Lewis inflected the war's challenge to modernistic form through a futuristic mandate (Perloff highlights it as "violence and precision") he simultaneously denied and enacted.

In advance of a gesture Jameson calls postmodernism's attack on "the Romantic valorization of organic form," Lewis demystifies the imperilling of artistic form by violence without precision when he limns what he calls the romance of war.[13] "It is commonly remarked that 'there is no romance in modern war,'" Lewis writes. "That is absurd, I am sorry to have to say" (*BB,* 121). He then proceeds to trope war as a form-making effect whose "romance" resides in refiguring what is seen as what is felt. As an artillery officer, Lewis refunctions the big guns as romantic artists: "Of course, it would be impossible to overstate the contribution of the guns to these great romantic effects. Even in such an essentially romantic context as war, they are startlingly 'romantic' accessories. . . . It is they who transform a smart little modern township, inside an hour, into a romantic ruin worthy of the great Robert himself, or of Claude Lorrain" (122). The guns re-produce landscapes already assimilated to prior sublimations, like the romantically idealized landscapes of Hubert Robert, "Robert des Ruines." But when he goes on to romanticize shell wounds, his demystification of the romance of war as nostalgia for a repressed and disavowed algolagnia, a secret and denied enjoyment of destruction and suffering (like Owen's "sucked sugar-stick," in Yeats's words), becomes apparent: "they give the most romantic and spectacular wounds of all—a bullet wound, even a dum-dum, is child's play to a wound inflicted by a shell-splinter" (122).

Lewis' sardonic inveighing against "the romance of war," which repeats the pre-modernist attacks on romanticism culminating in the work of T. E. Hulme, prepares the way for clarifying the formal and affective hardness of modernism. The sadism of his gestures—the "rational violence" of a cruelty in the service of the machine and reason—serves the production of the "vortex" well by transforming his intelligence and his writing into an energetic instrument of aggression without affect or malice. *Blast,* better than *Blasting and Bomardiering,* stages the formal implications of an epistemology that he himself implies is equivalent to the sculptural form that defines his paintings even more than his writings: "Give me the *outside* of things, I am a fanatic for the externality of all things" (9). In Henri Gaudier-Brzeska's *Blast* piece, "Vortex Gaudier-Brzeska (Written from the Trenches)," the double violence of sculpture—externalizing and disavowing what is inside or felt—becomes visible as the modernist aesthetics of war. Gaudier gives Lewis' fetishized obsession with externality or form the displaced logic of the objective correlative: "I SHALL DERIVE MY EMOTIONS SOLELY FROM THE ARRANGEMENT OF SURFACES, I shall present my emotions by the ARRANGEMENT OF MY SURFACES, THE PLANES AND LINES BY WHICH THEY ARE DEFINED."[14] Gaudier's formalistic epistemology—that is, his way of casting knowledge as form—allows him to limn the war into the hard angularity of one of his own sculptures. "THE BURSTING SHELLS, the volleys, wire entanglements, projectors, motors, the chaos of battle DO NOT ALTER IN THE LEAST, the outlines of the hill we are besieging." This description could virtually double as a historical referent for the Great War, in which unprecedented firepower failed over the course of a year to produce significant alteration in the trench lines. However, Gaudier extends the sculptural trope of the war to the shape of its army population as well: "HUMAN MASSES teem and move, are destroyed and crop up again." The war becomes for him the dynamic stasis of a Nietzschean eternal return of the same, that he internalizes as his own sculptural view: "Dogs wander, are destroyed, and others come along. . . . MY VIEWS ON SCULPTURE REMAIN ABSOLUTELY THE SAME" (B2, 33).

The figure of Gaudier's war writing is his carving of the enemy gun, a stolen German mauser, into *objet trouvé* art: "I broke the butt off and with my knife I carved in it a design, through which I tried to express a gentler order of feeling, which I preferred. BUT I WILL EMPHASIZE THAT MY DESIGN got its effect (just as the gun had) FROM A VERY SIMPLE COMPOSITION OF LINES AND PLANES" (34). Gaudier clearly intended his contribution to the 1915 War issue of *Blast* to function as a piece of verbal vorticist sculpture on the war, an intention emphasized, and foregrounded, by the exile of the historical referent to the prefatory note. Gaudier's sculptural effects depend not only on the suppression of the historical referent from his text but on the play of difference between the two. In a gesture borrowed from the ninth thesis of Marinetti's 1909 Futurist Manifesto, Gaudier's sculptural procedure abstracts the army's decimation as a prophylactic eugenics: "THIS PALTRY MECHANISM, WHICH SERVES AS A PURGE TO OVERNUMEROUS HUMANITY. . . . THIS WAR IS A GREAT REMEDY." In contrast, the historical reference restores to the killing the particularity of time and narrative: "In September he was one of a patrolling party of twelve, seven of his companions fell in the fight over the roadway."[15] In his sculptural text, Gaudier strips soldiering of all symbolic social or cultural reference: "IN THE INDIVIDUAL IT KILLS ARROGANCE, SELF-ESTEEM, PRIDE." In the prefatory note, however, he mentions his nomination for promotion to "sargeancy" (B2, 33).

The most strikingly indelible historical referent of the piece is one Gaudier didn't write: "Henri Gaudier-Brzeska: after months of fighting and two promotions for gallantry Henri Gaudier-Brzeska was killed in a charge at Neuville St. Vaast, on June 5th, 1915" (34). A modernist response was now required to explore the parataxis of its own aesthetic, in which the mass dead are "numbers upon numbers of unimportant units," and its historical doubling in the material death of its modernist artist (33). John Tytell writes, "News of Gaudier's death shocked Pound into an awareness of the closeness of the war. Gaudier had become for Pound a personal totem of the artist, a symbolic figure who had been sacrificed in a conflict that would prove nothing."[16] In "Hugh Selwyn Mauberley," Pound, in fact, both preserves the parataxis and sublates the loss of the artist into the loss of art. Poem IV preserves the insignificance of the mass dead who fought in the weak necessity and indeterminacy of "in any case" (a slippage from "in any cause") by investing their identity in a fragmentation and reduction of the proper noun that might have signed them into significance. The Somme, now become lower case, slips into the pronominal obliquity and indeterminacy of the "some":

> Some quick to arm,
> some for adventure,
> some from fear of weakness,
> some from fear of censure,
> some for love of slaughter, in imagination.[17]

Although the "some" outrageously understates the casualties of the Somme, where 12,000 soldiers are said to have fallen within the first hour, Pound uses its anaphoric repetition to break up the mass of men into smaller clusters, thus performing an ideological diaeresis. But given the flaccid catalogue—anti-epic in its bland abstractions, anti-imagist in its appeal to cliché—Pound's Juvenalian protest seems more likely aimed at trench poetry[18] ("Died some, pro patria, non 'dulce' non 'et decor' . . . hysterias, trench confessions") or at the democratic Whitmanesque catalogue than to the decimations of war. In V, Pound restores both the numbers and the style, in honor of Gaudier-Brzeska: "There died a myriad / And of the best, among them." In place of the scattered abstractions of jejeune motives (adventure, weakness, fear), he restores the bite of vulgar anger to his assault on the symbols of patriotism ("For an old bitch gone in the teeth, / For a botched civilization")—as he does again in Canto XVI ("And because that son of a bitch, / Franz Josef of Austria") and in Canto XXXVIII ("They began to kill 'em by the millions / Because of a louse in Berlin / and a greasy basturd in

Ausstria")[19] Gaudier's quality as artist is conjured up in sharp economy as a good bite, an ability to sculpt words with the chisel of teeth, and his death is invested in a double synecdoche: "Charm, smiling at the good mouth/Quick eyes gone under earth's lid." The sculptor's eye is extinguished and enclosed in the closing eye of a grave figured as a sculpture, Gaudier disappearing into the art of one of his own sculptural heads.

In Canto XVI, Pound makes the doubling of the death of sculptor and sculpture explicit: "And Henri Gaudier went to it,/and they killed him,/And killed a good deal of sculpture." The death of Gaudier posed a historical conundrum for Pound that he solved narratively by inserting Social Credit theory into his poetic history of World War I. The result, in *the Cantos*, is an excess of historical reference to arms and munitions manufacture and trade as the cause of a war recoded, after the death of Gaudier, as the war on art. In "Murder by Capital" Pound wrote, "I have blood lust because of what I have seen done to, and attempted against, the arts in my time" and referred to "sin against the best art of its time."[20] *The Cantos* become dotted with allusions and references to Basil Zaharoff, and Vickers, Ltd., and Krupp, Mitsui, Schneider-Creusot, and other armament firms and trades:[21]

> 500 to St Petersburg and 300 to Napoleon Barbiche
> from Creusot. At Sadowa
>   Austria had some Krupp cannon;
>   Prussia had some Krupp cannon.
> "The Emperor ('68) is deeply in'erested in yr. catalogue
> and in yr. services to humanity"
>   (signed) Leboeuf
>   (Canto XXXVIII)

The guns that were romantic accessories to Lewis, and *objets d'art* to Gaudier, become obsessively quantifiable and ennumerable commodities to the later Pound: "1885/1900 produced ten thousand cannon/to 1914, 34 thousand" (Canto XXXVIII). The myriad mass dead—though now listed ("Liste officielle des morts 5,000,000" [Canto XVI])—nonetheless slide under guns and art as referent of anger and anguish in the narrative of economic cause and aesthetic effect in Pound's history of early modernity.

The Great War became for Pound a war on art not only because Gaudier and Hulme served as proxies for art in the trenches, thereby giving Gaudier what Tytell describes as his "totemic" function for Pound. The term's literal image of a totem as a sculpture of primitive abstractness is appropriate because Gaudier carved himself, as he carved his trench experience and as he carved the German rifle, into a work of art, a sculptural text, like his piece in *Blast*. But Pound's later obsession with munitions manufacture makes it clear that he continues to narrativize the ideological relationship of the mass, violence, and form as an apologia for modernism's exemplary role in war's conduct. Pound's conception of mass psychology implicitly stresses the indiscrimination and indifference of the masses as constituting the intellectual and perceptual inanition that make them the enemy of art.[22] The mass-produced guns serve as instruments of mass-produced death, whose killing of the true artists leaves mass-produced art virtually uncontested in the field: "For two gross of broken statues,/For a few thousand battered books." The problem with war, then, is not its violence but the failure of its violence to conform to its artistic projections in futurism and vorticism as "violence and precision." The sin of guns in their production of mass death is not localized in their numbers of victims, but in their inability to function like art, their lack of discrimination, their failure to carve and cull the masses according to some formal principle that will reduce the formless mediocrity of populations while leaving their modernistic figures intact. Pound's selective mourning over the artist-casualties of the Great War, reckoning Rupert Brooke's death less as a loss to art than as the loss of a charming young man, makes less facetious his outrageous regret at military indiscrimination. "The real trouble with war," Tytell reports him as having told Harriet Monroe, "was 'that it gives no one a chance to kill the right people.'"[23] Lewis had no compunction, either, about preferring artists to live or die on the basis of their politics and poetics: "Why should Gaudier die, and a 'Bloomsbury' live" (*BB*, 182)? In this way and variously, the war's killing was textualized and valorized according to its repetition of the modernist poetic agenda.

The ninth thesis of the 1909 Marinetti manifesto programmatically links militarism to misogyny: "We will glorify war—the world's only hygiene—militarism, patriotism, the destructive gesture of freedom-bringers, beautiful ideas worth dying for, and scorn for woman" (*FM*, 22). Lewis elaborates the rationale of this ideological link when he creates an analogy between munitions production and human reproduction by explicitly troping childbearing during the war years as the manufacture of cannon fodder: "Women's function, the manufacturing of children (even more important than cartridges and khaki suits) is only important from this point of view. . . . It takes the deft women we employ anything from twelve to sixteen years to fill and polish these little cartridges, and they of course get fond of them in the process" (*B2*, 16). Lewis takes the sentimental icon of the soldier's mother whose form in Great War literature invariably figures her as a moribund Pietà, knitting socks for the boys at the front, and mechanizes and desentimentalizes her by restoring her to "the crowd" and the masses. His equation of the crowd with the inertia and mindlessness of Pound's "abuleia" makes it a figure for death—"Death is, however, only a form of Crowd"—that by the logic of a misogynistic algebra is deciphered as woman: "The Married Man is the Symbol of the Crowd: his function is to set it going. At the altar he embraces Death" (94). The fruition of this logic can be found in Ford Madox Ford's "From 'Antwerp,'" in which a series of paratactical translations fill Charing Cross with the masses of the Flemish dead: "There is a great crowd"; "that is a dead woman—a dead mother"; "That is another dead mother, and there is another and another and another"; "These are the women of Flanders"; "They await the lost that shall never again come by the train"; "the lost who lie dead in trench and barrier and foss" (*PB*, 145–46). The poem enacts an oneiric montage of time as well as place—return become departure, Flanders become England—in order to figure the war dead as an imbrication of losses, absences, and waitings.

Lewis' Nietzschean derision of "the crowd" in *Blast* was widely echoed in modernist representations of patriotic enthusiasm, as in Yeats's elegy for Major Robert Gregory, and the blind obedience of massed armies and the mass casualties they produced, as in Eliot's "A crowd flowed over London Bridge, so many/I had not thought death had undone so many."[24] But in *Blast* Lewis doubly politicizes the crowd by naming its desire as suffrage, echoing Nietzsche's excoriation in *Ecce Homo* of women's democratic movements as bids for cattle voting rights: "Their attitude is as though these universal crowds wanted some new vague Suffrage" (*B2*, 94). Of Cantleman, his alter ego in *Blasting and Bombardiering* running with the crowds at the Olympiad, Lewis writes, "he was very stupid. He was a suffragette." In "The Code of a Herdsman" Lewis writes, "As to women: wherever you can, substitute the society of men. Treat them kindly, for they suffer from the herd" (*BB*, 70). This feminization of the crowd brings modernism's contradictory discourse of population control into sharper focus, and exposes the logical strategy that lodges control with art. The 1915 war issue of *Blast* blasts "Birth-Control" and blesses "War Babies" (*B2*, 92–93). The logic of the etymological play—the blighting of birth control as enabling the breaking out of the embryo—is clearer than the political logic of a polemic that simultaneously despises the crowd produced by overpopulation and inveighs against the contraception that would reduce its size and proliferation. The issue is clearly the investiture of control: the indiscriminate population control by war preferred to the discriminate population control by democratic female suffrage, because the violence of the war at least releases energy and creates a vortex while feminism empowers the herd. Modernism ultimately enacted, in its own textual strategies, the function of the war as an imperfectly self-correcting machine that disciplined the masses and thereby institutionalized itself as the war's cultural counterpart.

The modernist text that becomes most conspicuously identified with the contradictory effects of this project is, of course, Eliot's *The Waste Land.* Canonized as the premier address to "the unprecedented death toll of the First World War," its historical reference encloses the illogical nexus of martial and feminist discourses of population control in order to sublate them wholly to the mythology of sacral fertility.[25] Upon the editorial pruning by Pound, the poem's opening introduces a montage of displaced historical codes for the outbreak and aftermath of World War I: the post-war haunting of watering places by the dislocated German aristocrats from eastern Europe, the ethnic chauvinisms and tensions of the Hapsburg Empire displaced from the Balkans to the Baltic, and the figure of the arch-duke careening downhill on a sled nearly out of control: "Bin gar keine Russin, stamm' aus Litauen, echt deutsch./And when we were children, staying at the arch-duke's/My cousin's, he took me out on a sled,/And I was frightened." The challenge of the poem may be sited in the insomniac reading of the baroness: "I read, much of the night, and go south in the winter." What does one read after the catastrophe of a war that murders sleep, and what writing replaces the peace foreclosed by historical nightmare? "Falling towers/Jerusalem Athens Alexandria/Vienna London." The fall and dispersal of the Austro-Hungarian Empire (Vienna) opens the text, and the deferred twilight of the British Empire (London), ingesting the religion of its colonies along with India's tea and spices, closes it in a cacophony of indigested and untranslated quotations that textually foreclose geopolitical peace. The poem's tacit attempt to reconstitute a third empire of polyglot and polymath culture—what Eagleton describes as "an alternative text which is nothing less than the closed, coherent, authoritative discourse of the mythologies which frame it"—becomes no more than another haunting, another invasion of the poem by the dead. "Eliot celebrates the voices of the dead," Maud Ellmann writes, "but he comes to dread their verbal ambush in *The Waste Land*."[26]

Ellmann's elegant rhetorical summation of the poem's compulsive attempt to remember and resurrect the dead through a doomed prosopopoeia—"*The Waste Land* strives to give a face to death"—endows the impossibility of representing the mass death and destruction of World War I with a compelling figure of poetic performativity.[27] But one might argue that there are two kinds of dead trying to appear in the poem, and that they are not equal: the poetic dead voices of the literary tradition, whose eloquence is the louder for the fragmentariness of their utterance, and the voiceless war dead. Indeed, even the figure of the spared, the demobbed returning soldier who gives the poem its most direct and specific historical reference, is not detachable from the repulsiveness of the mob. His wife, in fact, is given a face, or gives herself a face ("pulling a long face"), and it is the face of an anti-Helen; the face that launched a thousand ships becomes the young version of Pound's "old bitch gone in the teeth." Lil is a young bitch gone in the teeth, whose toothless face creates universal aversion: "He said, I swear, I can't bear to look at you./And no more can't I, I said." In attaching Lil's supreme ugliness to the unwholesomeness of her class, Eliot tracks highly specific causalities—the toothlessness of calcium deficiency from the multiparity of six pregnancies before the age of thirty-one ["You ought to be ashamed, I said, to look so antique./(And her only thirty-one)"]—back to the pullulating breeding of the masses.

The poem reverses the flow of the war dead to return them, by way of London Bridge, to the teeming slums from which they came. Eliot, like Lewis, tropes the war as a bridge between home and front, between living and dead—"The bridge, you see, is the war" (*BB*, 2)—and this bridge crosses, too, the discourses of population control that have cast their contradictory shadows upon other modernistic war writing. Reversing Gaudier's "good mouth," Lil's toothless head is carved into the barren landscape like a giant dead skull: "Dead mountain mouth of carious teeth that cannot spit" [l. 339] to be traversed by "the hooded hordes swarming/Over endless plain, stumbling in the cracked earth." But in spite of the industrial and urban pollution ("The river sweats oil and tar") they produce along with the "White bodies naked on the low damp ground/And bones cast in a little low dry garret," the poem blasts Birth-Control for the masses as surely as did *Blast*. "You are a proper fool," says Lil's interlocutor of her botched abortion, and Lil replies, "The chemist said it would be all right, but I've never been the same." As a form of population control, the war too was a botched abortion—of the sort that reduced her progeny, but left Lil ill, disfigured, and prematurely aged. World War I may have reduced some of Europe's unwanted masses, but at the price of leaving her countries weak, disfigured, and spiritually dessicated.

The conversation in the pub that retells the conversation with Lil is Eliot's Arnoldian demonstration that the discourse of the Populace is impervious to poetry because it lacks the porosity of other parts of the poem that let quotation leak in. For discourse to become art like sculpture requires the scission of metaphoric teeth. "I didn't mince my words," the speaker says, and her narrative is conspicuous in its seamless wholeness, unchopped by the parataxes that segment the poem's other speech. The masses produce a nearly perfect redundancy of citation, the episode suggests; culture and tradition are replaced by verbatim or unmasticated reproduction of earlier verbatim reproductions. This pullulation or regurgitation of trivial discourse—the speaker telling us what she told Lil Albert had said before he left—reproduces endless Heideggerean *Gerede* or idle talk deprived of teeth, "You have them all out, Lil, and get a nice set,/He said." The conversation's twice-told and triangular structure, whose parenthetical asides make a confidante of the poem's addressee, restores the implied reader herself to the masses. It is among the poem's projects to break up this mindless abulia of the masses by using the text's erudition to babelize its readership, carving its homeogeneous philistinism into polyglottal segments and cultural elites. By refusing to translate or reference many of its citations, the poem's cultivation creates borderlines of incommunication and minefields of incomprehension that recreate the conditions of geopolitical war and class revolution. The unified empire of culture the poem conjures up in its referenced appeal to the cosmopolitanism of Cambridge anthropology and the archetypalism of comparative religion becomes no more than a bogus sublation of the poem's politics into a myth of universal order that its own textual babelization ritually destroys.

The temptation to translate this ideological construction of Anglo-American high modernism's Great War into a historical narrative of rise and fall that implicates its political predilections in World War II is reductive, if not totally illogical, and must be resisted in the interest of preserving the complexity and overdetermination of historical causalities. But it is a temptation that the crude thematic outlines of the historiographies of both wars invite. One is tempted to blame modernism's obsession with nineteenth-century alarm over population control (Darwin, Nietzsche, Arnold) for its apocalyptic enactment in World War II, where its limited form became genocide, and its global form, the specter of atomic annihilation of the planet. One is tempted in emphasizing the Great War's competing poetic discourses to adjudicate them by lamenting modernism's institutional success in muting the naturalism of the trench poets and the politically subversive techniques of the German avant-garde. However dubious the assumptions behind such a move—for example, faith in the mimetic teleology of representation—one would like to impute to such tropes as Wilfred Owen's elemental figuration of a gas attack ("flound'ring like a man in fire or lime . . . Dim, through the misty panes and thick green light,/As under a green sea, I saw him drowning" [*PB*, 183]) the power to shut off the concentration-camp ovens in advance. And the German avant-gardists created a poetry of counter-assault that transformed Lewis' dramatic wounds and tropes of military romance ("the source of light is within your own belly" [*BB*, 122]) into numbing taxonomies of martial pathology that, like Wilhelm Klemm's "Clearing Station," turn the body of the war inside out—"Intestines hang out. From a ripped saddle of flesh/the spleen and stomach have welled. A rump-bone gapes/round an arse-hole./On the amputated stump flesh foams into the air" (*PB*, 235). Even the intractable representation of mass death is articulated in powerful syntactical deformations by August Stramm, when in "Battlefield" he pluralizes unquantifiable and indivisible substances ("bloods," "rusts," "fleshes") to transform an algorithm of murder into the elemental ontology of the battlefield as a mass subject:

> Yielding clod lulls iron off to sleep
> bloods clot the patches where they oozed
> rusts crumble
> fleshes slime
> sucking lusts around decay.
> Murder on murder
> blinks
> in childish eyes.
> (January, 1915)

> (PB, 237)

But such a historical construction of an abashed high modernism, conceding the dubiety of its victory over other war verse and the crumbling of its empire of poetry in the post-colonial era, sputters on the coda of its powerful reemergence as the chief critical intertext of the Vietnam War's canonical masterwork, Francis Ford Coppola's *Apocalypse Now*. Like the return of the repressed, high modernism reproduces itself in its own compulsion to intertextuality and quotation in *Apocalypse Now,* to repeat T. S. Eliot's own gesture when he calls for a "mythical method" to combat the futility and anarchy of modernity. In an age when poetry as an intellectual force retreated to the academy, modernism, in the form of Conrad's novella and Eliot's own poems and their archive, became ingested as a chief formal instrument (Eliot become his own mythical method) by the very media of mass culture its practitioners and theorists feared and fought throughout the period. But as ideological intertext of a mass medium, modernism is allowed to reproduce itself in Coppola's film with a complex set of differences. The allusions to the plot, characters, narrative frame, and snippets of dialogue from Conrad's *Heart of Darkness* are left uncited because they are extranarrative, and their reference is treated as familiar enough to be imputed to the general knowledge of a mass audience. But the citations and quotations from *The Waste Land* are treated in a way that differs from the occulting practices of Eliot's own poem. Where *The Waste Land* gives an externally referenced, but untranslated, set of lines from Wagner's *Tristan und Isolde,* the film internally provides translation, citation, and context— for example, *Die Valküre* referenced as Wagner's music and explained as a weapon in the "Psy-war." Eliot's poetry is quoted by the photographer and by Kurtz, but the paperback texts of the selected poems and their prolegomenae, Frazer's *Golden Bough* and Jessie Weston's *From Ritual to Romance,* are shown on the screen. The film's modernistic erudition is carefully made available to its mass audience in order to unify the American perception by reversing the babelizations with which Eliot sought to divide it. But at the same time, Coppola's film replicates the post–World War II transformation of modernism's discourses of population control by transferring its aversion to the masses from the European and American proletariat to the peoples of the Third World. The invisibility of the Vietnamese marks *Apocalypse Now* as a text whose empire of signs remains resolutely Western, even if one were to argue that the film stages and exhibits, rather than enacts, the Western occlusion of the Vietnamese.[28] But the film successfully meets the modernistic challenge of representing the mass dead with a stunning strategy of literalizing Eliot's sublation of the war dead into the mythology of fertility rituals. In the final Cambodian sequence of *Apocalypse Now,* the dead bodies fill the screen, dispersed through every element.

They hang from the trees like apples, protrude from the ground like tubers; their heads, like the Cook's, are tossed like cabbage, until dead bodies seem to be produced by the elements of war as naturally as vegetation. It is as though modernism made us wait until Vietnam before giving us, in a return of the repressed, its nightmare revisitation to the horrors of World War I.

CHARLES ALTIERI

A Tale of Two Modernisms, or Richard Rorty's Philosophy as Trojan Horse

I have had a lot of trouble deciding what I could write for this collection that would honor Joe Riddel and at the same time capture some of why Joe meant so much to me. Should I emphasize the arguments I had with Joe, taking this one last chance to set him right for eternity? Or should I try to show how his kindness, his intensity, and his critical seriousness helped shape my vision of professional life when I first came under his influence at Buffalo? (There is no way of showing how he deflated my ego as an academic athlete, but some aspects even of an academic's life are best left in forgetfulness.) I decided that it might be possible to address both concerns if I reverse the typical course of our conversations, where we were eager to get directly to our theoretical differences. Now I want to spend most of my time developing two themes with which I think Joe might agree, and whose import I still owe to him. The first concerns the importance of linking modernism in poetry to modernism in philosophy, and the second focuses on the inadequacy of the Anglo-American philosophical tradition to that task. Joe was especially bothered by philosophers like Richard Rorty who claim to be sympathetic to deconstruction, but whose eagerness to adapt it for an American context deprived it of most of its density and all of its complex negative playfulness. But my own engagement of Rorty is ultimately intended to provoke Joe yet once more. Without actually engaging Derrida, I want to suggest that the limitations in Rorty's relation to modernist literature stem from assumptions that also prove problematic when deconstructive theory tries to develop its own versions of what I will claim is the basic quest formulated by modernism in the arts. For deconstruction feeds so well as a parasite on empiricist binaries that it cannot sufficiently come to terms with philosophical gestures attempting to construct constructivist and expressivist alternatives to Anglo-American traditions.

It is now standard to view modernism in philosophy as a series of efforts to overthrow idealism, both as a metaphysics and, more important, as a vague commitment to developing through philosophy an authority capable of performing edifying roles for an increasingly decadent culture. But such efforts were not without substantial problems, and substantial consequences. Or so it seemed to that other modernism that tried to appropriate for itself the privilege and the responsibility of defining those possibilities for edification. This ambition, however, also exacted a substantial price. Faced with the vacuum created by the analytic demands that took over the empiricist tradition, modernist artists and writers had in effect to create a *bricoleur*'s version of philosophy. They had to find within their own medium versions of the psyche and of the forces at play in our emotional economies that could provide non-embarrassing modes and models for the entire process of idealization. Yet, because such work had to be done in resistance to the dominant philosophical practices, the early modernists at least (later ones had the benefit of Freud and sometimes Marx) made their own activity the basic vehicle for working out those desired versions of the psyche, and hence of establishing principles by which they could project shareable values and forge an improved social fabric. And such projections then brought them dangerously close to fascism, on the one hand, and to a radically individualist aestheticism, on the other. So we find a symmetrical irony almost worth idealizing in its own right: the empiricist philosophical modernism of Moore and Russell and Carnap offers a mode of thinking capable of representing a liberal political tradition that most of us honor, at the cost of reducing philosophy to something with minimal claims to shape the politics it liberates, while in poetry the ambitious effort to take on the concerns for models of the mind and of deep commitment that philosophy had rejected generates what are for the most part reprehensible political visions.

I think I like the symmetry of this picture too much to violate it by further analysis. So while I will fill in a few details, I will devote most of this essay to the closely related issue of how this ironic situation still affects contemporary literary culture. Clearly, those contemporary philosophers most influential on literary studies claim to provide a richer interplay with concerns basic to the arts. And Derrida in fact makes good on such claims, although he then seems to vacillate between letting the arts set values and trying to recapture the arts within his own philosophical vocabulary. But the case seems to me quite different when we turn to those American philosophers who now seek in literature various kinds of wisdom they feel lacking in their own disciplines. Here I will use as my example Richard Rorty because his work embodies the most complex repetition of the modernist dilemma. On the one hand Rorty is the most radical of philosophers trained in the Anglo-American tradition, since he renounces all foundational claims, and even all specific allegiances to philosophy as a disciplinary practice. Yet he is much more analytic and ascetic (one might also say "reductive") and reliant on traditional philosophical critiques like Davidson's than are thinkers like Cavell and Nussbaum (who turn to literature precisely because it allows them to take up edifying claims that are not possible within contemporary philosophy). One might even say that Rorty's postmodernism takes its license not from cultural multiplicity but from the positivist impulse to dismiss from metaphysics anything that cannot be absolutely demonstrated analytically. The power of philosophy clears the slate so that irony and solidarity become the only acceptable grounds for attributing values. But that reductive power proves woefully inadequate when it is applied to the edifying dimension of modernist writing. So it seems to me crucial that literary critics not be seduced by Rorty's invitation to solidarity. Instead we must look carefully at how thoroughly he is influenced by his roots in modernist empiricism, if only as a means of being wary of his comments on literary matters and of remaining open to competing versions of the roles literary education can be asked to play in contemporary culture.

Modernism in philosophy can be traced back to Bacon's, Descartes', and Hobbes's battles against scholasticism and the authority of religion. Twentieth-century modernism set itself a parallel opponent by turning against the Hegelian heritage that had come to dominate nineteenth-century academic philosophy in the West. On the continent this process takes a path through Nietzsche and Kierkegaard to thinkers as diverse as Bergson, Heidegger, and the Wittgenstein responsive to his native German philosophical traditions. For now, though, I want to concentrate on what the American and British modernists understood as the prevailing philosophical modernism in their own cultures. Here the major figures are Russell and Moore (with substantial parallels in the work of James and Dewey, so long as we let their principles of pragmatic judgment parallel what the British empiricists attribute to logic, and to the ideals of the natural sciences). All four of these thinkers began their philosophical careers attached to idealism, but it was an idealism that could be an easy target for empiricist methods because its primary representatives had turned from Hegel's *Phenomenology* to his *Logic* and had focused its attention on ontology, not on history or psychology.[1]

Three basic aspects of Russell's work must suffice here to summarize an orientation shared by almost all the Anglo-American philosophy coming to the fore early in the twentieth century. Russell's specific analyses are distinctive, but the purposes to which he put the analysis could be seen as participating in a common enterprise. He first took on the basic idealist claims about internal relations as a distinctive ontological category. As Russell put it, "The doctrine of internal relations held that every relation between two terms expresses, primarily, intrinsic properties of the two terms and, in ultimate analysis, a property of the whole which the two compose."[2] But then a good deal of metaphysical baggage becomes necessary. To jettison that baggage Russell insisted on a sharp distinction between properties and relations, with relations definable in terms of contingent circumstances that we order into propositions by using logical forms. Such moves greatly simplify ontology because we can handle what allows negation and subsists through change simply in functional terms whose ontology requires nothing more than the properties of language. And these properties in turn allow clear and distinct concepts of how logical form operates to establish what we can take as knowledge. Finally, such work seems to serve democratic interests by freeing value claims from any holistic necessity, instead casting necessity as another contingent property not predicable from facts or internal to any specific governing schema for experience.

The other two basic aspects follow easily. The second consists in Russell's realization that once properties are distinguished from relations and the internal made problematic, it becomes impossible to rely on organicist notions that treat form as growing out of content and shaping its distinctive internal relations. Form becomes logical form and matter becomes contingent facts to be read in terms of how they fit certain type-token relations or are defined within lawlike generalizations. Such an analytic philosophy need grant no purposiveness within the objects and relations that it analyzes, so there need be no claims about dialectical processes, even those that do not rely on assertions about teleological principles. Purpose comes from outside the phenomena analyzed.

Once concepts of internal purposiveness lose their appeal, we see that a third basic aspect becomes central. Philosophy turns out not to need much of a psychology. Spirit becomes mind, and mind becomes a phenomenon we understand in its immediacy as a mode of awareness or in its computational function. As an emblem of this shift we might think of the truth tables in Wittgenstein's *Tractatus* as a proto-Turing machine mapping what a mind must be to function within a language of truth and falsity. All the rest is mere attitude to be negotiated in social exchange.

Philosophy based on such principles is ideally contoured toward individualist versions of liberal values. The human world, too, is a matter of contingencies to be contained within a set of essentially formal constraints. So this mode of thinking emphasizes a freedom paralleling natural contingency, a creativity paralleling chance, and an ethics based on the kind of resistance involved in Enlightenment battles to avoid bewitchment by any external authority. But where in all this do literary ambitions fit, and what from all this can writers use? For most of the modernists, the only response available was bitter opposition. Convinced from their own art that there must be internal relations in life as well, they had to compose psychologies and ontologies making that belief plausible. However, they had to do so without any support from those whose discipline trained them in relating and testing ideas, so they tended to make their own activity the basic focus for their abstractions, as well as the only means of assessing the ideas they projected. The writer becomes culture hero; culture itself becomes material for the artist to shape according to *his* imaginings; and the resistance he experiences becomes prima facie evidence that culture needs the kind of total cure of its ground offered by authoritarian systems and strong leaders. And the failure of such dreams seemed sufficient reason to fall back on a radical individualism despairing of all social programs. Any liberal alternative seems co-opted precisely by its doctrinal alliances with a philosophy that had clearly betrayed the poets, and, according to the poets' logic, had hence betrayed the very possibilities of fostering civilized living conditions.

Almost any modernist writer will provide us some illustration of this struggle to supplement a philosophy turned alien and alienating. The most pronounced conflict took place in the protracted and cross-purposed letters exchanged between W. B. Yeats and T. Sturge Moore, G. E. Moore's brother.[3] Yeats tried his spiritualist fantasy that the objective world is mere appearance against Moore's resolute empiricism, less to explore possible grounds of agreement than to make articulate the contraries on which he could build his alternative vision. One might even say that for Yeats the philosophical contest was less a matter of argument than of provoking possible states of self energized by their refusal of prevailing doctrines.

For Eliot the same conflict takes very different form—both because Eliot wants a philosophical resolution and because the self that he musters for the conflict seems built on internalizing the warring ideas of the major contemporary representatives of idealism and empiricism. Writing on Bradley, Eliot directly takes on Russell in order to preserve an ontological place for internal relations, and hence in order to establish grounds for a dialectical psychology. But not only does his philosophical mind balk at the possibility of an Absolute capable of anchoring those internal relations, his lyric imagination seems to outdo Russell in its sense of the gulf between acquaintance and description and its feeling for the ways that objects pull apart from each other leaving only contingency experienced as an absence of underlying relatedness. No thinker and no system of thinking could successfully hold Russell and Bradley in a single thought, so it is no wonder that for Eliot both alternatives collapsed, leaving him convinced that philosophy itself could not be foundational but had to be grounded in a leap of faith. If the terms of idealism were to be preserved, they had to be redefined in terms that could command the assent of will. That then allowed a different contrast with secular liberalism: rather than attempt to refute it, Eliot could simply ask himself and his audience to register the evils he thought it produced, for that would be a sufficient contrast to drive the will to a transcendental faith securing a psychology and a political authority that purely secular values could no longer sustain.

My final example is considerably more entertaining. The relation between Bertrand Russell and D. H. Lawrence offers contrasts as sharp as those between Moore and Yeats, but the new personages bring a livelier human drama because each seems self-righteously to treat the flaws of the other as his own best self-defense. For Lawrence, the gulf between Russell the philosopher and Russell the moralist demonstrated the limits of rationalism and made visible the need for the alternative psychology that he proposed in *Fantasia of the Unconscious*. Russell, on the other hand, expresses his contempt for Lawrence in a way that exposes a problem he never quite faces. His *Autobiography* comes to his memoirs of Lawrence immediately after telling us how his own *Principles of Social Reconstruction* treated "liberation of creativeness" as "the principle of reform."[4] Then we find Lawrence proving all too creative in "the dream-like quality of all his thinking" that made him a "suitable exponent" of the cult of insanity that was Nazism: "I do not think in retrospect that [his ideas] had any merit whatever. They were the ideas of a sensitive would-be despot who got angry with the world because it would not instantly obey. When he realized that other people existed, he hated them. But most of the time he lived in a solitary world of his own imaginings, peopled by phantoms as fierce as he wished them to be."

However, all of Russell's analytic acuity would not save him from vapid theorizing about creativity, since his overall framework gave him nothing but vague pieties for describing the work such creativity might do. Those pieties nonetheless turned out to play a substantial role in reinforcing Wittgenstein's emerging suspicions about the entire empiricist enterprise. He could see no alternative to accepting its constraints on making positive assertions about matters of spirit, but that situation only made all the more clear the limitations of the overall empiricist program. To resist those limitations one could still turn to the positive potential of silence that gets framed by empiricism's limits on what could be asserted. The result, in my view, is a line of thinking on the mysteriousness of the "I" and of the possibility of a mysticism based on the notion of seeing the world as a limited whole that provides the richest philosophical framework we have for treating the arts.[5]

But at the time no significant philosopher followed Russell. In fact, the closest anyone in England came to those speculations was Dora Marsden, editor of the *Freewoman*.[6] Applauding philosophy's shift from pursuing the vague and indefinite to searching for the definable but unsound, she makes the analytic spirit itself the exemplar for a modernist version of the ideals of agency sought by the poets. Self-reflection can lead beyond the objects science deals with to an awareness of the powers of consciousness produced by pure concentration. Rather than surrender discourse about powers of mind to the idealist spiritualism fashionable in prewar London, she argued that in the very process of limiting a field, analysis establishes an "intensifying of the available attention." Analysis fosters movement from the simple to the complex while requiring the mind to stay tightly bound to the field that the movement establishes. And then, Marsden thought, one could recuperate spiritualist concerns on a new basis—by recasting, rather than rejecting, the concentrative power of empiricist analysis along lines soon to be elaborated in objectivist poetics.

I could proliferate examples of the crises shared by modern philosophy and literature. But we have seen enough to recognize a shared modernist sense that it had become necessary for art to take on the burden of philosophy by inventing, against the dominant philosophy, possibilities for reinterpreting the psyche and for developing emotional economies that could align subjective with collective interests. However, we have not yet paid sufficient attention to how such experiments can be evaluated. For that we need to take two further steps. We need a better understanding of the pressures put upon them by the dominant philosophical modernism, and we need a richer sense of how their struggles remain significant for our culture. I want now to turn to Rorty because I think he helps us take both steps. He insists on treating moral and political issues as if they could be subject to the same minimalist strategies adapted by modernist empiricist philosophy for questions of logic and epistemology. Yet he also uses that analytic intelligence to sustain claims for a postmodern, antifoundational alternative to empiricism's insistence on underlying "truths" that reduce the world to the logical structures imposed by philosophers, and that make it seem necessary to propose articulate principles of judgment capable of both demanding and justifying the individual's bonds to a public order. Rorty's alternative seems capable of sustaining a new "perfectionism" based on principles of poetic self-making: literature, and even literary criticism, both acutely attentive to multiple vocabularies, become central to the health of liberal culture. However, despite all this responsiveness to the arts, it is important to realize the costs involved in Rorty's continuing Russell's anti-phenomenological program and in his working with a psychology so thin that it confines his treatment of literary works to moralizing against cruelty or to pieties about creativity that cannot honor what most modernist writers think they are in fact creating. Creativity becomes a vague psychological cure-all rather than something we understand by sensitive attention to its complex products. It is difficult to "prove" such charges because they are so general. Suffice it to say that Rorty is rarely praised as a close reader of texts. And his distrust of all psychological claims is a constant theme, perhaps most evident in chapter five of *Contingency, Irony, and Solidarity,* where psychology collapses into claims about self-creation, with very little attention paid to what might resist or shape the creations. So it ought not seem surprising that one can show how Rorty's anti-foundational arguments nonetheless repeat four basic features of Russell's thinking. And that demonstration will then help establish by contrast the continuing power of modernism to provide alternatives to what haunts Rorty.

First, it is strange and significant that despite Rorty's distrust of all claims about underlying truths, he shares Russell's sense that one must recast arguments in order to display their underlying form. Only for Rorty this underlying form consists not in conditions of reference but in the hold of particular vocabularies. Vocabularies provide his "simples," his ground terms, and because of his effort to establish such a ground, he runs into problems quite similar to those Russell does. He ignores the phenomenology involved in particular uses of those vocabularies, with all the gaps and openings to adjustment that these involve. And he has no clear way to describe when one has arrived at what constitutes a vocabulary. Why do we identify certain statements as belonging to one rather than another vocabulary? How do we decide what makes a vocabulary specific to some cultural situation?

Rorty, I am sure, would claim that the boundaries of vocabularies are themselves rhetorically constituted by strong poetic acts among analysts, but this only doubles the difficulties. At one pole, vocabulary becomes little more than a synechdoche for what agents create, albeit a dangerously limiting one because it focuses only on the overt instruments without sufficient concern for the processes of exploring, testing, and negotiating the boundaries of such vocabularies. At the other pole, this emphasis on vocabularies can only have significant practical consequences if one treats vocabularies as providing evidence for determinate conceptual schemes. But, according to Rorty's hero, Davidson, that evidence is not likely to be convincing. Yet without faith in such explanatory power, Rorty could not sustain his claims for the ability of redescription to transform social conditions. Instead, he would have to admit that what matters is not vocabularies in themselves but what agents do in using, abusing, and modifying vocabularies. Correspondingly, history is rarely clear and distinct enough to be analyzed into the workings of discrete or policed vocabularies.

Let me make this point in more technical terms, if only to ward off (or offer ammunition to) philosophical objections. In his atomist phase, Russell developed a theory of description that required rewriting sentences so that the logical core of their propositional elements could be clearly assessed, properties distinguished from relations, and ontology replaced by functional semantics. Notice for example that the sentence "the present king of France is bald" seems to make sense even though it is false, so we seem to need hypotheses about subsistent elements allowing us to make negative judgments. Russell's recasting of the sentence instead dramatizes the strictly instrumental features of propositional form: "there is at least one present king of France," "at most one person is presently king of France," and "that person is bald." There is no need for any ontological claims about the instruments that carry denotation because the work of denoting is not a property of expressions per se but of their function as descriptions, a function that can be understood entirely as the working of logical forms.[7] There are then calculi operating within language that are not made visible in its ordinary form, so that philosophy must have the authority to recast the sentences so that the relation of form to function is manifest.

Rorty denies the ontology that sustains Russell's rewriting: the empirical conditions determining the truth of descriptions are not read off the world but are themselves conditioned by our practices. But to flesh out his case, he ends up licensing his own mode of redescribing sentences, justifying the practice by the general claim that the basic materials for theoretical analysis are our "final vocabularies" comprised of the words that we use to justify actions, beliefs, and lives.[8] Thus for Rorty the significant differences in our practices and beliefs come down to this question of conflict among vocabularies, conflicts likely to be resolved not by debate but by historical contingencies. However, although Rorty sometimes takes the Wittgenstein who analyzes language games as an ally, he seems to forget that those analyses depend on not proposing any underlying general forces that then tell us what is really going on. What is really going on is a matter for phenomenological analysis (loosely understood) that depends on specific uses and adjustments all too easily distorted if we try to specify abstractly what vocabularies they belong to and purposes they then must serve. Rather than deal directly with what a person proposes or how the agent's dispositions are expressed, Rorty shifts the focus to quite general containing classes. Once we do generalize to vocabularies and thus eliminate specific adjustments, we must conclude that differences become irreconcilable, but we do so because we have again put the claims of a single interpretive strategy over the possibility of contouring ourselves within the resources that cultural grammars afford. Rorty does see this danger, arguing that he does not ignore Davidson's strictures against the notion of conceptual schemes, but that very claim reveals the deep needs of Rorty's own version of empiricism that Davidson's emphasis on semantics enables him to finesse. Not only must Rorty have the possibility of analyzing so as to sanction redescription, he must authorize the analysis in terms of a generalized explanatory power that seems to me incompatible with his concern for rhetorical conflicts. That we cannot know the boundaries of vocabularies is precisely what keeps our rhetorics in enough contact, and more than enough difference, to require our attending, not to the vocabularies per se, but to what people do with them. There is at least as much reason to generalize about rhetorical acts and topoi as to rely on claims about vocabularies.

The second feature of the Russell-Rorty connection has a very different genealogy. Rorty thinks he can escape Russell's ontologizing, but he actively embraces the split between private and public realms central to Russell's thought, at a cost Rorty does not realize. Russell must maintain sharp distinctions between the public and the private because there is no way to move conceptually from the "simples" into which we analyze propositions to the bonds that unite communities or the properties that transform facts into values.[9] These gaps do not keep Russell from pronouncements on public issues. Quite the contrary, they force him to a painful admission of the gulf between the kind of reasoning one adapts in logical studies and the attitudinal principles that one tries to make vivid in one's writing for a public (*A*, II, 289). One might even claim that much of his *Autobiography* is structured by a process of marking the limits of what seemed to him a total conversion in 1901. Thus, in 1940, he tells us that his concurring with military involvement against Hitler "was the last stage in the slow abandonment of many of the beliefs that had come to me in the moment of conversion in 1901," to radical humanitarian principles (*A*, II, 287ff), and then goes on to summarize various aspects of his life where emotion and opinion had proven irreconcilable.

With Rorty the situation could be quite different, since his emphasis on rhetoric and vocabularies leads easily into idealist or Foucauldian schemes where the public inhabits and invades the private, and conversely where it makes sense to treat individuals as exemplars of attitudes a community might take on. But then Rorty's sacrosanct individualism is threatened. So Rorty develops a version of individualism even more insulated from public assessment than anything imaginable within Russell's world of noblesse oblige. He bases his individualism not on any set of private positive powers but on the ironist's ability to generate differences by using vocabularies and filiations without being chained to them. This route to individualism is necessarily divorced from any public life by its refusal to work within accepted categories and its insistence on difference as the mark of individuality separate considerations of agency from all thematized social bonds. However, for Rorty that lack of thematic bonds is to be embraced because it allows him a minimalist politics, not dependent on illusory abstractions and self-congratulatory notions of obligation and service. In his view, we need not work out positive theoretical principles for political life except insofar as we manage at once to protect the ironist's freedoms and to compensate for the cruelty and humiliations that such freedom creates. Our bonds to others depend simply on the solidarity that leads us to take their suffering as making claims upon us. Accordingly, social progress derives from the work imagination does in furthering that solidarity (*CIS,* xvi). In other words, when imagination is not ironic, it is in the service of solidarity. But Rorty still must explain why anyone whose freedom depends on irony would choose or even entertain the alternative focus for imagination that binds him or her to the political.

Modernist poetry provides one useful alternative to Rorty, since the careers of all the major modernists take the opposite tack. Early in their careers they become fascinated by the power irony gives to create individuality as a refusal of social filiations, but they soon treat that route as impoverished and turn instead to explore what Stanley Cavell calls a "generalized intimacy" allowing them to project values they hope can transform social life. In that work they imagine sociality depending on representative figures and articulated beliefs, while Rorty thinks he can keep freedom essentially negative and still find in solidarity a direct basis for social connections. Literature, for Rorty, could become social simply by stressing specific imaginative contents and their presumed effects, with no worry about how that content is mediated by the social construction of ideals that generate obligation and the means of self-representation by which agents internalize those obligations. Such a literature would be compatible with a morality that goes back before Kant to dreams of immediate empathy and imagined communities. But that model simply cannot work, since it has no way to handle conflict among groups or within psyches whose imagining of goods for themselves proves all too influential in how they use their imaginings about others.

To handle the difficulties Rorty faces, I suspect we need a more complex notion of freedom, where irony is at best only a partial means to certain self-representations. Correlatively, the public order cannot rely simply on a willingness to abide by contingency, supplemented by whatever people make of solidarity. Even if liberal society must accept whatever its processes generate, there is no reason to let such a general meta-vision prevent us from trying to determine how thinking might best affect those contingencies. Here I must leave it to others, preeminently Thomas McCarthy, to show how impoverished Rorty's political thinking is in its distrust of intellectually derived obligations, as if all theory had to be foundational.[10] I want to concentrate on how such politics also impoverish one's terms for appreciating literary experience. Rorty's text can offer us only a Nabokov redeployed in the service of exposing cruelty and a Proust reduced to the world of intimate personal relationships he cultivated. More generally, literature becomes once again moral example (as Russell himself viewed it, *cf. A,* III, 34), and the effort to compose psyches and develop constructive powers is dismissed in order to stress how we can recognize what constitutes cruelty.

Rorty's third basic link to Russell is manifest in this sort of response to literary works. He cannot do more with literature in large part because he accepts the tradition in empiricist philosophy that emphasizes working with the simplest possible versions of human psychology in order to trace the causal relations demanded by the theory. Rorty, of course, denies that he does so out of any scientism or commitment to physicalism, preferring instead to speak of allegiance to certain vocabularies and responsiveness to creative founding acts. But his analyses still seem to encounter the same problems facing those who are committed to empiricist principles. Rorty's fear of mysticism leads to what he calls a non-reductionist behaviorism characterizing human beings as "nothing more than sentential attitudes— nothing more than the presence or absence of dispositions towards the use of sentences phrased in some historically conditioned vocabulary" (*CIS,* 88). In this spirit, we are told that "what Hegel described as the process of spirit gradually becoming self-conscious of its intrinsic nature is better described as the process of European linguistic practices changing at a faster and faster and faster rate" (7). So much for Hegel's efforts to treat the negative force of irony as not simply a redescription but a deep marker of contradictions that must be worked through if agents are to establish significant personal identities and if the culture is to intensify its spiritual substance. This does not mean Rorty is wrong: making that judgment depends on what we can make of his notion of a disposition toward the use of sentences. There is, though, something worrisome in his distinguishing dispositions toward the use of sentences from Wittgenstein's more radical and more subtle sense that the use of sentences defines dispositions, and hence makes redescription and explanation extremely difficult because of the complex, indefinite states that can be involved.

The full price of Rorty's minimalism, as with Russell's, emerges when he turns to positive statements and thus has to rely on a psychology that he cannot even describe, let alone defend. Suppose we ask what motivates liberal ironists to seek freedom in creating new vocabularies? Rorty's answer is that the successful ironist can say "I willed it" (97), and hence, in the case of Proust at least, he can "free himself from the descriptions of himself offered by the people he had met" (102). That concern for freedom as expression resisting the expressive energies of others does play a central role in modernist art, but there the emphasis lies not on ironic negation but on what one can in fact make articulate. Rorty cannot go that far, since his psychology has no positive terms, and hence affords no place in its otherwise behaviorist framework for such naked voluntarism. Even if we grant him that there is such a power of will, he still has to tell us why the will puts such emphasis on vocabularies rather than actions or styles, and he would have to explain how those who are not intellectuals seek parallel satisfactions (or is this concern for will created by the contingencies of being an intellectual—in which case non-intellectuals need a different basis for their concerns about personal identity?). Once Rorty introduces such psychological issues, he is bound by his pragmatism to develop the relevant account, but within his vocabulary he simply lacks the resources to do that.[11]

Finally, the lack of a contoured or nuanced psychology leads Rorty to share Russell's tendency to rely on a vague ideal of creativity as his basic value term for the arts. It seems as if what both philosophers want to honor yet cannot describe as valuable in any detailed way they label as "creativity." In so doing they can transform a perspective based on treating freedom as negativity to one that promises positive models of value, and on that basis they can even project their work as helping to shape ends for political life. But as politics such theorizing seems to me far inferior to versions of liberalism that rely, as Joseph Raz's does, on more elaborate notions of wellbeing.[12] And, more relevant here, that idealizing of creativity seems to me largely responsible for Russell's and Rorty's inability to give textured readings or honor a modernism insistent on creativity as means rather than as end. To handle modernist theory and practice we need a sharp distinction between creativity as assertions of a will to power and creativity as articulate work shaping objects so that they actually do the work of defining values and exemplifying attitudes that other people can explore. Art that matters must put the creative will to work in exploring and testing specific values—that we regard as values, not simply as creations per se. In other words, it does not suffice to notice that something is created; what matters is how people can make the creation part of their lives. But Rorty can treat the making of fictions only as the ironic means for freeing contingent subjects, or as a reportorial mode helping to make public the sources and effects of cruelty. But the division between private and public makes it impossible to stress the use of private performances as providing exemplary strategies for attending to the world, or forming emotional economies, or imagining what personal powers can be, or forming tribunals like the eight to whom Nietzsche submitted his work for judgment.[13]

In conclusion, I want to insist, in the spirit of Rorty, that I have said nothing about the truth or falsity of modernist empiricism, but I hope I have said a lot about the limits we take on when we find ourselves adapting its strategies. If I am right about the limitations, two general warnings follow. First, since so many of Russell's problems reemerge in Rorty, and since both philosophers seem trapped within attitudes toward the arts that modernism tried to overcome, it seems plausible to argue that there are persistent problems and filiations that simply do not go away when we think we are changing vocabularies. Granted that problems can only be problems within a vocabulary. But if they persist through shifts in vocabularies, or if changes in vocabularies in fact repeat much the same basic ways of thinking, we must begin to seek reasons in the world, or in the ways a range of vocabularies get formulated, that explain the persistence. And in seeking those we are perforce seeking principles that allow us at least some ways of defining what functions the vocabularies must serve and what tests they must meet to earn authority. So, while the role of philosophy may no longer be to establish foundations, it has much work to do in clarifying the pressures on our different vocabularies and in defining what it might take for any one vocabulary to claim it has surpassed its competitors in relation to specific issues. And, since the power of literary works depends in large part on their sensitivity to such problems, it becomes quite dangerous to trust philosophers who come bearing gifts or praising their new hosts in literature departments. Imperious habits die hard, or fail to die because the empiricist bases of modernist philosophy prove remarkably flexible means of reestablishing the reductionist story about imaginative creativity on which philosophical authority has come to rest.

The second warning is that we be even more wary of philosophers bearing gifts with the designer label "post-modern." These gifts are in fact instruments in an undeclared war to establish whether the arts set the agendas for postmodernism or whether priorities will derive from the claims of philosophy and social theory. And in this struggle there is no better philosophical warrior than Rorty. By claiming to build a postmodern philosophy based on the example of writers and literary critics, Rorty in fact takes literature back before modernism when it could be content with edifying pieties about its creativity and mimetic truths, and before it had to do the work that philosophy has come to reject—first in the name of science, now in the name of "creativity." If the arts are to set agendas for postmodernism, artists and critics must begin by recognizing the work still to be done in shaping plausible secular psychologies and compelling images of possible selves—this time aware of the price to be paid if the arts let modernism in philosophy define what constitutes a liberal social order and thus trap them into pursuing hopelessly radical alternatives.

Joe Riddel turned to Derrida as his guide in preserving what could be philosophical in the arts from the versions of philosophy (not quite vocabularies) based on empiricist principles. It remains to be seen whether that path constitutes a hopelessly radical alternative defined too much by what it hopes to dislodge or a means of recuperating powers within the arts that our prevailing empiricist categories for thinking, willing, and writing, simply cannot credit. But Joe has done more than any other critic of modernist writing to show us how modernist writing seems to warrant our taking that path, and how in taking it we can preserve both the literariness of philosophy and the philosophical force of lyric constructions.

JOHN CARLOS ROWE

Whitman's Body Poetic

Behold me—incarnate me as I have incarnated you!
—Walt Whitman, "City of Ships"

Whitman's transcendental genius is best expressed in his extra-ordinary rhetoric of the body. He does not just faithfully represent nineteenth-century bodies; he makes possible the translation of the body into language, and convinces us that *this* is the American response to Wordsworth's claim that poetry ought to be the "language really spoken by men." What is really spoken by nineteenth-century Americans is still for Whitman the language of human labor, the basis for his visionary community. Repeatedly, he connects his own poetic activity to the everyday work of the nineteenth-century laborer, even though he knows how difficult it will be to convince his readers of this, accustomed as they are to the "pale poet-ling seated at a desk lisping cadenzas piano."[1] Human labor is sensuous, sexual, evocative, productive, and finally figurative. In this sense, the poet is merely one worker among many, "a strong man erect" with "sinewy limbs," but no more so than the smith or the mechanic.

In this spirit, Whitman's poetry implicitly criticizes Emerson's abstract-ness and the disembodied ideals that elude more ordinary, unphilosophical activities of daily life. Even in his best efforts to address directly the values expressed by the honest toil of the ordinary American or to protest loudly the violence slavery does to the body, Emerson consistently subordinates the materiality of human labor to what he had termed in *Nature* "man's power to connect his thought with its proper symbol, and so utter it."[2] However passionately Emerson insists that "Use, labor of each for all, is the health and virtue of all beings," he consistently subordinates such labor to "ideas," "Nature," "morality," and other key concepts in his transcendentalism.[3] In the face of the mounting casualties in the Civil War and the continuation of slavery's violence to African Americans, Emerson was certainly chastened by the knowledge that "ideas must work through the brains and the arms of good and brave men, or they are no better than dreams" ("American Civilization," 289). But even the "good and brave men" dying on the battlefields of the Civil War, however necessary Emerson insists they are, remain abstractions for him: "Better the war should more dangerously threaten us,—should threaten fracture in what is still whole, and punish us with burned capitals and slaughtered regiments, and so exasperate the people to energy, exasperate our nationality. There are Scriptures written invisibly on men's hearts, whose letters do not come out until they are enraged. They can be read by war-fires, and by eyes in the last peril" (282–83).

We must recall that Emerson's poetic rage is inspired by the crisis of the War and the continuation of slavery as an institution. His appeal for "immediate Emancipation" is unquestionably courageous, but his transcendentalism still neglects the *fact* of the human body and its damage in both war and under slavery. What appeals to us in Whitman's poetic concern for the human body is his refusal of such mystifying sentiments and his insistence that whatever is good in his poetry merely speaks to the body in its everyday struggle to express itself, in the toil of honest labor. In this regard, Whitman strikes me as an even more satisfactory revision of Emersonian transcendentalism than Thoreau.

Of course, Thoreau attempted to give concrete particularity to Emerson's abstractions, to follow as literally as possible the disciplines of transcendental man, if only to discover thereby the visionary connection of spiritual and material life. In reading Thoreau, this sense of concreteness is just what satisfies a sort of hunger left by Emerson's philosophical essays. Thoreau's writing is always autobiography, and his demand of the reader is equivalent to what Thoreau has *done*: the production in writing of a "body" that is also a self. This is what Stanley Cavell understands as Thoreau's deliberate confusion of the book with his body, of the figura for the figure: "The boon of Walden is *Walden*. Its writer cups it in his hand, sees his reflection in it, and holds it out to us. It is his promise, in anticipation of his going, and the nation's, and Walden's. He is bequeathing it to us in his will, the place of the book and the book of the place."[4] The rhetorical chiasmus Cavell employs here effectively captures the "imbrication" of self and text, object and idea, spirit and place that distinguishes Thoreau's transcendentalism. Beautiful as this entanglement is, it confronts a fundamental problem when the circumstances are shifted from the contemplation of Nature (either in Thoreau or Cavell) to the experience of war and physical injury. It is this problem I wish to explore in Whitman's *Drum-Taps*.

Thoreau's concreteness is an effect of his figurative language, not just of some naïve realism, but it is composed primarily of what Eliot termed "objective correlatives." The inner world assumes the dimensions of a landscape or a scene or the simplest object, richly charged with its significance in Thoreau's autobiographical purpose and thus with its careful placement in a narrative of self-representation. Thoreau's body is always there, but more often than not by implication, metonymically displaced by its proper extension—a hoe, an axe, the fields and woods, the pond itself. We see relatively little of Thoreau's actual body, even as he baptismally bathes in the pond each day; object-relations have replaced it, even if we are supposed to guess how that body has entered into those objects, extended itself, made itself by way of them. Near the end, in the famous Spring thaw of *Walden*, it is the railroad bank that becomes the ultimate metonymy for the transcendental body, the streams and mud figuring the circulation of the body. The Spring thaw is at once the birth of the poet, rebirth of Nature, and the origin of language. Nevertheless, the "nature" of language still requires Thoreau as interpreter; for Whitman, it promises simply to be there in the figural presence of the body. The woodcutter still has much to learn from the author of *Walden;* the mechanic, the "strong man erect," with "well-gristled body and sunburnt face and hands," is greeted on the open road by Whitman, who carries his burden of words with the same apparent ease as his companion bears "the trowel, the jack-plane, the black-smith's hammer." The difference between Whitman's democracy and the idealism of Emerson and Thoreau is that Whitman's utopian vision comprehends the equality of the labor of the poet and the mechanic.

My bits and pieces from Whitman have been from *Drum-Taps,* for the moment to demonstrate how Whitman's great revision of American Romanticism persists even here in the midst of the War's perverse invocation of the body. Of all human labor, the work of war insistently requires the most strenuous and urgent exertion; even more explicitly than other kinds of labor, war requires of the body symbolic as well as material expenditure. For these reasons, the Civil War posed the ultimate philosophical, as well as political, challenge to our greatest poetic celebrant of the human body and that diverse labor in which co-ordinated bodies make a community. *Drum-Taps* marks a crucial turn in Whitman's poetry that I shall interpret as Whitman's ultimate failure to sustain the democratic vision of the poet as merely one worker among many.[5] It is nonetheless a great failure, because it genuinely risks the poet's authority as neither Emerson's nor Thoreau's safer, qualified transcendentalisms would.

What Whitman risked in *Drum-Taps* was a poetic voice that could not incorporate war, even a war as just in the Union's cause as the Civil War— that is, a voice that despaired of transforming human pain into poetic meaning. The best parts of *Drum-Taps* spring from this refusal to render war "poetic," but it is a strong denial that even Whitman could not sustain. *Sequel to Drum-Taps* (1865–1866) charts the poet's return from the despair of "transcending" war in rhetoric and song, resulting in the two poems for which he is best known, "When Lilacs Last in the Dooryard Bloom'd" and "O Captain! My Captain!" The irony of Whitman's struggle with the ethics of poetically representing war and the violence it does both to the sacred body and human community is that the assassination of President Lincoln provided Whitman just the symbolic event necessary to overcome his pain regarding the suffering of the common soldier. The poetic genius of both poems in the *Sequel* is a consequence of Whitman's renewed ability to affirm poetic authority in the face of the absence of political authority left by the assassination of Lincoln. Empowered by this new sense of urgent responsibility for the poet to take up the "song" of the nation, Whitman may forget the terrible lessons of the hospital wards he visited in New York and Washington in 1863. By "forget," I do not mean, of course, to repress utterly the "everday" pain of those ordinary Americans addressed first and last by Whitman's democratic vision. I mean instead that Whitman rediscovers a poetic voice and authority in the *Sequel to Drum-Taps* that allows him to incorporate more easily thus more transcendentally the damage to the body in war.

I propose, then, to look at the first edition of *Drum-Taps* as distinct from its *Sequel* for the sake of understanding the internal conflicts of the former collection *before* Whitman found a way to overcome these problems in his elegies for President Lincoln. *Drum-Taps* was printed and ready for distribution when Lincoln was shot, and the conjecture that Whitman withdrew the volume "because of Lincoln's death" seems confirmed by Whitman's organization of the *Sequel to Drum-Taps* around his two great memorials for the President.[6] Yet, I do not want this close focus on *Drum-Taps* to suggest some special authority for the original text beyond its expression of Whitman's struggle with the realities of war and his ideals as a poet. In fact, Whitman's subsequent revisions of *Drum-Taps,* beginning with his decision to bind *Drum-Taps* and *Sequel to Drum-Taps* together for the 1865–1866 publication, support my thesis that Whitman was able to overcome the ethical problem of representing the physical suffering of individuals in the War by way of symbolic enactments that reaffirmed the authority of the poet and the value of his figurative language.

From the inclusion of *The Sequel* to his "final arrangement" of the poems in *Drum-Taps* and *Memories for President Lincoln* for the 1891–1892 edition of *Leaves of Grass,* Whitman rearranged the narrative of his Civil War experiences into a kind of poetic *Bildungsroman,* proceeding from the poet's initial patriotism through his disillusionment over the suffering of individual soldiers to the reaffirmation of the redemptive powers of the poet, both in his testament to the otherwise anonymous Union dead and his ecstatic substitution of his own authority for the dead President in the two great elegies. These revisions of the last twenty-five years of Whitman's life seem to confirm Timothy Sweet's thesis that the threat posed by the Civil War to the political union was understood by Whitman as equally a threat to his democratic poem, *Leaves of Grass,* and that *Drum-Taps* "presents itself as a recuperative political-poetic response."[7] In effect, Whitman was reaffirming the ethics and aesthetics of American romanticism in the course of these revisions. In doing so, he produced one of the greatest poems of American nationalism, "When Lilacs Last in the Dooryard Bloom'd" and thereby legitimated the romantic concept of the poet as spokesman for a nation.[8] Whitman's rediscovery of his transcendentalist roots, however, was purchased at the expense of his earlier commitments to the "equality" of material and intellectual labor in the building of community. The renaissance of Whitman's idealism after the War also resulted in the vainglory of the egotistical sublime expressed in poems like "Passage to India" and "Prayer of Columbus"—works that helped legitimate culturally the emerging imperialism of the United States in the Western Hemisphere and the Pacific.[9]

The narrative I wish to trace in *Drum-Taps* begins with the patriotic strains that Whitman sings with only the most troubled voice. Beating the drum and flying the banner of the Union, he acknowledges the justice of the Union cause, even as he recognizes how easily such sentiments transform the critical edge of the poet into war-time clichés, mere propaganda. From the first, he is troubled with the ineffectiveness of poetry to address History:

> Words! book-words! what are you?
> Words no more, for hearken and see,
> My song is there in the open air, and I must sing,
> With the banner and pennant a-flapping.
> ("Song of the Banner at Day-Break," *DT,* 458)

Yet the image of the active, militant poet, some medieval troubadour leading his troops in battle, singing defiance on the battlefield, is equally unacceptable, since the poet in such circumstances must sing only the military general's command. Despite the performatives, so often in the volitive mood, Whitman doubts the capacity of his words to act, to carry the agency and urgency of the poet, rather than the general or statesman:

> I'll pour the verse with streams of blood, full of volition, full of joy,
> Then loosen, launch forth, to go and compete,
> With the banner and pennant a-flapping.
> ("Song of the Banner at Day-Break," *DT,* 458)

From the first poems of *Drum-Taps,* such lines ring false, and Whitman is intent upon reclaiming some natural or divine authority that will liberate him from mere service to the government's cause without forgetting his commitment to the justice represented by that cause.

The chief propaganda of the war poem has often been the rhetoric of sacrifice, that perverse appeal to mothers and fathers to surrender their children to the noble purposes of war. From the outset, Whitman identifies his poetic voice with the banner of the Union and the pennants of its military units. But already he claims for that poetic voice a *generative* power that both exceeds the parent's natural authority over the child and antedates the Union's leadership. The visionary authority of the poet does not simply gather together communally the labor of others; throughout *Drum-Taps,* it claims a superiority that stems from both Whitman's panoptic view of historical purpose and his prior knowledge of the inevitability of war. The opening lines of "Rise O Days from Your Fathomless Deeps," "probably composed in the early days of recruiting" for the War, suggest that the poet's entire career, especially the rhetorical travels of *Song of Myself,* has been simply preparation for the War: [10]

Long for my soul hungering gymnastic I devour'd what the earth gave me,
Long I roam'd the woods of the north, long I watch'd Niagara pouring,
. . . .
I heard the wind piping, I saw the black clouds,
. . . .
Noted the slender and jagged threads of lightning as sudden and fast amid
    the din they chased each other across the sky;
These, and such as these, I, elate, saw—saw with wonder, yet pensive and
    masterful,
All the menacing might of the globe uprisen around me,
Yet there with my soul I fed, I fed content, supercilious.
            ("Rise O Days from Your Fathomless Deeps," *DT,* 483–84)

In the concluding stanza of this same poem, the poet claims to have returned from his long preparation in the colder northern climates, where he had "waited the bursting forth of the pent fire—on the water and air I waited long," only to be satisfied now with the realization of his prophecy: "But now I no longer wait, I am fully satisfied, I am glutted,/I have witness'd the true lightning, I have witness'd my cities electric,/I have lived to behold man burst forth and warlike America rise" (*DT,* 485–86).[11]

Whitman's claim for foreknowledge of the War's necessity not only reaffirms his prophetic powers, it also becomes the occasion for recalling the historical purposes of revolutionary America.[12] *Drum-Taps,* like all serious poetry of war, is obsessed with the problem of memory, for it appears to be the hopeless task assigned the poet either to memorialize gloriously war or simply remind us of its pain. The "old man bending" who arrives "among new faces" in "The Wound-Dresser" is the poet reduced to failure, "To sit by the wounded and soothe them, or silently watch the dead," even as he is charged to "witness again, paint the mightiest armies of earth," and answer the questions: "What stays with you latest and deepest? of curious panics,/Of hard-fought engagements or sieges tremendous what deepest remains?" ("The Wound-Dresser," *DT,* 479, 480). As Sweet argues, Whitman's questions in *Drum-Taps* reflect the self-doubt manifested both in Whitman's physical and emotional breakdowns while serving as volunteer in the army hospitals and the poetic struggle in *Drum-Taps* to reaffirm the Self of his antebellum poetry.[13]

Neither the transcendental Self nor the patriotic purpose of the Union quite serves the poet's effort to reaffirm his own voice and prophetic mission. As if searching for a more profound justification for the human damage he witnesses, Whitman returns to the original revolutionary purpose of the nation. To be sure, this is by no means unique to Whitman's Civil War poems; it was commonplace for abolitionists to make the call to arms in terms evocative of the Revolution, often insisting that the Civil War must complete the unfinished work of our first war against tyranny.[14] What distinguishes Whitman's appeal to the revolutionary past, however, is his claim that only poetic vision can turn that past and the present carnage of the war into an optimistic future. In "The Centenarian's Story," for example, the aged veteran of the Revolution is an alter-ego for the poet, who in "The Wound-Dresser" is reduced nearly to the feeble condition of the blind Centenarian. Both are left apparently with nothing more than their powerless memories, but in "The Centenarian's Story" this poetic recall is finally transformational. The veteran claims that "as I talk I remember all," and what he remembers for the sake of the "Volunteer of 1861–2," "assisting the Centenarian," is initially conventional war propaganda:

> As I talk I remember all, I remember the Declaration,
> It was read here, the whole army paraded, it was read to us here,
> By his staff surrounded the General stood in the middle, he held up his
>   unsheath'd sword,
> It glitter'd in the sun in full sight of the army.
>   ("The Centenarian's Story," DT, 471)

Whitman's invocation of General Washington reading the troops the Declaration of Independence at the Battle of Long Island (August 27, 1776) is metamorphosed from patriotic lore into a resource for the poet himself, who concludes the poem abruptly and with surprising authority:

> Enough, the Centenarian's story ends,
> The two, the past and present, have interchanged,
> I myself as the connecter, as chansonnier of a great future, am now
>   speaking.
> And is this the ground Washington trod?
> And these waters I listlessly daily cross, are these the waters he cross'd,
> As resolute in defeat as other generals in their proudest triumphs?
> I must copy the story, and send it eastward and westward,
> I must preserve that look as it beam'd on you rivers of Brooklyn.
>   ("The Centenarian's Story," DT, 473–74)

Whitman has not quite displaced Washington, as he will attempt later to fill the absence left by the death of Lincoln in "Lilacs," but the active purpose of poetic memory to construct a positive future out of the chaos and damage of the present is clear enough.[15]

Whitman's entanglement of poetic and political *genii loci* is evident throughout *Drum-Taps,* as if he were struggling to take over the sites of the war, with both their verbal conventions and physical horrors, for the sake of some finer poetic vision. In "City of Ships," the Union's naval strength is quickly subordinated to the poet's imaginative powers, especially as the latter have been identified with Whitman's Brooklyn and New York throughout *Drum-Taps.* Once again, the rhetoric of *Song of Myself* is employed primarily for the sake of restoring to the poet his special authority to be more than a mere chronicler of war. This is also the poem in which Whitman makes his most direct, albeit still figuratively disguised, address to the true moral purpose of the War: the abolition of slavery. For all the patriotic enthusiasms of *Drum-Taps,* there is scant evidence of this issue in the collection, strangely, since this issue seems the justification of the poet's claim to "prior knowledge" of the necessity of war. They are "black ships" and thus "fierce ships" in this "City of the world! (for all races are here,/All the lands of the earth make contributions here;)" ("City of Ships," DT, 490). It is above all, however, Whitman's poetic city: "City of the sea! city of hurried and glittering tides!/ . . . Proud and passionate city—mettlesome, mad, extravagant city!" that is indistinguishable from the poet's imagination:

> Spring up O city—not for peace alone, but be indeed yourself, warlike!
> Fear not—submit to no models but your own O city!
> Behold me—incarnate me as I have incarnated you!
>
> ("City of Ships," *DT,* 490)

This power of incarnation is achieved by way of imaginative identification with military power, the *genius loci* of the democratic northern city, and the revolutionary history of the republic. It enables Whitman to substitute his own egotistical sublime for the conventional propaganda of war poetry. What emerges in *Drum-Taps* is Whitman's reaffirmation of the poet's ability to redeem what has been destroyed in war, thus answering those who ask: What has the poet to tell us of war? In effect, Whitman answers by insisting that the poet bring the indispensable vision of what will redeem the pain and damage of war.

In some poems, Whitman merely continues to compete with the generals and statesmen for authority. Even in those poems Matthiessen praised for their painterly impressionism, such as "Cavalry Crossing a Ford," "By the Bivouac's Fitful Flame," and "Bivouac on a Mountain Side," Whitman is doing more than merely poetically describing armies in the field.[16] In such poems, the process of perception itself is often problematized, suggesting some division between the military strategists and the poet, who in most instances subordinates the terrible practicalities of battle to his larger, often redemptive vision. The speaker in "By the Bivouac's Fitful Flame," for example, reviews his own troops while the real troops sleep, drawing on the rhetoric of that much-revised poem from *Leaves of Grass* whose final version was "The Sleepers" (1871, 1881):[17]

> A procession winding around me, solemn and sweet and slow—but first I
>   note,
> The tents of the sleeping army, the fields' and woods' dim outline,
>
> . . . .
>
> Like a phantom far or near an occasional figure moving,
>
> . . . .
>
> While wind in procession thoughts, O tender and wondrous thoughts,
> Of life and death, of home and the past and loved, and of those that are
>   far away;
> A solemn and slow procession there as I sit on the ground,
> By the bivouac's fitful flame.
>
> ("By the Bivouac's Fitful Flame," *DT*, 466)

In keeping with the conventions of the dramatic monologue Whitman used so often, the reader is tempted to understand this poem (and others like it in *Drum-Taps*) as spoken merely by a soldier in the field.[18] Yet when connected with the rhetoric of poetic aspiration in the rest of *Drum-Taps*, the "voice" of even the most realistic war poems takes much of its resonance from that of the poet's distinctive identity. Indeed, the mark of Whitman's poetic genius is just such ventriloquism and subsequent confusion: Who is not a poet when the urgencies of history provoke significant speech? Thus the funereal procession that fades into the poet's own dreamy reflections marks the sort of transformation he desires—from a "solemn and slow procession" declaring death—just what the soldier of the field fears—to the respect paid the poet (whether he be Whitman or the soldier turned poet) for his "wondrous thoughts."

Whitman's appropriation of military and political authority reaches its romantic limit when the power of "incarnation" quite literally becomes the power of parental generation and divine regeneration. Poems like "Come

Up from the Fields Father" and "Vigil Strange I Kept on the Field One Night" complement the "Wound-Dresser" by claiming for the poet not simply the voice of mourning but also the power to resurrect the dead. The Ohio farming parents who receive the message that their son has been wounded read the official lie, *"At present low, but will soon be better,"* which is not unlike the patriotic enthusiasm for war the poet himself expresses in poems such as "Pioneers! O Pioneers!" and even "Beat! Beat! Drums!" that immediately precedes "Come Up from the Fields Father" in the first edition of *Drum-Taps*.[19] The mother is stricken with grief and thus "catches the main words only,/Sentences broken," but the unpoetic character of the message is not just an effect of her emotion, but of the manner in which the official word betrays the natural affections of a family for its wounded son: "O this is not our son's writing, yet his name is sign'd,/O a strange hand writes for our dear son, O stricken mother's soul!" ("Come Up from the Fields Father," *DT,* 489). Even as the daughter attempts to console her mother by repeating the official lie—*"Grieve not so, dear mother, . . . the letter says Pete will soon be better,"* the poet answers honestly; "Alas poor boy, he will never be better. . . ./While they stand at home at the door he is dead already" (489). What appears to be Whitman's substitution of his own poetic truth for the official lie in sympathy with this family's grief turns quickly in the direction of poetic legitimation at the expense of the family. "While they stand at home at the door he is dead already" is concluded with: "The only son is dead." Sympathy gives way to poetic identification of this dead child with Christ, His "only son," and this "sacrifice" now serves not the war effort but the visionary aim of the poet. In the final stanza, the mother wastes away, yearning "silent from life escape and withdraw,/To follow, to seek, to be with her dear dead son" (489).[20]

Neither the farmer nor his wife can address the loss of their son, only the poet replaces the "strange hand" signing the official message with their son's "name" with the allusion to Christ that allows *Whitman* to substitute his forgery for that of the War Department. Such a perverse reading would be strained were it not for the development of this Christological imagery in the subsequent poem, "Vigil Strange I Kept on the Field One Night," in which the substitution now involves not the poet for the grieving parents but the poet for the corpse of a soldier. In the first edition of *Drum-Taps,* this poem is preceded by "Mother and Babe," a two-line lyric without apparent relevance for the War: "I see the sleeping babe, nestling the breast of its mother;/The sleeping mother and babe—hush'd, I study them long and long" ("Mother and Babe," *DT*, 491). In later editions of *Leaves of Grass*, the poem was moved out of *Drum-Taps* to find its eventual place in *By the Roadside* in the 1881 edition, as if Whitman recognized that his invocation of mother and child could serve no other purpose in *Drum-Taps* than reinforce his own bid for authority as the redemptive father of a new, postbellum order of things.

Read in this way, "Vigil Strange" nearly provides the "story" behind the official message of "Pete's" wounding in the earlier poem, although it is clear enough that the two poems refer to different events and characters. Even so, "Vigil" substitutes an intensely personal account of a soldier's death in the field for the "Sentences broken" that announce Pete's wounding to his family in "Come Up from the Fields Father." And the "son" of this poem is also the poet's "comrade," allowing the poet to claim the special intimacy that only veterans of war have for each other:

> When you my son and my comrade dropt at my side that day,
> One look I but gave which your dear eyes return'd with a look I shall
>   never forget,
> One touch of your hand to mine O boy, reach'd up as you lay on the
>   ground.
>   ("Vigil Strange I Kept on the Field One Night," *DT*, 491)

The poet's vigil is earned as a consequence of shared battle, and the body he views so lovingly is inspired by his own sense of miraculous escape from death. As he contemplates this double, "leaning my chin in my hands," the poet has discovered the certain purpose that escaped the more emotional response of the parents in the previous poem: "Passing sweet hours, immortal and mystic hours with you dearest comrade—not a tear, not a word,/Vigil of silence, love and death, vigil for you my son and my soldier" ("Vigil," *DT*, 492). Even as the poet acknowledges the impotence of mere words before actual death, he does so only parenthetically and within the same aside recognizes what seems to contradict the claim that he cannot save this boy: "(I could not save you, swift was your death,/I faithfully loved you and cared for you living, I think we shall surely meet again,)" ("Vigil," *DT*, 492). Ritually wrapping his comrade in his blanket, the poet "envelop'd well his form," and "bathed by the rising sun, my son in his grave, in his rude-dug grave I deposited,/Ending my vigil strange with that"

(492). Sweet reads this poem in conjunction with others that invoke the father for the sake of recalling "the healing power of adhesiveness," including "Quicksand Years" and "The Wound-Dresser."[21]

"Vigil" is a strange combination of compassion and arrogant assertion through which "my son" quite literally becomes Christ buried by the poet/god just as the dawn announces not his "son's" resurrection, but that of the poet transfigured: "I rose from the chill ground and folded my soldier well in his blanket,/And buried him where he fell" (492). It is not, of course, Whitman's purpose to rationalize the carnage of the Civil War by invoking some vague reference to Original Sin and our collective "fall," but rather to suggest how the poetic voice can redeem all those who have fallen in the War. It is the form of the poetry that will not simply chronicle the War but claim the memorializing function that will quite literally "resurrect" poetic vision from the terror of History. By the end of the poem, the fallen comrade has become "my soldier," and he marches for the sake of the poet's triumphant resurrection.[22]

For me to claim that Whitman's *Drum-Taps* has as its ultimate purpose the reaffirmation, even resurrection, of poetic power, rather than an address to the problem of remembrance occasioned by the bloodiest American war, tends to trivialize the compassion that his rediscovered poetic voice expresses. "Many a soldier's loving arms about this neck have cross'd and rested,/Many a soldier's kiss dwells on these bearded lips," Whitman writes in "The Wound-Dresser" (*DT*, 482). Few poems of any war are as powerful in their evocation of sheer human suffering, of the waste of the body occasioned by war. Even in the *Sequel to Drum-Taps,* written expressly to elegize Lincoln and, I contend, to assert more forthrightly than *Drum-Taps* the regained voice of the romantic poet, the nightmare of war's injury to the body remains untranscended, as in "Old War-Dreams":

> In midnight sleep of many a face of anguish,
> Of the look at first of the mortally wounded, (of that indescribable look,)
> Of the dead on their backs with arms extended wide,
>   I dream, I dream, I dream.
>
> ("Old War-Dreams," DT, 550)

Yet, there is still something disturbing in the poet's rediscovery of his voice, of his capacity to wander from the maimed to the dead to receive his blessing. Thus that troubling line at the end of "Long, Too Long America" is more than just the customary bravura of the poet who previously had taken into himself the whole of America. Now there is a note of a "poetic voice" that must remain always before and after the knowledge of fathers and mothers, of comrades and lovers, of sleepers and readers:

> But now, ah now, to learn from crises of anguish, advancing, grappling
>   with direst fate and recoiling not,
> And now to conceive and show to the world what your children en-masse
>   really are,
> (For who except myself has yet conceiv'd what your children en-masse
>   really are?)
>
> ("Long, Too Long America," *DT,* 495)

From the end of *Drum-Taps* to the end of his career, Whitman speaks of those "bodies" that can "make" themselves only in the redemptive language of *his poetry.* The egotistical sublime of "Passage of India" and "The Sleepers" may be the understandable consequence of this working-out of the problem of death in the face of war. What other answer could allow the poet to keep singing? How survive those hospital wards and witness such wounds without the consolation that poetry could redeem them? Sweet concludes that *Drum-Taps* performs rhetorically the "re-union" that War can only require but not itself achieve. Quoting "Reconciliation" from *Sequel to Drum-Taps*—"Beautiful that war and all its deeds of carnage, must in time be utterly lost" (*Sequel,* 555), Sweet claims: "Discourse itself is represented as possessing the aesthetic power to make war disappear."[23] In the back of our minds, heard with the compassion we feel for Whitman's struggle to preserve poetry in *Drum-Taps,* there is the other knowledge that the body poetic soon allows us to forget the body politic, which is perhaps why Whitman had repeated in the 1871 and 1876 editions the lines from "The Wound-Dresser" as an epigraph for the whole: "But soon my fingers fail'd me, my face droop'd and I resign'd myself./To sit by the wounded and soothe them, or silently watch the dead" ("The Wound-Dresser," *DT,* 480). As Whitman's romantic voice "rose from the chill ground" of the battlefield and the hospital, it arrived in time to sing the most extraordinary elegy of our nationality, "When Lilacs Last in the Dooryard Bloom'd." It did so nonetheless at the cost of what Whitman's more truly democratic vision recognized as the proper song of ourselves—the common work of community fractured by slavery, by war, and sometimes by its most exquisite poetry, as well.

JOHN JOHNSTON

Jameson's Hyperspace, Heidegger's Rift, Frank Gehry's House

Surely one of the chief lessons of what has come to be known as poststructuralist theory is that virtually everything comprehensible to us is somehow implicated in language, and that no interpretation can be detached or extricated from what it seeks to interpret. In other words, every act of interpretation necessarily remains blind to its own status and functioning as discourse as long as it is content to offer itself as an objective or even self-reflexive account of what is "already out there," silently waiting to be revealed and given a meaning. In contrast, poststructuralist theory conceives of discourse—of which interpretation is a highly regulated instance—as "a violence we do to things, or in any case a practice which we impose on them," as Michel Foucault succinctly puts it. Since phenomenologically oriented interpretation in particular naturalizes and effaces this violence by assuming that "things are already murmuring meanings which our language has only to pick up," Foucault strenuously opposes it by shifting attention to the active, constitutive power of discourse.[1]

Foucault's recognition of interpretation as a discourse that cannot gain critical access to its own internally regulated mechanisms through the phenomenological epoche compels him to develop a radical alternative. According to Gilles Deleuze, Foucault converts phenomenology into epistemology by challenging Heidegger's (and Merleau-Ponty's) assumption that the order of visibilities and the order of statements (determined historically by a "regime of light" on the one hand and a "regime of language" on the other) both open upon the same world, as if "signification haunted the visible which in turn murmured meaning," as if "it is the same world that speaks itself in language and sees itself in sight."[2] Foucault challenges such an *entrelacement* between the two regimes and the entire structure of intentionality that it supports by elaborating a different conception of knowledge (*savoir*), according to which seeing and saying—the two forms of "knowing" that correspond to these two regimes—are irreducible to one another. (One thinks, of course, of Magritte's *Ceci n'est pas une pipe.*) By envisaging relationships of non- *rapport*, capture or contestation between *le visible* and *l'enoncable,* Foucault moves beyond Heidegger toward a radically Heraclitean epistemology.

Foucault's insistence that the relationship between the visible and the sayable is a reciprocally determined historical variable has potentially significant consequences for the analysis of works of visual art. In fact, for an art criticism that tends to treat art exclusively in terms of perception in a visual field, a field assumed to be free of discursive restraints, Foucault's effort to articulate language with space in a way that does not support intentionality presents a rigorous challenge. To be sure, Foucault was not the first to do this, even among the French poststructuralists. In *Discours, figure,* published in 1971, Jean-François Lyotard argues that language and space cannot be separated, that each always already inhabits the other. Just as language is structured by diacritical differences, so perception is structured by the difference between foveal (*i.e.,* centered and focused) and peripheral vision, a difference that cannot be reduced to an opposition. However, when Lyotard turns to analyze specific works of visual art in these terms, the results tend to be disappointing (with the exception of his book on Duchamp), for the simple reason—and this is true of Foucault as well—that he never confronts any contemporary art as challenging and complex as his theory.

In the United States, where complex and challenging visual art has been abundant since the 1950s, the many recent attempts to expropriate poststructuralism, above all for a theory of "postmodern art," continue to be the order of the day. Fredric Jameson probably represents the best-known example of this effort, both for his attempt to offer a general theory of postmodernism based on art's putative "distorted reflections" of a third stage of capitalism, and for his proposal that a distinctively new kind of space or "hyperspace" is one of its characteristic features.[3] For Jameson, John Portman's Bonaventure Hotel in Los Angeles, with its voluminous lobby and complex of central column and miniature lake, rising balconies, and four symmetrical residential towers, serves to illustrate a new spatial dynamic recognizable by its tendency to go beyond "the capacities of the individual human body to locate itself, to organize its immediate surroundings perceptually, and cognitively to map its position in a mappable external world" (*P*, 44). In this new postmodern "hyperspace," Jameson argues, "distance in general (including 'critical distance' in particular)" has been abolished: "We are submerged in its henceforth filled and suffused volumes to the point where our now postmodern bodies are bereft of spatial coordinates and practically (let alone theoretically) incapable of distanciation" (*P*, 48).

But if postmodern hyperspace not only eludes phenomenological determination but also problematizes or even abolishes "critical distance," then one would expect that the language and the very operations which enable the critic to "read" and interpret the work of art should also come under critical scrutiny. Yet for all his insistence upon the disorientations and confusions of hyperspace and his urgent plea for the necessity of "cognitive mapping," Jameson remains oddly detached, as if this "hyperspace" unfolded outside of his own "scene of reading" and interpretation. It is all the more striking then that Jameson should ignore or dismiss the "lesson" of poststructuralism, precisely at the moment when the art he wants to consider appears to lead him in its direction. Of course, by reducing poststructuralist theory to a series of symptomatic themes and attitudes, Jameson avoids confronting the challenges it might pose to his own Marxist hermeneutical enterprise. This latter may be understood as an act of interpretation in which, in Jameson's words, "the [art]work in its inert, objectal form is taken as a clue or symptom for some vaster reality which replaces it as its ultimate truth" (*P*, 8). But who or what draws the line between symptom and ultimate truth? Here, the word *replaces* hides an entire chain of metaphoric substitutions, and the discursive mechanism that allows the interpreter to move from "symptom" to "ultimate truth" is never put into question. From a poststructuralist viewpoint, the whole machinery of interpretation thus appears as a totalizing metaphorical system that reduces a multiplicity of cultural givens to a dominant scheme in order that this multiplicity can be ordered and controlled, that is, made meaningful. But doesn't the very attribution of meaning—whether positive or "oppositional"—to what Jameson calls "the newer cultural production" (*P*, 49) further the purposes of the capitalist system? Jean Baudrillard, another poststructuralist, suggests as much when he points out that by privileging production as a self-imposed "principle of reality," capitalism and Marxism actually share the same totalizing cultural code.[4]

Thus we might question whether Jameson's "hyperspace" does not hint at something that cannot be decoded and interpreted according to his Marxist scheme, and whether the tendency of hyperspace to exceed phenomenological limits does not also bespeak the limits of Jameson's Marxist hermeneutic and its dialectical underpinnings. Yet if this is indeed the case, then Jameson is surely right in his assertions concerning the novelty of hyperspace, but just as surely wrong about how it should be understood. Since these questions resonate more insistently through Jameson's interpretation of Frank Gehry's Santa Monica house as another signal instance of a postmodern hyperspace, I want to consider his reading of it in some detail.[5]

What is striking about the Gehry house is the novel articulation of space brought about by Gehry's decision to wrap three sides of an already existing "pretty pink shingled 1920s house"—as Gehry himself described it—with a corrugated metal shell. (See Figure 1.) In an interview Gehry speaks of his

1. Street view of the Gehry house
   Photo © Tim Street-Porter/Esto

decision to wrap the old Santa Monica house as a way of establishing a dialogue with it:

> I got fascinated with the idea that the old house should appear to remain totally intact from the outside, and that you could look through the new house, and see the old house as though it was now packaged in this new skin. The new skin and the windows in the new house would be of a totally different aesthetic than the windows in the old house. So they would constantly be in tension, or whatever, with each other. I wanted each window to have a different aesthetic, which I couldn't accomplish at that time.[6]

When Gehry "wraps" the house, the old wooden frame remains but is allowed to protrude in certain places as a strikingly visible inner scaffolding, while "outside" or beyond the latter a new dining area and kitchen expand the space into what was formerly the driveway and yard. These new areas between the older frame and the wrapper are mostly glassed in and therefore visually open to and even continuous with the former "outside" or "outdoors." (See Figure 2.)

What fascinates Jameson is not only the space formed by the architectural wrapper but also the "stark effect of the corrugated metal frame which seems to cut ruthlessly across the older house and brutally stamp the mark and sign of 'modern art' on it . . ." (*P,* 112). Accordingly, Jameson insists on the connotations of the new materials added on to the older construction—corrugated aluminum, steel mesh, raw plywood—which not only "annul the projected syntheses of matter and form of the great modern buildings" but also inscribe economic and social themes in the work. The most obtrusive of the new house's identifying features are the new outer wall of corrugated metal and the glass, cube-like structure referred to by Gehry himself as the "tumbling cube," which actually forms a skylight over the kitchen that when seen from the street appears suspended precariously between the upper roof whose outline it echoes and this new outer wall. (See Figure 3.) "These ostentatious markers," Jameson says, "planted in the older building like some lethal strut transfixing the body of a car crash victim, clearly shatter any illusions of organic form that might be entertained about this construction (and that are among the constitutive ideals of the older modernism)" (*P,* 113). In sum: "These two spatial phenomena make up the 'wrapper'; they violate the older space and are now both parts of the newer construction and at a distance from it, like 'foreign bodies'" (*P,* 113).

Ignoring the modernist Constructivist tradition, a tradition obviously rel-

2. Inner scaffolding in the Gehry house
Photo courtesy Frank O. Gehry & Associates, Inc.

3. The "tumbling cube" skylight
Photo © Tim Street-Porter/Esto

evant to Gehry's entire architectural project, Jameson proceeds to interpret the house indirectly and self-reflexively by way of a prior commentary in *The Secret Life of Buildings*. There Gavin Maccrae-Gibson concentrates on another aspect of the house's visuality, its disorienting, "defamiliarizing" effects: "The tilting of planes expected to be horizontal or vertical and the converging of studwork members cause one to feel suspended and tipped in various directions oneself. . . . For Gehry the world vanishes to a multitude of points, and he does not presuppose that any are related to the standing human being. The human eye is still of critical importance in Gehry's world, but the sense of center no longer has its traditional symbolic value."[7] In Maccrae-Gibson's reading, the numerous contradictory perspective lines and absence of right angles produce a spatial disorientation not unlike the loss or alienation of the older phenomenological body (with its right/left, front/back, up/down orientation) that characterizes the new postmodern "hyperspace" as Jameson defined it earlier in relation to Portman's Bonaventure Hotel lobby. Yet Jameson rejects the validity of Maccrae-Gibson's analysis, precisely because of its reliance upon a modernist aesthetic, specifically Russian Formalism, according to which the purpose of art is to defamiliarize and restimulate perception. Such an aesthetic has become meaningless, Jameson boldly proclaims, because, "in an environment of sheer advertizing simulacra and images," there is no reason "why we should even want to sharpen and renew our perception of those things" (*P*, 122). Instead of dismissing Maccrae-Gibson's analysis outright, however, Jameson appropriates and re-writes it in dialectical terms, in order to propose his own allegorical reading of Gehry's house. But not without having to confront a series of interpretative obstacles along the way.

First, we should note that the connotations of violence in Jameson's descriptive language, as in the formulations quoted above where the "exterior" elements come to penetrate and plant themselves as virtual "foreign bodies" on the more "organic" form within, seem at odds with a feature of the house that noticeably interests Jameson: the fact that the wrapper functions as a semi-transparent skin that allows the older part of the house to remain visible, as a persistent reminder of the past, indeed of history itself as a "content" that can still be glimpsed through the space articulated by the newer elements. In this we see an apparent contrast between modernist and postmodernist artistic strategies. Whereas modernist art, according to Jameson, defines itself through its radical negation of traditional art and its repression of history, as we see in Maccrae-Gibson's exclusive concern with

4. Exposed structural features of the Gehry house
   Photo courtesy Frank O. Gehry & Associates, Inc.

the perception of purely formal relations, Gehry's postmodernist art performs a kind of *Aufhebung* in which historical referents can be subsumed
and cancelled out but remain visible nonetheless as parts of a new spatial
articulation.

However, the attempt to read the Gehry house as a supposed dialectical
Aufhebung has to ignore its evident spatial complexites. The architectural
wrapper and the addition or grafting of new architectural elements transform the entire space of the house, and not simply through the addition of
new and adjacent spaces, as in the case of the kitchen and dining room,
which now exist where before there was only an "outside," more specifically, a driveway. First and foremost, the addition of this new space permanently displaces the structural center of the house when we consider that in
both the traditional and modern house the kitchen and dining room are centrally located and often constitute the heart (or indeed hearth) of the house.
In other words, this de-centering becomes a permanent feature because
Gehry's kitchen will always remain to a certain extent "outside." Furthermore, the opening up of the house tends to dissolve the older solidity of its

walls, within which the centered bourgeois ego could luxuriate in privacy. Of course, one might reply that this "opening up" is a common feature of a generalized California architectural style. But here it achieves a singular articulation in several senses. In exposing the inner structural features of the old house at the same time that new structural features are added and grafted on, Gehry initiates a certain play or destabilization between what we might call the house's endo- and its exo-skeleton. (See Figure 4.) This play or de-stabilization is further articulated in the passageways and windows connecting the rooms, as in the case of the living room, which on one side communicates traditionally with entrances to bedrooms and a stairway to the second story (which, from the kitchen level, would be experienced as the third story) and on another side looks "out" through a window into the kitchen. Finally, there is the paradoxical novelty of the traditional bedroom upstairs. Jameson insists that this room, apparently untouched, has been transformed by virtue of its context into a quotation of its former self, and now exists both inside and outside the temporal frame in which we experience it. But here we may wonder if the "quotation effect" does not override/overwrite the logic of the dialectic, if indeed the room is now an eerie simulacrum of what was formerly an ordinary room.

In any case, it should be evident why the wrapper—that is, the cube and corrugated slab—but also the tilted planes of glass and steel mesh, the windows that look "out" into or interface with other rooms, all produce not only a complicated play of inside and outside, interior and exterior, old space and new space but also, as Jameson puts it, "some radically new spatiality beyond the traditional and the modern alike which seems to make some historical claim for radical difference and originality" (P, 120). My point, however, is that Jameson fails to account for the "radical difference and originality" of this new space, and defers instead to the presumably more important question of its allegorical meaning. In other words, the problem with Jameson's dialectical dismissal/rewriting of the modernist aesthetic is that it forces him to displace and re-situate the spatial problematic of the Gehry house in order to assign it a meaning, without really making sense of that space, that is, without making it fully "readable." Moreover, by ascribing an allegorical meaning to several elements that Gehry employs—above all the corrugated wall and cube-like structure—Jameson allows the critical question of the unity of this new space to be superseded by the at once practical and utopian question of whether or not it can be lived in, or perhaps we should say "lived out" in. But even so, as Jameson must admit, his allegorical reading cannot tell us whether or not the new space of the house is livable and meaningful in its own right; it can only provide the terms for bringing into focus the dilemma for which this new space would constitute something like a "solution."

The problem, simply put, is how the Gehry house relates to the space surrounding it. Jameson flatly rejects Maccrae-Gibson's modernist answer that the house positions itself in relation to Santa Monica through various marine allusions and imagery, that it anchors itself to the sea and coastline on one side and the city and mountains on the other through a set of subtle symbolic references. For it is Jameson's contention that the phenomenological sense of place on which such a reading is based, while not exactly absent, is noticeably giving way and being superseded in the United States by a more powerful and more abstract sense of space, present or evoked not just by the proximity of Los Angeles as some new hyper-urban configuration but beyond it by the "increasingly abstract (and communicational) networks of American reality whose extreme form is the power network of so-called multinational capitalism itself" (*P*, 127). Thus, while acknowledging that "Gehry's space is . . . far more precise and sculpted" than Portman's "crudely melodramatic" hotel lobbies, Jameson finds that the space of the Gehry house nevertheless "confronts us with the paradoxical impossibilities (not least the impossibilities of representation) which are inherent in this latest evolutionary mutation of late capitalism toward 'something else' which is no longer family or neighborhood, city or state, nor even nation, but as abstract and nonsituated as the placelessness of a room in an international chain of motels or the anonymous space of airport terminals that all run together in your mind" (*P*, 116).

Not surprisingly, then, Jameson will read Gehry's tumbling cube not as an allusion to the work of Malevich, a reading, he says, "that would oblige us to rewrite the fundamental contradiction in the house as one between traditional American life and modernist utopianism" (*P*, 126). Rather, he reads the cube as a figuration for what is an impossible mental puzzle or paradox: that although we are all caught up and immersed within the complex networks of global capitalism we have no way of representing that situation in a concrete and meaningful way. In short, because the cube exists simultaneously in two types of incommensurate space (tract house and corporate monolith) it demands what it also displaces or stands in for: a cognitive map that would enable us as individuals to position ourselves in relation to those "prolongations of corporate space" that intrude everywhere into our daily lives and from which we palpably suffer.

In my rather bald summary, Jameson's equation of Gehry's cube with precisely what is unrepresentable in our living space will no doubt appear somewhat arbitrary. (Maccrae-Gibson, as Jameson notes, observes in contrast that the cube "marks the junction of the streets with what during the day is a receding void and at night is an advancing solid, like a beacon" [5].) However, the apparent arbitrariness of Jameson's reading diminishes considerably when he opposes the cube to another set of architectural features, the corrugated aluminum wrap, and the chainlink balcony above it. Here, what counts for Jameson are the associations that these materials— so essential to what Gehry calls "cheapskate architecture"—evoke: "the junk or Third World side of American life today: the production of poverty and misery, people not only out of work but without a place to live, bag people, waste and industrial pollution, squalor, garbage, and obsolescent machinery" (P, 128). But in order to complete his allegorical scaffolding, another representation of America, "equally unquestionable" Jameson says, must be set beside this one: the America of awesome wealth and military power, extraordinary scientific and technological achievement, with its "inconceivable" financial system. What then emerges are "the two antithetical and incommensurable features of abstract American space, of the superstate or multinational capitalism today, which the cube and the wall mark for us (without offering representational options for them)" (P, 128). In other words (for this last phrase is rather obscure), the opposition between cube and corrugated wall does not exactly represent the opposition between our abstract knowledge of the superstate and our existential daily experience, but it allows Gehry to think this opposition in spatial terms. If the new living space articulated by these elements proves to be livable, and opens up new and original ways of inhabiting a space, Jameson concludes, then not only has the conceptual dilemma the space poses been resolved experientially, but its utopian dimension has also been affirmed.

Yet Jameson's desire to read the Gehry house as a utopian space would seem to work against any precise understanding of its relationship to capitalism in postmodern terms. According to the latter, contemporary capitalism functions as a desiring machine in which use-value is subordinated to exchange-value, and the production and distribution of information supersedes that of objects. If Gehry's house is "about" American capitalism, it is because the house itself is a small desiring machine located at the interface of two inseparable economies: the American middle-class desire to own a personalized house and the global workings of capitalism that Gehry as an internationally acclaimed architect necessarily represents (in the sense of "works for"). Of course, one can say that capitalism both functions as the Gehry house's condition of possibility and establishes its limit, that the house only opens up a pocket of alterity within the largely monolithic precincts of corporate capitalism. But, for that very reason, the house also becomes a site of both domestic and aesthetic desire, whose conflicting codes are not easily reducible even to the always expanding terms of capitalist regulation and exchange.

Thus far I have argued that Jameson's allegorical method, according to which spatial and material oppositions are transcoded into a single semantic opposition, allows him to assign a meaning to the new space of the Gehry house without actually enabling him (or us) to read it. I now want to push this claim further by proposing a reading of Jameson's essay that will open up this new space to another line of questioning, which, in its turn, will indicate how Jameson's allegorical interpretation of the way in which the Gehry house figures the "unrepresentable" may actually be read as a displacement of Jameson's own failure or inability to come to terms with the kind of space the Gehry house embodies. Moreover, I mean this failure to be understood not as Jameson's personal failure but as a failure within the larger modernist project to theorize abstraction adequately. And by abstraction I mean not only non-representational art (especially painting and sculpture) but abstraction as the necessary and essential part of any cultural or semiotic process whatever.

In this latter sense, at least until fairly recently, abstraction has been theorized in entirely negative and derivative terms, beginning with Marx's notion of commodity fetishism and alienation, followed by Max Weber's notion of rationalization, Georg Lukacs' translation of the latter into the concept of reification, and Jurgen Habermas' utilization of the opposition between system and life-world. Basically, these thinkers all assert that modernization is best explained as an increasing process of abstraction and rationalization according to which traditional, "natural" unities (social groups, institutions, cultural events and activities, religions, forms of authority, human relations, and so forth) are broken down into their component parts or functions in order to be re-organized or "Taylorized" into more efficient systems grounded in an instrumental or binary, ends/means logic. In the process of abstraction, activities and functions which before were "organically" integrated are now allowed a certain quasi-autonomy, but as a result human experience becomes ever more compartmentalized and fragmentary.

Jameson situates himself squarely within this tradition of interpretation. "We can think abstractly about the world only to the degree to which the world itself has already become abstract," he asserts in *The Political Unconscious,* where he argues that within this process of modernist reorganization art assumes a new function by "constitut[ing] a Utopian compensation for everything lost in the process of the development of capitalism—the place of quality in an increasingly quantified world, the place of the archaic and of feeling amid the desacralization of the market system, the place of sheer color and intensity within the grayness of measurable extension and geometrical abstraction."[8]

In Jameson's critical scheme, "hyperspace" now occupies the place formerly occupied by modern abstract or non-representational art, and therefore must be characterized as a new "by-product" of an increased level of abstraction achieved in the functioning of contemporary global capitalism. As art, however, this "by-product" would serve as both "figure" for these new processes and utopian compensation for their dislocations and disorientations. In short, postmodern art makes hyperspace available for aesthetic consumption, but the new experiential intensities it makes possible are paid for by the cognitive blockage it both effectuates and stands (in) for. Finally, because Jameson understands hyperspace only as symptomatic effect, the cognitive mapping he calls for can be traced out only within the contours of a Marxist hermeneutic.[9]

Thus, even though the language of Jameson's allegory—particularly the thematized absence of cognitive maps—tends to suggest that the individual's relationship to global capitalism augurs some new or postmodern sense of the sublime and the inhuman, and despite his earlier disavowal, Jameson does in fact bring into his interpretation of the Gehry house a version of "modernist utopianism." What he seems to be arguing is that in the lived continuity between new experiences and new meanings we broach or gain access to a utopian dimension in which the "political unconscious" is overcome, an argument with a pronouncedly modernist ring to it. The alternative, as Jameson formulates it, is therefore particularly revealing: "There must be a relationship between those two realms or dimensions ['the abstract space of the superstate and the existential daily life of people in their traditional rooms and tract houses'],'" Jameson asserts, *"or else we are altogether within science fiction without realizing it"* (*P*, 128, my emphasis). To many, no doubt, this latter prospect will sound distinctively more "postmodern." In any case, the rhetoric here alerts us to the possibility that the utopian theme does not simply offer compensation for the reifications of modernization (according to the logic of Jameson's dialectic) but actually sutures over a threatening disjunction between experience and meaning, or vision and language, and thus provides Jameson's discourse with a means of "closure."

Despite his avowed Marxism, Jameson's numerous references to Martin Heidegger suggest a certain affinity for or at least a proximity to another strand of modernist hermeneutic. However, in relation to certain of Heidegger's formulations, which is where I now want to situate Jameson's remarks about the Gehry house, Jameson's tendentious allegorizing will appear in a somewhat different light. For both Heidegger and Jameson, art is essentially historical, but for Heidegger its historicity derives from its foundational, rather than expressive function. In his essay on "The Origin of the Work of Art," Heidegger asserts: "As founding, art is essentially historical. This means not only that art has a history, in the purely exterior sense that in the course of time it, too, appears side by side with many other phenomena and is subject to processes of transformation whereby it emerges and disappears, offering thus to the science of history a series of changing aspects. Art is history in the essential sense that it grounds History."[10] Heidegger's claim that "great art" grounds history, rather than standing in some representational or expressive relationship to it, forms part of his attempt to find an alternative to subjective and aesthetic understandings of art, and thus to move beyond both Kant and Hegel. As Heidegger sees it, art forces a historical opening between "earth" and "world," an "event" that he conceives as a clearing or lighting (*Lichtung*) that possesses all the inaugural force of the birth or origin of a new world. As the site of primal, originary language (*Dictung*), art is political in the strong sense because it essentially opens a world—it holds itself in the clearing of Being, Heidegger says—and does this in a way specific to each historical epoch. The epoch of modernity, Heidegger argues, has realized itself most fully in and as our technological world, and this impells him to attempt a *Destruktion* or Deconstruction of this epochal way of thinking, and to formulate a theory of art that exceeds in its very terms the metaphysical assumptions of modernity as usually defined.[11]

What, then, does Heidegger think of modern art, particularly of the avant-garde art that emerged in the 1920s and 30s only to be virulently denounced by the Nazis as a "Jewish-Bolshevick conspiracy" intended to undermine morality and destroy nations? To answer we must proceed carefully, not only because except for a few fleeting remarks Heidegger never confronted the question directly but also because, retrospectively, it is clear that the question itself goes right to the heart of a dilemma inherent in his entire thinking about art.

On the one hand, Heidegger clearly agreed with Adolf Hitler's denunciation of modern art—in *Mein Kampf*, for example—as an international art that, like speculative finance and the stock exchange, had nothing to do with a specific people rooted in a specific place and language (and race, as Hitler added ominously). On the other hand, Heidegger could never accept the understanding of art that undergirds this condemnation, an understanding that Hitler elaborated in a speech at the House of German Art in Munich in 1937. There Hitler argued that modern art, lacking a popular base or foundation, could only be "the expression of a particular year," like the changing fashion for impressionism, then futurism, cubism, and so on, whereas "the Germany of national-socialism, for its own part, desires a new 'German art,' and this, like all the creative values of a people, must be and will be eternal."[12] With this last assertion, a crucial point of difference clearly emerges, since for Heidegger art was essentially historical, not eternal. But the real problem is Hitler's simple notion of art as expression, according to which art would arise from and give concrete form to the "creative values of a people." For Heidegger the reverse is closer to the truth: it is art that serves as a ground out of which and by means of which a people comes to identify itself collectively with a particular destiny or myth and can thereby achieve their historic identity. This is precisely the kind of importance that Heidegger attributes to Homeric epic and the Greek temple.

We can now formulate the contradiction that modern art poses for Heidegger: in perfect accordance with the demands of his own theory, modern art offers no other ground or justification than itself; indeed, it proclaims its own autonomy (its "pure self-subsistence," in Heidegger's words) as a condition of its functioning as art. In this way modern art cuts itself off from any popular determination and becomes an elitist experiment, no

longer conceivable as the expression of the soul of a people or nation. However, Heidegger worried that, as a consequence, Hegel may have been right
when he said that "great art" was a thing of the past. The other side of the
contradiction makes this more explicit: insofar as modern art no longer
assumes any direct rapport with an individual nation or people and can
therefore be said to be truly trans-national, then it must be seen to accord in
some essential and fundamental new way with the present "era of techno-
science." In contrast to Hitler and the Nazi ideologues, then, Heidegger
acknowledges the legitimate historical necessity of modern art and its necessary correspondence with the new and decisive role assumed by advanced
technology and science. Heidegger's caveat, however, is that this new science and no longer art now seem to define or frame human existence. This
would be the "truth" that modern art reveals through its own historically
distinct mode of presencing.

Returning to Jameson, I would like to suggest that his allegorical reading
of Gehry's house simply substitutes for Heidegger's "techno-scientific
world" the space defined by current international capitalism, whose infinite
networks of power and communication have become more or less indistinguishable from today's advanced technological order. Of course, Jameson
does not make this substitution explicit, largely because for him the new
technology that defines and shapes our world is a development within capitalism, and not the inevitable outcome of a certain kind of epochal thinking, as it was for Heidegger. But whatever the merits of this distinction, it
should now be clear that Jameson's interpretation is a weaker formulation
of a tension within modern art that Heidegger, sensitive to the grounding
function of art, hesitated to reduce simply to a symptomatic expression of
the historical context. Moreover, whereas Jameson's discourse is motivated
by an attempt to close the gap modern art opens between experience and
meaning, Heidegger seeks to address the more fundamental question of how
art actually "opens" a new space. Heidegger's attention to art's grounding
function through its opening of a new space of de-concealment can thus
lead us to a very different reading of Gehry's house.

To explore the grounding function of art let us return to the point in "The
Origin of the Work of Art" where Heidegger introduces his crucially important notion of "the rift" (*der Riss*). The rift is what marks or traces the
opening between earth and world that allows the "working of the work."
Heidegger describes this working as follows:

World demands its decisiveness and its measure and lets beings attain to the Open of their paths. Earth, bearing and jutting, strives to keep itself closed and to entrust everything to its law. The conflict is not a rift [Riss] as a mere cleft is ripped open; rather, it is the intimacy with which opponents belong to each other. This rift carries the opponents into the source of their unity by virtue of their common ground. It is a basic design, an outline sketch, that draws the basic features of the rise of the lighting of beings. This rift does not let the opponents break apart; it brings the opposition of measure and boundary into their common outline. . . . The rift-design is the drawing together, into a unity, of sketch and basic design, breach and outline. . . . The strife that is brought into the rift and thus set back into the earth and thus fixed in place is *figure, shape, Gestalt*. Createdness of the work means: truth is being fixed in place in the figure. Figure is the structure in whose shape the rift composes and submits itself. This composed rift is the fitting or joining of the shining of truth.[13]

Heidegger's notion of the "rift" might be glossed as follows: The conflictual opening between earth and world is traced out in the rift, which, in turn, is fixed in place and set up in the work as a tracing of a figure or shape (*Gestalt*).[14] In this relationship between the rift and the figure the truth of Being is both revealed and concealed. This is because the rift itself is not posited or presented directly; it is, strictly speaking, unpresentable, for it is not a thing or an existent. It appears only in the movement of repetition by which the setting forth of the earth is drawn out of the rift itself as the opening and gathering of the conflict of earth and world. The artwork essentially retraces this opening trace that makes possible any delimitation of form; more precisely, the Gestalt or figure of the work visibly re-marks an originary differentiation (this is the work's createdness and the source of its strangeness). At the same time, in setting forth and composing the conflict of earth and world, the work comes to bear and manifest in its very composition their intimate belonging. In sum, the artwork's "working" consists in figuring the rift, and in the process it achieves the special gathered unity and self-sufficiency that first strikes our attention when we behold the work of art.

Let us return to Gehry's house and consider it more explicitly in these Heideggerian terms. The question is how the space of that house—specifically the space created by wrapping the little house on three sides with corrugated aluminum—is to be described. We might be encouraged by the ease with which Jameson's oppositional terms—the corrugated wall and the tumbling cube—seem to rewrite or translate, respectively, Heidegger's notion of earth and world. But the "rift" poses more difficult, "linguistic" problems. Derived from the German verb *reissen,* which means both to separate or tear apart and to grasp or hold together, the "rift" names for Heidegger the initial opening and tracing of a space, and thus a differentiating between earth and world that at the same time brings them into their essential natures, or their "common ground." While the term is clearly intended to ensure that their "intimate conflict" is not riven by any true discord, we might well wonder precisely what kind of "unity" the rift figures. The question is all the more pressing in relation to the Gehry house, whose spatial novelty results precisely from the way Gehry's "additions" challenge conventional notions of architectural unity. How should the rift there be characterized? By the doubling and reinscription of a prior rift? But what would this imply about the presumed unity of the new structure? Thus, if Heidegger's notion of the rift is to provide the basis for a more precise account of the "radical difference and originality" of Gehry's postmodern space, it would seem necessary that we first allow the house to question Heidegger's terms. In other words, perhaps we can best move toward characterizing this space by first establishing the limits of Heidegger's notion of the rift—limits that Gehry's house itself forces us to confront.

Let us look again at Heidegger's word, *der Riss.* In order to get the sense he wants into the word, Heidegger has obviously jammed or forced one set of meanings (tear, rent, breach, rupture, rift) onto another (plan, design, or outline drawing). It would appear, then, that Heidegger's use of the word *Riss* in "The Origin of the Work of Art" is itself a kind of rift, a split or rupture between two different meanings that are drawn together into a deeper unity. In this sense it could be said that Heidegger forces the word to become an example of itself, to perform itself, to take on a kind of performative meaning. This is more clearly visible in the original German text, where immediately after defining *der Riss* Heidegger insistently repeats it in the words *Aufriss* (a vertical projection or elevation), *Umriss* (an outline or contour), as well as in the more familiar *Grundriss* (a ground plan or layout).

Heidegger's jamming of one meaning onto another can be analyzed further as an operation that makes the word itself the site of a particular trope, that of catachresis. In traditionally accepted accounts, catachresis occurs when a word or sign already assigned to a first idea is assigned to a new idea for which there is no expression, that is, no existing literal expression that the figurative designation is replacing, as in the obvious examples of the leg of a chair or a head of lettuce. Catachresis thus appears as a kind of stand-in for a default in language, particularly when compared to other tropes like metaphor, metonomy, or synechdoche, which (again in traditional accounts) embellish or extend or shift meaning on the basis of an already constituted language which thereby functions as their "ground." This difference perhaps accounts for the marginality of catachresis as a trope, which has been relegated to a curious intermediary status between true metaphor and the proper or non-figurative use of language.

But following Jacques Derrida's commentary in "White Mythology" on Pierre Fontanier's explanation of tropes, we might want to say that the oppositional difference between proper and figurative language is undermined or de-grounded by the very structure of catachresis.[15] Derrida first cites Fontanier: "Tropes occur, either by necessity and extension, in order to supplement the words for certain ideas which are missing from language [here Fontanier is referring specifically to catachresis], or by choice and figure, in order to present ideas with more vivid and striking images than their own signs [here he is referring to metaphor proper]." Fontanier then draws the conclusion that there are two different kinds of tropological sense: the extended tropological sense (*i.e.*, catachresis), and the figurative tropological sense (*i.e.*, metaphor). "The first," he says, "stands between the primitive sense and the figurative sense, and can hardly be regarded as anything but a new kind of proper sense." What matters here, Derrida notes, is this "production of a proper sense, a new kind of proper sense, by means of the violence of a catachresis whose intermediary status tends to escape the opposition of the primitive and the figurative, standing between them as a 'middle'." When "the middle of an opposition is not the passageway of a mediation," Derrida concludes, "there is every chance that the opposition is not pertinent."

Derrida's analysis of Fontanier's treatment of catachresis is especially revealing in regard to Heidegger's philosophical use of the term "Rift." Derrida is interested in how certain "irruptive tropes" and other "nontrue figures"—which "no code of semantic substitution will have preceded"—both trouble and prove indispensable to a rhetorical classification. (For example, in his *Supplement to the Theory of Tropes*, Fontanier explains how catachresis is both excluded and serves "as the foundation of our entire tropological system.") Furthermore, many of these "violent, forced, or abusive" tropes turn out to be essential to philosophical language ("a system of cat-achreses, a fund of 'forced metaphors'"), as in the case of expressions based on "light" and "blindness." For how, Fontanier asks, "without these forced metaphors, without these catachreses, could one have come to retrace these [philosophical] ideas?"

The question leads Derrida, very quickly, to demonstrate two things. First, that the assumption here is that these "ideas" already existed ("already in the mind like a grid without a word"), but that "they could not have been retraced, tracked down, brought to daylight without the force of a twisting which goes against usage, without the infraction of a cat-achresis." And second, that "this is also how philosophy traditionally has interpreted its powerful catachresis: the twisting return toward the already-there of a meaning, *production* (of signs, or rather of values), but as *reve-lation,* unveiling, bringing to light, truth."

In view of Derrida's analysis, it hardly seems arbitrary or accidental that Heidegger's notion of the Rift should assume the form of a catachresis. But prior to that, we must consider how the Rift allows Heidegger both to pose and obscure the sense in which art is a grounding, for it is by means of this primordial "idea" that Heidegger can assert that two things—earth and world—are both riven apart and joined at the same time. To put it another way, the question of the grounding of the ground or the originating of the origin does not have to be posed, since Heidegger's very terms presuppose a primal unity or ground that would guarantee the unity-in-tension or difference-in-sameness of earth and world. In Heidegger's formulation, therefore, there is no question of a primal rift, since the very possibility that the rift may be the site of an original or originating discord or divergence is excluded. Hence the necessity of Heidegger's effort to give his notion of the Rift a semantic unity grounded in the word's etymology. Furthermore, by virtue of this exclusion and this necessity, the entire interpretive machinery of *Lichtung*—"of revelation, unveiling, bringing to light, truth"—slides into place as an apparent event of language, or poetic saying (*Dictung*). How-ever, once we see that this machinery is governed by the altogether differ-ent logic of catachresis, the excluded possibility—that this "ungrounded" trope may bridge a truly threatening or discordant rift—can no longer be pushed aside or denied.

We can now return to consider Gehry's house in light of Heidegger's notion of the Rift. In its initial condition, before the house was "wrapped,"

5. The house in its original condition
   Photo courtesy Frank O. Gehry & Associates, Inc.

the Rift could be said to refer to the way in which the house sets itself up in relation to the ground and sky, the way it establishes itself as a Gestalt and identifies itself as a dwelling. (See Figure 5.) In extending the house by adding the wrapping wall, the cubic skylight, and other new elements, Gehry retraces, displaces and re-inscribes the Rift, but in such a way that he literalizes it: the *Riss* becomes a rift, an adjoining that is also a disjoining, which throws any presumed unity into question. Perhaps more important, Gehry's wrapping implies a vantage point or space from which we can question the adequacy of the Heideggerian conceptual framework by questioning both the "ground" or grounding function of art and the adequacy of the opposition between earth and world which follows from it. Gehry opens this space, quite simply, by assuming not the modernist, Heideggerian model of artistic origination but a model of transformation or metamorphosis of the already-there through a process of displacement and reinscription. Gehry thus brings about not a grounding but a de-grounding, not an abolishing of the ground but a de-privileging of it (as merely the condition of one type of spatial orientation). In this gesture, the "ground" itself becomes a figure, and the paradoxical expression "figure of the ground" suddenly becomes meaningful.

Yet perhaps all this has been a roundabout way of affirming what may have been apparent all along: that Gehry's wrapping of the old house is first and foremost a radically linguistic act, an act of displacement and reinscription of architectural elements that makes a new kind of sense architecturally precisely by discovering an alternative to the visual opposition between spatial continuity and spatial juxtaposition (visible in the old and new styles, respectively) through the inherently linguistic notion of "an extended tropological sense." Just as a new statement can always be produced by adding new elements to an older statement, or by displacing and reinscribing elements already available within language, so Gehry articulates a "radically new spatiality" not by creating a new space but by extending and inflecting a space that was already there, but that was closed in upon itself rather than articulated to "the outside." Yet in this very articulation, the outside must be seen as a new inside, or rather as a kind of middle space (like the "new proper sense" produced by the violence of catachresis Derrida describes), which no longer serves as the passageway of a mediation and thus acquires an importance in and for itself.

On this account, the basis for a semantic reading of Gehry's house would seem to be contested by its very articulation of space. As we have seen, through a process of allegorical substitution Jameson ascribes a figurative sense or meaning to this new kind of architectural space. Motivating Jameson's allegorical reading is his argument that this new space or hyperspace cannot be made intelligible in phenomenological terms, and that something "unrepresentable" is figured there. Yet what does not make sense at the level of physical, perceptual space, Jameson claims, can be made meaningful nonetheless through "cognitive mapping," which turns out to mean thematizing the material and spatial opposition between the glassed-in cubic skylight and the corrugated aluminum wrapper as the "spatial equivalent" of—and therefore means of "thinking" architecturally—the abstract space of current multinational capitalism.

However, as we have also seen, the space of the Gehry house is not fully intelligible in oppositional terms, inasmuch as its space is built or constituted not merely of oppositions but works as an attempt to de-ground and put into play the very structure of opposition itself, not by denying opposition but by relativizing it, so that the oppositions now appear as inflections within what we might call lines of continuous variation. In other words, the house embodies a new spatial syntax that puts into question or makes indeterminate the basis or "ground" of the opposition between inside and outside, old and new (but also literal and figurative, perceptual and semantic). This syntax might be described as a spatial catachresis that produces an extended tropological sense or "new proper sense" which escapes or proves irreducible to the oppositional structure that defines the visual context in which it occurs. In effect, stark visual opposition is belied and overcome by tropological extension as an essentially linguistic form.

Consequently, and fatally for Jameson's reading, the new space can be said to support a semantic opposition only if we ignore the syntax of its articulation. If the Gehry house presents "a spatial equivalent," therefore, then surely it is that of an aporia, the site of a radical adjoining that at the same time is a disjoining—not only of the old and new, the inside and outside, but also of the visual and the linguistic. And it is precisely at the site where these different orders converge and conflict, where the differences between the visual and the linguistic are remarked or traced within the same space, that something like a hyperspace can be said to emerge.

But finally, I wonder if this spatial extension in which oppositions are put into play does not also harbor but at the same time contain a far more radical impulse than the house itself as a material structure can realize. I want to say, simply, that the Gehry house strives for the condition of "false work." In the language of architectural construction, "false work" denotes "both a temporary support (for a building under construction) as well as a structure added to an existing building (as addendum or exergue). Neither 'bearing wall' nor 'core' nor 'ornament,' false work may be extricated from the structure whose existence it makes possible and reinserted elsewhere. It is, therefore, a nomadic type of construction, temporarily occupied yet permanently uninhabitable." [16] But if "false work" usually stands outside or to the side of an emergent structure, perhaps one can say that in the Gehry house it has been internalized or collapsed into the house itself, which it now inhabits from within as a matrix of structural transformation. The connotations of transience and transparency evoked by the materials which Gehry adds to the house support this reading, as does the fact that recently, I am told, the house has undergone still further modifications. In other words, as an ultimate consequence of the house's de-stabilizing of oppositions the house has become a fundamentally transitory structure. But far from being in transit toward some more stable or enduring structure, it is toward this condition of "false work" that the Gehry house gestures, but to which of course it cannot attain.

Finally, to recapitulate, my intention has not been simply to argue for the relevance or cogency of the language model to contemporary architecture but also to trace something like a structure of entanglement that Jameson's attempt at allegorical reading necessarily brings about. Schematically, the story I have tried to tell would go something like this: Gehry produces a new architectural structure by displacing and reinscribing a prior structure; and it might be pointed out that the first structure—a 1920s "tract house"—was hardly an "original" in any sense. As I hope to have shown, Jameson's discourse repeats the operation it is analyzing through its own displacement and reinscription; more specifically, in Jameson's analysis the "postmodern spatiality" of Gehry's house is displaced by an inscription of the wrapper into an allegory about the abstract space of contemporary global capitalism. I have repeated Jameson's analysis by displacing and reinscribing it in turn within Heidegger's discourse on "The Origin of the Work of Art." Within Heidegger's essay, I have suggested, when we finally move to its center—the question of the grounding of the ground—we witness a catachrestic displacement and reinscription of a threatening difference (a primal rift) into a unity that holds differences together in their sameness.

From this perspective, finally, we can view Gehry's house as a critique or at least a "reading" of Heidegger—and of Jameson as well—that allows something like a distinctively postmodern space to emerge. In theoretical terms, as I suggested at the outset, such a space is opened through a disjunction of vision and language, which are no longer intricated in such a way as to open upon "the same world." In this sense the Gehry house is like a sentence that "contains" a quotation re-articulated within an utterly new and foreign context. More precisely, it is a construction in which an "extended tropological sense" (Fontanier's catachresis) syntactically bridges the gap between two completely antagonistic visual styles: the small-scale functional harmonies of the modern American middle-class house and the obtrusive modernist clash of visual elements in juxtaposition. These styles are not resolved into a unity, for the house no longer makes sense at the level of style; instead, a new kind of consistency is discovered through syntactical lines of continuous variation which "concretize" at various places in one style or the other. The complexity of the resulting "post-phenomenological space" simply does not yield to analysis in experiential or dialectical terms. In Heideggerian terms, on the other hand, the house presents a disarticulation of *Lichtung* and *Dictung* through a literalization of the Rift. What the space of the Rift, as Gehry's house figures it, then opens up is not so much the possibility of a postmodern arhitecture as a postmodern way of thinking about architecture.

JOSEPH G. KRONICK

Afterword: Joseph N. Riddel (1931–1991)

After the publication of *The Inverted Bell: Modernism and the Counterpoetics of William Carlos Williams* (1974), Joseph Riddel turned his attention to nineteenth-century writers and that intractable problem of defining an "American" literature. Repressing its past and yet obsessed with imported traditions, America has sought to reinvent itself in a literature whose primary subject matter has been its own invention. Riddel came to identify this reflexive engendering of an origin as a performative, a writing that is inseparable from its acts (of "creation," "destruction," "retrospection," "quotation"). "America" performs its origin "as a reflection on its unique difference; yet, even this very difference is a projection of what American thought and literature would be if they could but realize themselves."[1] This need to invent an original literature reveals itself, therefore, in those acts that stage "America" in a scene of writing that upsets and upstages the Cartesian subject, exposing any genealogy or theory of origination to be a construction, a performance of what will have been. Only, thus, do we have the "making" of Americans.

Riddel's understanding of America as "future anterior . . . a prospective writing of what will have been" (*CE*, 280), echoes the paradox that, from Emerson to Stein, American writing allegorizes itself as self-engendering quotation, the repetition of what is to come. "American literature" is an oxymoron; it must be critical if it is to be new, but as critical it is retrospective, dreaming of what it will someday be. If American writing, in canonical accounts, meant the ideal of a perfect self-reflection wherein the creator is mirrored in the work as act, Riddel's notion of performative self-quotation as the originary condition of American literature exposes the self-reflexive ideal to the iterative force of writing. That is, self-reflection posits a uniquely singular event wherein the subject is present in the object, but insofar as the event is unique it cannot be read. The possibility of an American literature or, for that matter, any communication depends upon iterability, repetition and difference. Hence, it is most original when it quotes.

Riddel's reflections on American writing as quotation or the "performative displacement by reinscription" were spurred by his readings of Jacques Derrida. In translating and transposing deconstruction and the name of Derrida into America, Riddel discovers in Poe and Williams deconstruction "ventriloquized in an American idiom" (*IB*, 309). Few critics have so rigorously thought through the implications of deconstruction for American literature. In displacing the canonical principle of American literature as a world elsewhere and reinscribing "America" as another name for "writing," he is most American. Those who were close to him might say that Riddel's name bears within it the oxymoronic condition of American literature as original quotation. "Riddel" is a provisional name, a paleonym, for "American" criticism.[2]

In writing *The Inverted Bell*, Riddel recognized that Derrida's critique of the metaphysics of presence hinged upon the principle that any utterance is conditioned by repeatability. He went on in subsequent essays to call the characteristic American motif of self-invention "original repetition."[3] To write the past as one's future means that writing is not to be interpreted literally but is a generalized repeatability which structurally determines the possibility of literature, history, and self. In Derrida's reading of J. L. Austin in "Signature, Event, Context," the performative speech act is shown to be fissured by the iterable structure of language. Any utterance is conditioned by the possibility of the absence of a receiver or sender, as well as by citationality; that is, it is structurally determined by the possibility of its disengagement from a signature, event, or context. This disengagement is the condition for the possibility of communication. This is why Derrida says in his afterword to *Limited Inc* that the "pure realization of self-presence" is death. The self-presence of the totalizing utterance—totalizing because it is present to and complete unto itself—would consume itself in the very event of the utterance, if an absolutely unique event were imaginable. Paradoxically, the very condition for communicability, and therefore of "identity" and "presence," is the possibility of absence (of referent, receiver, sender) that permits an act of language to be repeated in altered contexts.

This principle of iterability describes an aporia between creation and repetition that exists at the beginnings of American literature. When we turn to classic formulations of the position of the American writer, such as the opening sentence of Emerson's *Nature*—"Our age is retrospective. It builds the sepulchres of the fathers. It writes biographies, histories, and criticism"—we find that we are asked to overcome retrospection and invent an "original relation" to God, nature, and history. Riddel notes that this dual act of acknowledging and denying belatedness marks "American" thought and literature as self-reflexive. American writing is both "the end and fulfillment of history and yet the 'beyond' of history, a powerful exception to what it represents" (*HS*, 77). Although the thematics of American exceptionalism, the characterization of America as self-originating, have been dealt with by numerous critics, few, if any, have recognized that self-reflexivity is a problematic, preferring to treat it thematically or as a formal property of the text. As a problematic, self-reflexive discourse is a critical intervention or disturbance of the totalizing ideal of self-consciousness. This ideal must suffer the same fate of absolute self-presence, if it were not at once conditioned by its belatedness. That is, a representation adequate to absolute self-consciousness would be something like an apocalypse, a dissolution of the object in pure self-presence; but forced to invent its origins, American literature stages itself proleptically as what will have been. There can be no identity, therefore, between language and history because there is no "original" language in which to embody a national identity: "'American literature' is deferred in the very moment of its writing" (*IB*, 305).

The "American" writer is doomed to invent or, as Riddel would say, perform her- or himself in a borrowed language. The performative is not the singular event of Austin's self-reflexive speech act—that is, the present statement grounded in a self-conscious subject—but is determined by iterability. In "To Perform—A Transitive Verb?" Riddel recalls Derrida's intervention at the 1966 Johns Hopkins colloquium after Roland Barthes delivered his essay "To Write: An Intransitive Verb?" Derrida remarks that the possibility of saying "I" lies in its always already being repeated. That is, the "I" pronounced by the speaking subject in the present instance of discourse functions as "an act of language" only insofar as it is "already constituted by the possibility of repetition."[4] This mark of my self-identity must be repeatable in altered circumstances, as well as by other speakers, if its identity is to be preserved. Identity, however, is impure because repetition implies both identity *and* difference. Thus, when I say "I," I cannot refer to something absolutely unique and singular but to something, an "I," that must be constituted by the possibility of repetition if it is to function as an act of language. It is an original repetition. When I say "I," I am already absent from my utterance, that is, from the supposed originality and singularity of what I say. How, indeed, can I say "I" if the "I" did not already contain in itself the possibility of being repeated in different contexts? In other words, how can I say "I" if the I is not always already said and did not contain within it a reference to a future "I"?

Riddel was provoked by Derrida's deconstruction of the conventional structures of intelligibility and his concept of iterability to speculate that American literature always already exists in a movement of interpretation. Therefore, American literature has been underwritten by the old names and the tradition it would transcend or destroy. The opposition between old and new world cannot be sustained once the irreducible alterity that conditions writing is seen to resist the canonizing gesture of this historical narrative. We can say, therefore, that Riddel is concerned with history throughout his work, for he recognizes that the crux of historical time is discursive time or language. The condition for inventing America "begins" in the paradox that "America" is always deferred at the very moment of its writing. This condition of deferral/invention is what Riddel calls "performative self-quotation" (*IB,* 306).

It is necessary, however, to distinguish "original" self-quotation from self-reflection. If the ideal of self-reflection posits the identity of the creator in his or her creation, then American literature is, indeed, self-reflexive insofar as it characteristically stages itself as reflecting upon its origins. However, as the spur to such self-reflection is belatedness, American writing, like deconstruction, "could never write in any language but the text it was inhabiting [or quoting], since that text was always already two languages at least" (310), critical and poetic, "American" and other. As Emerson noted, "Literature is now critical. Well, analysis may be poetic."[5] This is why Riddel can say America appears most "original" when it quotes and thereby exposes, as do Poe's self-plagiarisms, the ideal of self-reflection to iterability. "America" is not the name for a new literature but a strategic positioning of its literature within several languages. And to those who lament the translation of French theory into the pragmatic environs of American literature, we can reply that America "was always already the writing space of deconstruction" (*IB*, 310). Riddel was an original and historically minded critic because he recognized that the need to invent an "American" writing or a national identity means to think its impossibility. "America" is deconstruction.⁶

It is, I might confess, tempting to find in *The Clairvoyant Eye: The Poetry and Poetics of Wallace Stevens,* even in his study *C. Day Lewis,* Riddel writing what will have been, a prospective deconstructive criticism.⁷ Such a discovery of Riddel writing deconstruction "before the letter"—let us avoid foreign phrases, even if American criticism has been in a foreign phase at least since the 1966 conference on the human sciences at Johns Hopkins—would constitute a scene of reflection, a performance, if you will, wherein Riddel will have proven to have known all along what he came to articulate in terms indebted to, but not derivative of, Derrida. Such a retrospective reading would turn the text into an "act of finding/What will suffice."

Perhaps this may, after all, describe Riddel's texts, for if they are marked, as his critics may say, by repetition, this makes them all the more American. They quote "originally": "Quotation becomes a kind of originality to the degree that it adds or supplements, translates and transforms. Quotation is hermeneutical, and in a sense, it is pre-original because it breaks the law of genealogical succession by its additions. If every man is a quotation from all his ancestors, he is nevertheless not determined by the past any more than quotation repeats the earlier text" (*HS*, 83). Therefore, those who lament the imposition of theory in American literary studies fail to perceive that the literature is already self-divided—American writers are nothing, certainly not creative, if not critical.

This critical condition makes American writing a problematic of self-reflection because the text doubly marks itself as an object, a work of language, and an act, a production or performance that undoes the self-reflexive closure wherein the work becomes the subject of itself. The performative is the temporalizing of the spatial work, and the work is the spacing of time, such that the "present" work, the poem or critical text, is possible only by its carrying within itself the mark of some past work and a relation to some future work.⁸ The performative is not a matter of retrospection and anticipation, which are mental faculties, but of writing and "America." It is, finally, a condition of criticism, even a critical condition, for the performative means "American literature" is vitiated by what it is not—a future that will have been. Thus, when Riddel reflects in his postscript to the 1991 reissue of his Stevens' book, he cannot but see himself caught in a scene of self-reflection wherein "the very idea of 'self' . . . [is] precipitated into the abysses of speculation and retrospection" (*CE,* 279).

If Riddel's postscript undoes his earlier dialectical reading of Stevens' self-reflexive poetry, it does so as performance, not by an exhaustive self-analysis. Moreover, the performative is not a theory of literary composition applied to Stevens' texts but is a property of those texts themselves, which endlessly displace their key terms, "reality" and "imagination," in a self-reading that turns them into "figures for the poem's act of self-production" (288). In 1965, Riddel viewed Stevens' poetry as a dialectical unfolding of the mind, as acts of self-creation. His thesis claims "that Stevens' total work constitutes metaphysically the act of creating oneself" (vi). This thesis, circumscribed as it is by a phenomenological language of consciousness, bears scrutiny for the way it negotiates the Emersonian notion of a "central man." Riddel argues for the self-creating force of reflection in Stevens' poems, thereby situating the self at the center of the poem; however, he allows for a more complex reading of Stevens' Americanism by suggesting, after Roy Harvey Pearce, that "the role of the American experience [is] to be a metaphor of the history of the modern self" (271). Although ensconced in a language of consciousness, Riddel's text approaches the notion that the fall into self-consciousness and the subsequent loss of the world the poet would realize is already a problem of language.

Neither Stevens nor Riddel allowed himself to be deceived by the idealist epistemology of the mental act; the ontological priority of nature haunts Stevens' verse and makes of every poem an epitaph—a phrase of Eliot's but eminently descriptive of Stevens. "This life of mind . . . is constantly brought into question by the world it did not create, even though it knows only the world of its own creation" (273). Riddel's reading of Stevens' last works as a heroic effort to sustain the self as an act of the mind might represent the most significant difference between his early work and the later turn toward a problematizing of language and, therefore, of the self, mind, and act.

We can find such a critical reading of the self in his original afterword where, paraphrasing Georges Poulet, Riddel writes "of the paradoxical condition of the modernist who exists so fully in his act that he does not exist otherwise, mind cannot both *be* and *know* of its *being,* for what it knows is the past, what it *was*" (274). Riddel anticipates his later critiques of self-presence or the transparency of the self-reflexive subject. Here, in his conclusion, Riddel begins to problematize the American desire for origins. We have seen how Riddel later defined this Adamic theme of the search for an absolute origin as quotation, or repetition as origination, but here the failure of self-reflexivity is read in phenomenological terms as the resistance of materiality or, rather, the thing itself to consciousness. In composing its own world, Riddel says, the mind loses the thing itself. The paradox of self-creation, then, is that of the resistance of non-being to thought. The rock upon which Stevens would found the world and the self proves a trope serving for the truth, but as trope, it turns, averts, language away from what it would name; hence, "It was difficult to sing in face/Of the object. The singers had to avert themselves/Or else avert the object" (Wallace Stevens, "Credences of Summer").

Riddel is very close to a rhetorical reading of Stevens by virtue of his attention to Stevens' self-reflexivity, but he confesses he failed to recognize "that critical understanding is structured by an *aporia* and problematic that condemns it to a limit. More importantly, I now think that it is this very *aporia* that lies at the heart of poetry—of Stevens' poetry and of something we call 'modernism' (sometimes with a 'post')—that makes poetic discourse critical, or effaces the margins between the creative and critical" (*CE,* 281). In *The Inverted Bell,* Riddel calls this problematic a "poetics," which he distinguishes from a study of poetry: "For my argument is that a poet's poetics cannot exist before the poem as a cause of that 'object,' or even inhere or be incarnated in the body of any one particular poem or canon of works. A poet's poetics is his discoveries, his interpretations, which in turn can only be known by interpretation" (*IB,* xi–xii). Even as he acknowledges the hermeneutic circularity of poet, work, and critic, Riddel undoes the totalizing design of hermeneutic circularity, first by insisting that "a poet's poetics, like his individual poems, can never be complete" and then by equating interpretation with transgression, taking as his figure for violation the hunt of the unicorn in *Paterson,* Book Five.

For Riddel, poetics is an "art forced to reflect on itself and thus on its own act of reflection" (*IB,* xiii). It is this reflection to the second degree that distinguishes Williams' poetry from the self-reflexivity we have come to associate with certain versions of modernism. It is what makes self-reflexivity a problematic. As a hidden site from which the poem issues, a poetics has the status of a *mise en abyme,* to use a phrase current in 1974; that is, as the "'deep structure' of utterance," a poetics comes into being only in the poet's utterance but cannot be recovered from it. A poetics is merely "the residue, the sign or trace of some lost origin . . . and finally a profound questioning of the 'origin' itself" (xiv, xiii). In other words, a poetics is an origin to come, disclosing itself only in interpretation.

Criticism is not an act of consciousness set over against yet another consciousness, that of the poet, but is language, and reading is the agon between one language (the poem) and another (criticism). Riddel writes, "Criticism is an act of interpretation, and thus, to use Heidegger's terms, an act of violence, of translating, or carrying over. It is a carrying over of language by language into language—an interpretation (the poem) by interpretation (criticism) into interpretation (poetics)" (xvii). The transgressive act of interpretation does not self-reflexively resolve the poem into a perfect whole. Were presence or transparency achieved, there would no longer be poems or reading. This is implied by Riddel's calling poetics the "deep structure" of poetry. Reading or interpretation then becomes the thinking of differences or, as he says elsewhere, of "the undetermined relation of things" (14).

The Inverted Bell has been rightly recognized as the first significant full-length work of American deconstructive criticism. Riddel's study in poetics offers a distinctive take on Derrida and poststructuralism, one that has not been adequately explored by critics. Following its publication he went on to write a number of essays on modern poetics, giving particular attention to Pound, H.D., Crane, Stein, Olson, as well as Stevens and Williams.[9] Although his work is most closely associated with modernist poets, Riddel also wrote a number of essays on Poe, Emerson, Hawthorne, and Adams for a projected book, *Purloined Letters*.[10] These last works resulted in a dual reading of America and an American reading, the reading of American literature as the staging of its self-engendering. Distancing himself from the thesis of Stevens' creation of the self in poetry, he argues, "The self is never simple, or singular. It is dialogical and interpretative. And is already constituted by what Emerson has called quotation" (*HS*, 87). Basing his argument upon a reading of Emerson's "Quotation and Originality," he came to see repetition as the key to the American writer's problematic— how can he or she produce a new literature without destroying the old? And how can literature be produced without a past? It would seem by a performative quotation that stages the past as an event to come.

American writing, Riddel argues, is caught in a double bind wherein the renunciation of authority and tradition means the renunciation of the very modernity in which it finds itself. Compelled to reject Europe, to "begin again," the American writer confronts "the problem not of the absence of origins or even the challenge of being *sui generis,* but of adjusting the 'self' to the crisis of modernity, that its origin lies in the Hegelian moment of self-reflection or self-production and thus in a moment of a 'self' irreducibly doubled and originally without identity" (*IB,* 303). The reflexive engendering of a self that is without identity, Whitman's "'Simple separate person' as 'En-Masse,'" means "a pure possibility whose being 'will be' performed, acted out" (304). The performative self, "at once an original and a counterfeit," undoes the self-reflection that would proleptically found itself in the self-conscious act of projecting an identity. Where self-reflection implies a founding act of self-representation, the performative exposes every self-representation as quotation.

Quotation acts as a guiding thread in Riddel's deconstruction of the "American self" and in his theorizing of an "American" literature. Riddel calls quotation a "performative modality" that displaces the self and undoes the search for closure in reflexive self-identity. The process of naming and renaming, or quotation, inscribes self-reading in a chain that resists closure not because of an unreachable goal but because of a structurally de-centered origin, a self that can never be present to itself. The self is "originally without identity," Riddel suggests, because it is engendered in an act of quotation (303). Its "identity" is already Other; the fate of the American self is to sign itself in a future anterior—America is what will have been. Therefore, the American writer has always to begin again in a performative act of self-engendering. "If the 'American self' and 'American verse' are performative, then, they might appear most 'new' when they repeat, even quote, the old, like the iteration of a speech act" (304).

Riddel developed this concept in his series of readings focusing primarily on Emerson and Poe in what is perhaps a singular linking of the two as the original name for "American" poetry. He perceived a similarity between Emerson's self-quotations—his epigraph for "Quotation and Originality" is from "Plato"—and Poe's self-plagiarisms. Both Emerson and Poe have provoked interpretations that define and organize American literature but through a trans-Atlantic detour: Emerson through German philosophy via Nietzsche, Poe through French thought via Baudelaire, with both readings returning "home" with an uncanny force. And at a time when it has become fashionable to decry canonization, we can say that what makes Poe and Emerson unavoidable in any reading of "America" is their capacity to provoke readings, particularly readings that share their own decanonizing gestures.

Riddel's own work partakes of this decentering of "American" writing. Some, of course, would charge him with having imported a foreign text and reading America through the writings of Derrida, but this implies a naïve notion of originality that is consistently belied by American writers. To the charge Riddel "quotes" Derrida, I can only reply, "But, of course!" We can say of Riddel's criticism what he once wrote of Williams: "how repetitively original he was, how anxious to destroy . . . 'the whole of poetry [we can say "criticism"] as it has been in the past.' How metaphysically anti-metaphysical. How 'American'" (xx)!

Notes

Joseph N. Riddel, "To Perform—A Transitive Verb?"

1. Roland Barthes, "To Write: An Intransitive Verb?" in *The Structuralist Controversy: The Languages of Criticism and the Sciences of Man,* ed. Richard Macksey and Eugenio Donato (Baltimore, 1970), 135. Hereinafter cited in the text as *SC*.

Paul A. Bové, "Anarchy and Perfection"

1. The great exception to this general statement is, of course, R. P. Blackmur, fragments of whose incomplete manuscript study appear as *Henry Adams,* ed. and with an introduction by Veronica A. Makowsky, foreword by Denis Donoghue (New York, 1980). This version of Blackmur's efforts at a lifelong study of Adams derives from manuscripts in the Firestone Library at Princeton. The book's dust jacket misrepresents it as "A Leading Critic's Account of a Great American Figure." It would have better been called the greatest wreck to be found on the shoals of Henry Adams' career. There are, of course, innumerable academic essays on Adams; none are of the status of either James on Hawthorne or Matthiessen on Melville. With the exception of Blackmur, Adams has had no critic whose work must be read along with Adams himself in any effort to come to grips with the significance of that mind. While Ernest Samuels' three-volume, Pulitzer Prize-winning biography of Adams provides essential information, it is not critically distinguished—nor is its one-volume redaction (Cambridge, Mass., 1948–64, 1989).

2. See *The Education of Henry Adams,* in *Henry Adams: Novels, Mont-Saint-Michel, The Education* (New York, 1983), 774. For this edition, Ernest Samuels and Jayne N. Samuels edited the text of *The Education.* Hereinafter cited in the text as *Education.*

3. For example, the dust jacket to the Library of America edition refers to *The Education* as autobiography. James D. Hart, in the fifth edition of *The Oxford Com-*

panion to American Literature, begins his entry on *The Education* typically calling it the "autobiography of Henry Adams" (New York, 1983), 222. The complex publishing history of *The Education* gives some evidence of this public perception as well—no matter how troubled that perception might be. From at least as early as 1918, when Houghton Mifflin Company published *The Education,* until 1964, when Time Books published a two-volume edition, *The Education of Henry Adams* appeared with the published subtitle *An Autobiography.* Critics who have been troubled by the fact that Adams' text does not "fit" genre expectations were correct to be troubled but should have given more attention to material details such as these when commenting on the "status" of Adams' text as "autobiography." To the best of my knowledge, Samuels does not speak of the text specifically as "autobiography," but in his Introduction to the Riverside Edition, he does call the book a "record of his [Adams'] experiences." Ernest Samuels, "Introduction," *The Education of Henry Adams* (Boston, 1973), viii.

4. Samuels sees himself as doing this from the very opening of *The Young Henry Adams* (Cambridge, Mass., 1948).

5. One matter needs to be mentioned and kept in mind as we go along. As he aged, Adams became increasingly anti-Semitic, siding with the army against Dreyfus, speaking constantly of "Jew bankers." This is a bizarre and horrendous element in Adams. It is not to be excused as it sometimes is as being "of his time" or "of his class," since it was neither, at least not in the United States—as the example of Henry James and other friends of Adams indicate. I am not going to make the anti-Semitism central to my remarks today, and were I to do so I would try to locate it in terms of two things: first, Adams' opposition in the 1890s to what is called in the United States, "The Money Trust," a cartel of enormously powerful bankers led by Morgan, Guggenheim, Gould, Fiske, and the agents of the Rockefellers at what is now Citibank; and second, his increasing preoccupation with Greek as opposed to Hebraic intellectual sources at the very same time as he was engaged in his study of the Gothic.

6. I use the word *productivist* here not to refer to the common Marxist or post-Marxist understandings, but rather to a sense more usefully found by Deleuze in Spinoza: "This is what Spinoza calls Nature: a life no longer lived on the basis of need, in terms of means and ends, but according to a production, a productivity, a potency, in terms of causes and effects." Gilles Deleuze, *Spinoza: Practical Philosophy,* trans. Robert Hurley (San Francisco, 1988), 3.

7. It would be foolish to think of Adams as an historicist, of the old or even "new" variety. Such thinking would put much more confidence in historical knowledge and give too little thought to the nature of history writing than Adams does himself. Another extended essay would be needed to take up Adams and the question of history.

8. Following Thomas Pynchon in a reading of Adams' preoccupation with chaos

and entropy raises questions beyond the scope of this essay. They touch on the problem of order in and from chaos. It raises the initial question "What is chaos" for Adams, and it begs for the answer to that question to be situated in relation not only to current theories of chaos in physics and dynamics but also to problems of philosophy, especially regarding the nature of the singular. Above all, it suggests as I try to hint by means of reference to pre-Socratic atomists, a rethinking of materialism as a form of intelligence. The most obvious references here are to Spinoza, Deleuze, Democritus, and Lucretius, although more contemporary thinking about artificial life and complex systems theory are also crucial.

9. As a rather compact example of most of these tendencies, see T. J. Jackson Lears, *No Place of Grace: Antimodernism and the Transformation of American Culture, 1880–1920* (New York, 1981), esp. 286ff.

10. See Manuel de Landa, *War in the Age of Intelligent Machines* (New York, 1991), *passim*. De Landa nicely theorizes the importance of War Department rationalization of systems and production, even from the period before the Civil War, and makes evidently clear the increasing role of the War Department in the emergence of scientific management and rationalization during and after the war.

11. At this point, Antonio Negri's reading of Spinoza in *The Savage Anomaly*, trans. Michael Hardt (Minneapolis, 1991), esp. 137ff., will throw some light on Adams' sense of how force and power, taken as production, relate to politics.

12. Less severely, contemporary culture-critics, following Raymond Williams, refer to this outmodedness as "residual formations." More predictably, President Clinton thinks of them as Americans in need of state-sponsored retraining.

13. Were there space, it would be worth pursuing the implications of Adams' intense interest in photography—his wife was an accomplished amateur photographer and he himself worried the technologies of reproduction over and against coal power—and architecture to understand how he analyzed the relations between the ordered intelligence of American heavy industry in the time of railroads, newspapers, and cartels and the newer intelligence of automobiles, photography, and radiation.

14. Perhaps another reason for Adams' relative absence from current critical debates is his antihumanist denunciation of the importance of what even or especially "oppositional" critics call "subjectivity." Adams simply does not think it to be very important at all.

15. I hope it is clear that if one were to graph this argument on some map of recent debates, Adams would be closer to Foucault than to Althusser, Lacan, Lukacs, or Jameson.

16. As an illustration, take the relatively clumsy case of Dreiser: in *Sister Carrie*, as my students always point out, Hurstwood is constantly called "the manager." Yet, his chief feature is his "dumbness." He can articulate nothing. By contrast, Ames, the entrepreneurial engineer and educator of the "higher Carrie"—he has her

read Balzac!—seems able to speak well and about a great deal; yet, even Ames does not and cannot speak about the United States or about capital. We get no sense from him of the nature of the system he runs; we merely get a sense of his "higher values." A better contrast with Hurstwood would be Gerald Crich, from Lawrence's great novel *Women in Love,* but that takes us outside "America." Innumerable examples of the "dumb" appear throughout Dreiser, Norris, and even Howells, whose Silas Lapham has little understanding and even less speech. Perhaps the best example of such silence is James's Goodwood character in *The Portrait of a Lady.* Contrast him with Warburton, who can and does speak of England and politics, as well as something of his roles within them both.

17. This is not to say that we "have" knowledge only of the past; it is rather to say that whatever knowledge that is "had" is "had" within an order whose regulating conditions that knowledge cannot grasp and in which, normally, it plays a defining part.

18. Michel Foucault's great essay "A Preface to Transgression" makes a great deal of the fact that while the line that is transgressed has no dimensions, the transgressor can do no more than remain caught "within" that line in the act of transgression. To put it simply, "transgressors" never get across to "the other side." Michel Foucault, *Language, Counter-Memory, Practice,* ed. and trans. Donald F. Bouchard and Sherry Simon (Ithaca, 1977), esp. 36 and Foucault's discussion of "contestation."

19. See Paul A. Bové, "Reclaiming Criticism: Willful Love in the Tradition of Henry Adams," in *Mastering Discourse: The Politics of Intellectual Culture* (Durham, 1992), 180–82. These pages attempt to outline one part of Adams' use of the figure of Gallatin.

20. See especially W. Edwards Deming, *Quality, Productivity, and Competitive Position* (Cambridge, Mass., 1982).

21. This is, I contend, the serio-ironic burden of his *History of the United States,* reinforced by his novels, especially *Democracy.*

Mark Bauerlein, "Henry James, William James, and the Metaphysics of American Thinking"

1. Henry James to Thomas Sergeant Perry, September 20, 1867, in *Letters,* ed. Leon Edel (4 vols.; Cambridge, Mass., 1974–84), I, 77.

2. Quoted in F. O. Matthiessen, *The James Family* (New York, 1947), 339. For more on the brothers' relationship, see Ross Posnock, *The Trial of Curiosity: Henry James, William James, and the Challenge of Modernity* (New York, 1991); Richard Hocks, *Henry James and Pragmatistic Thought* (Chapel Hill, 1974); and Howard Feinstein, *Becoming William James* (Ithaca, 1984).

3. William James, *Pragmatism* (Cambridge, Mass., 1978), 32. In this essay, quo-

tations are taken from volumes in the standard edition published by Harvard University Press under the general editorship of Frederick H. Burkhardt and appearing as follows: *Essays in Radical Empiricism* (1976); *A Pluralistic Universe* (1977); *Essays in Philosophy* (1978); *The Will to Believe* (1979); *The Principles of Psychology* (1983); and *Manuscript Essays and Notes* (1988).

4. While the scholarly literature that broaches James's pragmatism makes up a significant segment of contemporary cultural criticism, studies relating his pragmatism to a philosophy of consciousness have been no less numerous and often more rigorous and comprehensive. These include Charlene Haddock Seigfried, *William James's Radical Reconstruction of Philosophy* (Albany, 1990); Gerald E. Myers, *William James: His Life and Thought* (New Haven, 1986); Ellen Kappy Suckiel, *The Pragmatic Philosophy of William James* (Notre Dame, 1982); Marcus Peter Ford, *William James's Philosophy: A New Perspective* (Amherst, 1982); Daniel Bjork, *William James: The Center of His Vision* (New York, 1988); and Hilary Putnam, *Realism with a Human Face*, ed. James Conant (Cambridge, Mass., 1990), 217–51.

For detailed phenomenological readings of James, see Hans Linschoten, *On the Way Toward a Phenomenological Psychology: The Psychology of William James*, trans. Amedeo Giorgi (Pittsburgh, 1968); Bruce Wilshire, *William James and Phenomenology: A Study of "The Principles of Psychology"* (Bloomington, 1968); John Wild, *The Radical Empiricism of William James* (New York, 1969); and James M. Edie, *William James and Phenomenology* (Bloomington, 1987). Each of these studies finds in James a form of pre-Husserlian insight, one bearing upon the intentional structure of consciousness.

5. James, *Essays in Philosophy*, 12. The essay on Spencer appears in *Essays*, 7–22. "The Sentiment of Rationality" appears in the same volume (32–64), hereinafter cited in the text as "Sentiment." In regard to the putative givenness of sensation, James says, "No one ever had a simple sensation by itself. Consciousness . . . is of a teeming multiplicity of objects and relations, and what we call simple sensations are results of discriminative attention" (*Principles*, 219). That is, a sensation is an abstraction, a disruption of the same "relations" constituting a sensation as such.

6. "Ontologic wonder" is not to be confused with the "ontological wonder-sickness" cited in a later piece published as a chapter in *The Will to Believe* under the same title, "The Sentiment of Rationality." The latter chapter condenses and heavily revises the first and last few pages of the earlier essay into eight introductory pages. There, James defines "ontologic wonder-sickness" as "the craving for further explanation" (63). But "ontologic wonder" is precisely the absence of such craving.

Henry Sussman, "At the Crossroads of the Nineteenth Century"

1. Walter Benjamin, "Theses on the Philosophy of History," in *Illuminations*, ed. Hannah Arendt, trans. Harry Zohn (New York, 1969), 257–58.

2. Irony is at once an ongoing (*i.e.,* ahistorical) and a historically specific aesthetic achieving prominence at moments of demonstrated sensitivity to differentiated levels of knowledge (configured spatially) in artifacts. Some of the current cutting-edge theoretical work on irony has been done by Paul de Man. See his *Blindness and Insight* (2nd ed.; Minneapolis, 1983), 208–28. The American Romantic epoch, whose major artifacts "Benito Cereno" joins, was conditioned by meditations on irony undertaken by the likes of Friedrich Schlegel, Hegel, and Soren Kierkegaard. Romantic deliberations on irony revolved around such issues as fragmentation and its aesthetic and metaphysical implications and the parallelism between linguistic play and sexual understandings. Kierkegaard, for example, finds close affinities between Socrates' disputational devices and the sexual and aesthetic issues of his own epistemological moment. For important source materials on irony, see Philippe Lacoue-Labarthe and Jean-Luc Nancy, *The Literary Absolute,* trans. Philip Barnard and Cheryl Lester (Albany, 1988), and Friedrich Schlegel, *Friedrich Schlegel's Lucinde and the Fragments,* trans. Peter Firchow (Minneapolis, 1971). Also see Soren Kierkegaard, *The Concept of Irony,* trans. Lee M. Capel (Bloomington, 1968), 85, 120–25, 155–56.

3. I wish to note here additionally only the parallelism between sublime (quantitative) expansion and ironic debunking and the aspect of borderline psychopathology designated "omnipotence and devaluation" by Otto Kernberg. There will be more on the derivation of the current rhetoric of borderlinity in note 4. The aesthetics of Romanticism serves as an instance of a cultural phenomenon dramatizing the sudden shifts between idealization and contempt observed by contemporary psychologists in patients diagnosed with narcissistic or borderline personality disorders. Clearly, there needs to be a contemporary literary translation of phenomena that clinicians can only situate in subject-based, personal, and, implicitly, moralistic spheres. For a powerful contemporary articulation of "omnipotence and devaluation" as a clinical phenomenon, see Otto Kernberg, *Borderline Conditions and Pathological Narcissism* (New York, 1975), 33–39. For a preliminary attempt to translate into literary discourse the observations of contemporary subject-conditions made by Kernberg and other object-relations theorists, see Henry Sussman, *Psyche and Text: The Sublime and the Grandiose in Literature, Psychopathology, and Culture* (Albany, 1993), 45–92, 157–205.

4. Herman Melville, *Moby-Dick,* ed. Harrison Hayford, Hershel Parker, and G. Thomas Tanselle (Evanston, 1988), 3–7, 188–95, 411–14. In its widest parameters, the psychoanalytical discourse of the borderline continues a general reorientation by object-relations theory away from the vicissitudes of drives and their fulfillment or repression so pivotal to the Freudian universe and toward the interpersonal domain of human relations. This redirection received its first substantial articulation by Harry Stack Sullivan. Subsequent theorists in the field of object relations proper placed borderline phenomena within a context of human interactions char-

acterized by, among other things: the persistence of fundamental narcissistic wounds (Heinz Kohut), sharply polarized values (Melanie Klein and Otto Kernberg), damaged attachments (John Bowlby), "false self" (D. W. Winnicott), and a notable dearth of psychological integration (Kohut) at the crux of a battery of defensive reactions and life-strategies including projective fantasies, persistent acting out, and "the subjective experience of emptiness" (Otto Kernberg). Also see Kernberg, *Borderline Conditions and Pathological Narcissism,* 3–44, 69–151, 213–23.

5. Joseph Conrad, *Lord Jim,* ed. Morton Dauwen Zabel (Boston, 1958), 153: "The way is to the destructive element submit yourself."

6. Herman Melville, *The Confidence-Man,* ed. H. Bruce Franklin (Indianapolis, 1967), 3–9.

7. Immanuel Kant, *Critique of Pure Reason,* trans. Norman Kemp Smith (New York, 1929), 257–75, 384–409, 436–58.

8. Sussman, *Psyche and Text,* 22–44.

9. For the concept of original genius, see Immanuel Kant, *Critique of Judgment,* trans. J. H. Bernard (New York, 1951), 150–64, 189.

10. All citations of "Benito Cereno" refer to Herman Melville, *The Piazza Tales and Other Prose Pieces, 1839–1860,* ed. Harrison Hayford, Alma A. MacDougall, and G. Thomas Tanselle (Evanston, 1987), Vol. IX of Hayford, Parker, and Tanselle, eds., *The Writings of Herman Melville,* 9 vols. to date. Hereinafter cited in the text as *PT.*

11. For Melville's elaboration of the ideology of confidence, see *The Confidence-Man,* 8, 12, 40, 42–48, 67–72, 88–93, 164–79, 291–307. I have commented extensively on the literary and metaphysical dimensions of this ideology in *High Resolution: Critical Theory and the Problem of Literacy* (New York, 1989), 88–114.

12. See Sigmund Freud, *The Standard Edition of the Complete Psychological Writings of Sigmund Freud,* trans. James Strachey (19 vols.; London, 1953–74), II, 85, 136–37; VI, 157.

13. See such paintings as *Morning in the Riesengebirge* (1810–11), *The Traveller over the Sea of Mist* (1818), and *The Frozen Ocean* (1823–24), all reproduced in *Caspar David Friedrich,* ed. Jorg Traeger (New York, 1976), 17, 22–23, 38–39.

14. Martin Heidegger, "The Origin of the Work of Art," in *Poetry, Language, Thought,* trans. Albert Hofstadter (New York, 1975), 43–49, 60–64.

15. Jacques Lacan, *The Four Fundamental Concepts of Psycho-Analysis,* trans. Alan Sheridan (New York, 1978), 42–79, 203–15, 279–80.

16. Jacques Derrida, *The Truth in Painting,* trans. Geoff Bennington and Ian McLeod (Chicago, 1987), 17–24, 29–34, 61–82, 134–47.

17. D. W. Winnicott, *Playing and Reality* (New York, 1989), 14, 68, 87, 102. Also "The Theory of the Parent-Infant Relationship," in *Essential Papers on Object Relations,* ed. Peter Buckley (New York, 1986), 233–53.

18. Lacan, *The Four Fundamental Concepts of Psycho-Analysis*, 24–25, 45, 165, 169, 193.

19. See Max Weber, *The Protestant Ethic and the Spirit of Capitalism*, trans. Talcott Parsons(London, 1991), 13–31.

20. Citations derive from Georg Wilhelm Friedrich Hegel, *The Philosophy of History*, trans. J. Sibree (New York, 1956), cited in the text as *PH*.

21. Karl Marx, *Capital: A Critique of Political Economy*, trans. Ben Fowlces (Vol. I), David Fernbach (Vols. II, III) (3 vols.; New York, 1977–81), I, 125–244, 709–72; II, 436–67; III, 170–99, 998–1016.

22. James Joyce, *Finnegans Wake* (New York, 1986), 117, 121.

23. Freud, *The Standard Edition*, VIII, 18–21, 41–42, 163–71.

24. Helene Deutsch is responsible for coining this term. Annie Reich elaborates it and applies it to attachment in women in "Narcissistic Object Choice in Women," *Journal of the American Psychoanalytic Association*, I (1953), 22–44, reprinted in Buckley, ed., *Essential Papers on Object Relations*, 297–317.

Edgar A. Dryden, *"Mute Monuments and Doggerel Epitaphs"*

1. Herman Melville, *Pierre; or, The Ambiguities*, ed. Harrison Hayford, Hershel Parker, and G. Thomas Tanselle (Evanston, 1971), 141, Vol. VII of Hayford, Parker and Tanselle, eds., *The Writings of Herman Melville*, 9 vols. to date. Hereinafter cited in the text as *Pierre*. Subsequent references to Melville's works, except as noted, will be taken from the Northwestern-Newberry Edition series *The Writings of Herman Melville* (Evanston), as follows: *Billy Budd, Sailor*, ed. Harrison Hayford and Merton M. Sealts (Chicago, 1962); *The Confidence-Man*, ed. Harrison Hayford, Hershel Parker, and G. Thomas Tanselle (1984), Vol. X; *Journals*, ed. Howard C. Horsford and Lynn Horth (1989), Vol. XV; *Moby-Dick*, ed. Harrison Hayford, Hershel Parker, and G. Thomas Tanselle (1988), Vol. VI; *The Piazza Tales and Other Prose Pieces, 1839–1860*, ed. Harrison Hayford, Alma A. MacDougall, and G. Thomas Tanselle (1987), Vol. IX (abbreviated as *PT* in the text); *White Jacket*, ed. Harrison Hayford, Hershel Parker, and G. Thomas Tanselle (1970), Vol. V.

2. Paul de Man, *The Resistance to Theory* (Minneapolis, 1986), 30.

3. John T. Irwin, *American Hieroglyphics: The Symbol of the Egyptian Hieroglyphics in the American Renaissance* (New Haven, 1980), 69.

4. Paul de Man, *The Rhetoric of Romanticism* (New York, 1984), 74.

5. William Wordsworth, "Essays upon Epitaphs," in *The Prose Works of William Wordsworth*, ed. W. J. B. Owen and Jane Worthington Smyser (3 vols.; London, 1974), II, 50. For discussions of Melville's knowledge and use of Wordsworth see Michael Davitt Bell, "The Glendinning Heritage: Melville's Literary Borrowings in Pierre," *Studies in Romanticism*, XII (Fall, 1973), 741–62; Thomas F. Heffernan, "Melville and Wordsworth," *American Literature*, XLIX (November, 1977), 338–51;

Hershel Parker, "Melville and the Berkshires: Emotion-Laden Terrain, 'Reckless Sky-Assaulting Mood,' and Encroaching Wordsworthianism," in *American Literature: The New England Heritage,* ed. James Nagel and Richard Astro (New York, 1981).

Melville owned a complete Wordsworth, *The Complete Poetical Works of William Wordsworth Together with a Description of the Country of the Lakes in the North of England, Now First Published with His Works,* ed. Henry Reed (Philadelphia: James Kay, Jun. and Brother; Boston: James Munroe and Company; Pittsburgh: C. H. Kay & Co., 1839), which he took with him on his 1860 voyage to San Francisco. As Parker notes, "We do not know how long he had owned it or whether it was the first or last copy he ever owned" (75), but Merton Sealts speculates that he may have bought the Wordsworth volume in 1849 (*Melville's Reading* [Columbia, S.C., 1988], 45). Melville refers to Wordsworth as early as *White Jacket,* where he describes him as the "gentle and sequestered Wordsworth" (40), and by 1853 he had read "Resolution and Independence" and parodied several lines of it in "Cock-a-Doodle-Doo!"

The first of Wordsworth's "Essays upon Epitaphs" was printed in *The Friend* in 1814 without Wordsworth's name and was reprinted in 1814 as a note to *The Excursion*—a poem that Melville marks and annotates (Heffernan, "Melville and Wordsworth," 349–51; Parker, "Melville and the Berkshires," 75–79)—and it appears as Appendix V in the Henry Reed edition.

6. Paul de Man, "Time and History in Wordsworth," *Diacritics,* XVII (Winter, 1987), 9.

7. Wordsworth, "Essays upon Epitaphs," 54.

8. William Wordsworth, *The Prelude,* V, l. 12, in *Poetical Works of Wordsworth,* ed. Thomas Hutchinson, rev. Ernest de Selincourt (London, 1960).

On April 4, 1850, Evert Duyckinck, who was visiting Melville in Pittsfield, wrote to his wife as follows: "I dropped you a line yesterday in a parcel to the office which Melville says I must have been tempted to make up by the Yankee atmosphere. I had the proof sheets of Appleton's edition of Wordsworth's posthumous poem 'The Prelude' with me to read & use at leisure in the paper. Mathews told me that Griswold was about to publish a whole book of it in his next week's magazine, so I concluded that my next week's paper should have its share & made up a parcel of mail with necessary directions at once" (Eleanor Melville Metcalf, *Herman Melville: Cycle and Epicycle* [Cambridge, Mass., 1953], 80).

9. De Man, "Time and History in Wordsworth," 9.

10. Jacques Derrida, *Margins of Philosophy,* trans. Alan Bass (Chicago, 1982), 83.

11. Derrida, *Margins of Philosophy,* 82.

12. Wordsworth, "Essays upon Epitaphs," 52.

13. *Ibid.,* 54, 56.

14. De Man, *The Rhetoric of Romanticism,* 78.

15. Wordsworth, "Essays upon Epitaphs," 60, 57.

16. Wordsworth, *The Excursion*, VII, ll. 409–15.

17. Cynthia Chase, *Decomposing Figures: Rhetorical Readings in the Romantic Tradition* (Baltimore, 1986), 59.

18. *Ibid.*, 61.

19. For a detailed discussion of quotation and allusion in Melville, see Edgar A. Dryden, "From the Piazza to the Enchanted Isles: Melville's Textual Rovings," in *After Strange Texts: The Role of Theory in the Study of Literature,* ed. Gregory S. Jay and David L. Miller (University, Ala., 1985), 46–68.

20. Philippe Lacoue-Labarthe and Jean-Luc Nancy, *The Literary Absolute: The Theory of Literature in German Romanticism,* trans. Philip Barnard and Cheryl Lester (Albany, 1988), 62.

21. The second and third "Essays" remained unprinted until they appeared in A. B. Grosart's edition of *The Prose Works of William Wordsworth* (3 vols.; London, 1876).

22. De Man, *The Rhetoric of Romanticism,* 80.

Michael A. Beehler, "Riddle the Inevitable"

1. Joseph N. Riddel, "Decentering the Image: The 'Project' of 'American' Poetics?" in *Textual Strategies: Perspectives in Post-Structuralist Criticism,* ed. Josue V. Harari (Ithaca, 1979), 323. Hereinafter cited in the text as "Decentering." Other of Riddel's works cited in this essay are "The Anomalies of Literary (Post) Modernism," *Arizona Quarterly,* XLIV (Autumn, 1988), 80–119, and "The Crypt of Edgar Poe," *boundary 2,* VII (Spring, 1979), 117–44.

2. Emmanuel Levinas, *Ethics and Infinity,* trans. Richard A. Cohen (Pittsburgh, 1985), 76. Abbreviations for Levinas' texts cited in this essay are: "Trace"—"The Trace of the Other," in *Deconstruction in Context: Literature and Philosophy,* ed. Mark C. Taylor (Chicago, 1986); *OB—Otherwise than Being; or, Beyond Essence,* trans. Alphonso Lingis (Dordrecht, 1981); *LR—The Levinas Reader,* ed. Sean Hand (Cambridge, Eng., 1989).

3. T. S. Eliot, *The Complete Poems and Plays, 1909–1950* (New York, 1958). Hereinafter cited in the text as *CPP.* The following abbreviations will be used for citations of other Eliot works: *TCC—To Criticize the Critic* (New York, 1965); *MC—Murder in the Cathedral* (New York, 1963); *SE—Selected Essays* (London, 1951).

4. Jacques Derrida, *Mémoires for Paul de Man,* trans. Cecile Lindsay, Jonathan Culler, and Eduardo Cadava (New York, 1986), 29, 37.

5. Derrida, *Mémoires,* 56.

6. *Ibid,* 35.

7. *Ibid,* 61.

8. Jacques Derrida, "How to Avoid Speaking: Denials," in *Languages of the*

Unsayable: The Play of Negativity in Literature and Literary Theory, ed. Sanford Burdick and Wolfgang Iser (New York, 1989), 132; Derrida, *Mémoires,* 132.

9. Emmanuel Levinas, *Difficult Freedom: Essays on Judaism,* trans. Sean Hand (Baltimore, 1990), 293.

10. Levinas, *Collected Philosophical Papers,* trans. Alphonso Lingis (Dordrecht, 1987), 48.

Margot Norris, *"The Trace of the Trenches"*

1. Paul Fussell, *The Great War and Modern Memory* (London, 1977), ix, 70 (hereinafter cited in the text as *GW*); Elaine Scarry, *The Body in Pain* (London, 1985), 85; Wyndham Lewis, *Blasting and Bombardiering* (London, 1937), 94 (hereinafter cited in the text as *BB*); Gertrude Stein, *Picasso* (London, 1946), 11.

2. William M. Chace, *The Political Identities of Ezra Pound and T. S. Eliot* (Stanford, 1973), 145.

3. Marianne De Koven, "History as the Supressed Referent in Modernist Fiction," *ELH,* LVIII (Spring, 1984), 137–52.

4. Martin Stephen, ed., *Never Such Innocence* (London, 1988), 6. Jean Baudrillard describes *hyperreality* as "the generation by models of a real without origin or reality: a hyperreal. The territory no longer precedes the map, nor survives it. Henceforth, it is the map that precedes the territory—precession of simulacra—it is the map that engenders the territory and if we were to revive the fable today, it would be the territory whose shreds are slowly rotting across the map." Jean Baudrillard, *Selected Writings,* ed. Mark Poster (Stanford, 1988), 166.

5. For a discussion of the problem of memory and forgetfulness in Pound, see Michael North, "Where Memory Faileth: Forgetfulness and a Poem Including History," in *Ezra Pound: The Legacy of Kulchur,* ed. Marcel Smith and William A. Ulmer (Tuscaloosa, 1988).

6. Scarry, *The Body in Pain,* 121.

7. Chace, *The Political Identities of Ezra Pound and T. S. Eliot,* 145.

8. Marjorie Perloff, *The Futurist Moment* (Chicago, 1986), 187.

9. *The Oxford Book of Modern Verse, 1892–1935,* chosen by W. B. Yeats (New York, 1937); Jean-François Lyotard, *The Differend: Phrases in Dispute,* trans. Georges Van Den Abbeele (Minneapolis, 1988).

10. See Yeats's letter to Dorothy Wellesley of December 21, 1936 in *The Letters of W. B. Yeats,* ed. Allan Wade (New York, 1955), 874.

11. Jon Silkin, ed., *The Penguin Book of First World War Poetry* (New York, 1981), 186, 182. Hereinafter cited in the text as *PB*. Fussell argues that the battle of the Somme ("destined to be known among the troops as the Great Fuck-Up" [12]) had among its causes "the class system and the assumptions it sanctioned" concerning the rapidly trained army "largely recruited among workingmen from the

Midlands. The planners assumed that these troops—burdened for the assault with 66 pounds of equipment—were too simple and animal to cross the space between the opposing trenches in any way except in full daylight and aligned in rows or 'waves.' It was felt that the troops would become confused by more subtle tactics like rushing from cover to cover, or assault-firing, or following close upon a continuous creeping barrage" (13).

12. W. B. Yeats, *The Poems,* ed. Richard J. Finneran (New York, 1983), 135.

13. Fredric Jameson, *Fables of Aggression: Wyndham Lewis, the Modernist as Fascist* (Berkeley, 1979), 30.

14. Wyndham Lewis, ed., *Blast 2* (Santa Barbara, 1981), 34. Hereinafter cited in the text as *B2.*

15. See Filipo Marinetti, "The Founding and Manifesto of Futurism 1909," in *Futurist Manifestos,* ed. Umbro Apollonio (London, 1973), 22: "We will glorify war—the world's only hygiene." Hereinafter cited in the text as *FM.* John Tytell attributes this "shocking recapitulation of the eugenics theory that was prevalent at the time" to Winston Churchill, among others: "Winston Churchill was a believer in eugenics and the idea that the earlier stages of the industrial system had created work for an enormous mass of inferior Europeans who were less and less required as the system evolved." See John Tytell, *Ezra Pound: The Solitary Volcano* (New York, 1987), 119. Gaudier applies this economic argument to the prophylaxis of war, "IT TAKES AWAY FROM THE MASSES NUMBERS UPON NUMBERS OF UNIMPORTANT UNITS, WHOSE ECONOMIC ACTIVITIES BECOME NOXIOUS AS THE RECENT TRADE CRISES HAVE SHOWN US" (*B2,* 33).

16. Tytell, *Ezra Pound,* 119.

17. Ezra Pound, *Personae: The Collected Shorter Poems of Ezra Pound* (New York, 1971), 140.

18. Fred D. Crawford, *British Poets of the Great War* (London, 1988), 83.

19. Ezra Pound, *The Cantos of Ezra Pound* (New York, 1970), 71, 188, 191.

20. Ezra Pound, *Selected Prose, 1909–1965,* ed. William Cookson (New York, 1973), 229, 228.

21. Christine Froula, *A Guide to Ezra Pound's Selected Poems* (New York, 1983), 167.

22. See Chace, *The Political Identities of Ezra Pound and T. S. Eliot:* "Lacking both perception and a basic curiosity about the workings of the world, the masses could only subside into 'abuleia'" (44).

23. Tytell, *Ezra Pound,* 120.

24. T. S. Eliot, *Collected Poems, 1909–1962* (New York, 1963). All Eliot quotations in the text come from this edition. Lewis (who wrote in the editorial of the war issue of *Blast* that "Nietzsche has had an English sale such as he could hardly have anticipated in his most ecstatic and morose moments" [5]) produced his own important Nietzschean texts dealing with the crowd and herd mentality. These

include a 1915 Vorticist painting called *The Crowd,* "The Code of a Herdsman" published in the *Little Review* in 1917, and the 1926 book *The Art of Being Ruled,* with its explicit references to Arnold's *Culture and Anarchy.*

25. Maud Ellmann, *The Poetics of Impersonality* (Cambridge, Mass., 1987), 101.

26. Terry Eagleton, *Criticism and Ideology* (London, 1976), 149–50; Ellmann, *The Poetics of Impersonality,* 101.

27. Ellmann, *The Poetics of Impersonality,* 109.

28. Frances FitzGerald blamed the administration policy failure in losing the war on this inability or refusal to recognize the reality of the Vietnamese: "For the Americans to discern the enemy within the world of the Vietnamese village was to attempt to make out figures within a landscape indefinite and vague—underwater, as it were." See *Fire in the Lake: The Vietnamese and the Americans in Vietnam* (Boston, 1972), 142.

Charles Altieri, "A Tale of Two Modernisms"

1. Bradley's theories of tragedy do preserve the intricacy of dialectics, but significantly by limiting attention to works of art. Both his and McTaggart's metaphysics give up Hegel's ambitions to place history within philosophy, so that dialectic is at most a way of working through mediations in an epistemological sphere.

2. Russell, *My Philosophical Development,* 54, quoted in Ronald Jager, *The Development of Bertrand Russell's Philosophy* (New York, 1972), 63. I found Jager quite helpful for clarifying Russell's various projects and the pressures leading from one to the other.

3. Ursula Bridge, *W. B. Yeats and T. Sturge Moore: Their Correspondence, 1901–1937* (London, 1953).

4. Bertrand Russell, *Autobiography* (3 vols.; Boston, 1968), II, 10. The extended quotation is from p. 15. Hereinafter cited in the text as *A.*

5. For Wittgenstein's increasing sense of Russell's hollowness see Ray Monk's biography, *Ludwig Wittgenstein* (New York, 1990), and see the marvelous contrast between the two philosophers developed in Bruce Duffey's novel, *The World as I Found It* (New York, 1987). On the mysteriousness of the "I," see Wittgenstein, *Notebooks, 1914–1916,* trans. G. E. M. Anscombe (Oxford, 1961), and on the mystical see Monk and Wittgenstein's *Tractatus Logico-Philosophicus,* trans. D. F. Pears and B. F. McGuiness (London, 1961).

6. Dora Marsden, "Lingual Psychology: A New Conception of the Function of Philosophic Inquiry," *Egoist,* III (July, 1916), 7. Bruce Clarke, who is writing a book on Marsden, pointed out this essay to me.

7. Jager, *Bertrand Russell's Philosophy,* 231.

8. Richard Rorty, *Contingency, Irony and Solidarity* (New York, 1989), 73. Hereinafter cited in the text as *CIS.*

9. Jager, *Bertrand Russell's Philosophy,* 378ff and 472, argues convincingly that logical atomism can have no ethics because it allows no conceptual space for principles and for corresponding modes of judgment.

10. Thomas McCarthy, "Private Irony and Public Decency: Richard Rorty's New Pragmatism," *Critical Inquiry,* XVI (1990), 355–70.

11. Rorty uses Freud as an exemplar of the power to change our moral vocabulary by showing how contingent forces affect our possibilities for acting. But having said that, he cannot go on to assess that vocabulary, or assess how we might assess that vocabulary's relevance for our world, beyond pointing out that certain vocabularies prevail in those assessments. He cannot locate by theory provisional criteria within the nesting of vocabularies and principles.

12. Joseph Raz, *The Morality of Freedom* (Oxford, 1986).

13. Friedrich Nietzsche, *Human All Too Human: A Book for Free Spirits,* trans. R. J. Hollingdale (Cambridge, Eng., 1986), 299.

John Carlos Rowe, "Whitman's Body Poetic"

1. Walt Whitman, "Eighteen Sixty-One," *Drum-Taps,* in *Leaves of Grass: A Textual Variorum of the Printed Poems,* ed. Sculley Bradley, Harold W. Blodgett, Arthur Golden, William White (3 vols.; New York, 1980), II, 467. Further references to *Drum-Taps* will be cited in the text as *DT* and to *Sequel to Drum-Taps* as *Sequel.*

2. Ralph Waldo Emerson, *Nature,* in *Nature, Addresses, and Lectures,* ed. Robert E. Spiller and Alfred R. Ferguson (Cambridge, Mass., 1971), 20, Vol. I of *The Collected Works of Ralph Waldo Emerson,* ed. Joseph Slater and Douglas Emory Wilson, 4 vols. to date.

3. Ralph Waldo Emerson, "American Civilization" (1862), in *Miscellanies* (Boston, 1904), 297, Vol. XI of *The Complete Works of Ralph Waldo Emerson,* 12 vols., ed. Edward Waldo Emerson. Hereinafter cited in the text as "American Civilization." See also my discussion of Emerson's treatment of labor in "Man, the Reformer," in "Romancing the Stone: Melville's Critique of Ideology in *Pierre,*" in *Theorizing American Literature: Hegel, the Sign, and History,* ed. Bainard Cowan and Joseph Kronick (Baton Rouge, 1991), 221–23.

4. Stanley Cavell, *The Senses of Walden* (expanded ed.; San Francisco, 1981), 119.

5. As Betsy Erkkila demonstrates in *Whitman the Political Poet* (New York, 1989), Whitman's utopian vision was communitarian and thus far more demanding in terms of what the poet had to acknowledge and incorporate into his thinking and poetic practice than the ego-centered transcendentalisms of Emerson and Thoreau, in which the "representative man" could stand metonymically for a people, community, or nation.

6. F. DeWolfe Miller, Introduction to *Drum-Taps* (1865) and *Sequel to Drum-Taps* (1865–66), facsimile edition, ed. F. DeWolfe Miller (Gainesville, 1959), xxxi. It

is worth pointing out that the first edition of *Drum-Taps* did include reference to Lincoln's assassination in "Hush'd Be the Camps To-Day," with its title note, "A. L. Buried April 19, 1865." Sculley Bradley and Harold W. Blodgett point out in *Leaves of Grass*, Norton Critical Edition (New York, 1973), 338*n*, that this original title note was included "evidently under the misapprehension that interment, as well as the funeral, was to take place in Washington. In the 1871 and 1876 editions he corrected the note to the present reading ["May 4, 1865"], and also made a number of changes in the final stanza."

7. Timothy Sweet, *Traces of War: Poetry, Photography, and the Crisis of the Union* (Baltimore, 1990), 11.

8. In *Walt Whitman and the Citizen's Eye* (Baton Rouge, 1993), James Dougherty argues that Whitman adapts the dramatic monologues of "Song of Myself," in which he had "spoken on behalf of slaves and criminals, to draw them back within the spiritual commonwealth," to his own situation in *Drum-Taps:* "Now Whitman speaks as an outsider himself: a citizen whose democratic anarchism was affronted by the Union's suppression of political dissent and by the elitism of its military leadership, and whose human impulses were enraged by the suffering and human wastage he saw in the hospitals. . . . He begins to speak not as the president of regulation (as he had called himself in the 1855 Preface), but as the perpetual revolutionary" (82). It is just this difference between his marginal poetic authority and the authority represented by Lincoln that he can no longer sustain in "Lilacs" and most of the *Sequel*. As Sweet points out, Whitman collapses his poetic purposes in "Lilacs" with a heroic Lincoln, who has been thereby "dehistoricized" and thus depoliticized (*Traces of War*, 77). In this regard, see also Mark Edmundson's "'Lilacs': Walt Whitman's American Elegy," *Nineteenth-Century Literature*, XLIV (1990), 465–91.

9. Although he makes the case a bit too reductively that "Whitman *was* an imperialist poet," Walter Grünzweig connects effectively Whitman's cosmopolitanism and internationalism, especially in the poetry of the 1870s and later, with U.S. expansionist policies in the later nineteenth century. See Grünzweig, "Noble Ethics and Loving Aggressiveness: The Imperialist Walt Whitman," in *An American Empire: Expansionist Cultures and Policies, 1881–1917,* ed. Serge Ricard (Aix-en-Provence: Université de Provence, 1990).

10. Bradley and Blodgett, eds., *Leaves of Grass*, Norton Critical Edition, 290*n*.

11. As Kent Ljungquist points out in "'Meteor of War': Melville, Thoreau, and Whitman Respond to John Brown," *American Literature*, LXI (December, 1989), 679, Whitman identifies his poetic voice with a meteor in "Year of Meteors" (the twenty-ninth poem in the first edition of *Drum-Taps*), probably in reference to the meteor shower reported in the Northeast in December, 1859, and cited by many as a portent of war: "In typical Whitman fashion, he appropriates this image of the 'I' of the poem and asks: 'What am I myself but one of your meteors?'"

12. Of course, Whitman's various appeals in *Drum-Taps* for poetic foreknowl-

edge of the war's necessity serve also to divert attention from his ambivalence regarding war in the early months of the Civil War. See DeWolfe, Introduction to *Drum-Taps* and *Sequel to Drum-Taps*, facsimile, ix–xvi, for an account of how Whitman's ambivalence about the war was treated by his contemporaries up to his death and by Thomas Wentworth Higginson in his obituary on Whitman in the New York *Post*.

13. See Sweet, *Traces of War*, 44: "In the context of the war Whitman found his own 'self' to be unstable. During his years as volunteer nurse in army hospitals he suffered physical and emotional breakdowns, in 1863 and again in 1865. . . . The grounding of poetics in 'myself' or in the 'body electric' as constructed in the first edition of *Leaves of Grass* was brought into question by the violence of the war."

14. As Eric Sundquist points out in "Slavery, Revolution, and the American Renaissance," in *The American Renaissance Reconsidered*, ed. Walter Benn Michaels and Donald Pease, English Institute Essays, n.s., No. 9 (Baltimore, 1985), 3–9.

15. The appropriation of General Washington's authority by the poetic voice is perhaps subtly reinforced by the Whitman family's tradition that "one of the sons of Nehemiah Whitman, W[alt] W[hitman]'s great grandfather, lost his life fighting as a rebel lieutenant in this action," as Bradley and Blodgett note in *Leaves of Grass*, Norton Critical Edition, 295*n*.

16. F. O. Matthiessen, *American Renaissance: Art and Expression in the Age of Emerson and Whitman* (New York, 1941), 599–600. Matthiessen's purpose, of course, in stressing Whitman's impressionistic techniques in these short lyrics, was to establish a connection between the later romantic and early moderns, especially T. S. Eliot. Dougherty's treatment of Whitman's pictorialism is a later and better interpretation, in part because Dougherty recognizes the narrativity of the impressionist lyrics in *Drum-Taps* and in part because he does not push Matthiessen's formalist thesis. See Dougherty, *Walt Whitman and the Citizen's Eye*, 108–16.

17. Bradley and Blodgett, eds., *Leaves of Grass*, Norton Critical Edition, 424*n*: "The Fourth of the untitled twelve of the first edition, this poem was called 'Night Poem' in 1856, 'Sleep-Chasings' in 1860 and 1867, and 'The Sleepers' since 1871."

18. This is how Dougherty reads these short poems in *Drum-Taps* about soldiers' experiences in the field. See *Walt Whitman and the Citizen's Eye*, 110–11. I don't disagree with this more literal treatment of Whitman's dramatic monologues, but I would argue that Whitman wants the reader to be confused about the speaking voice in these poems, such that the soldier's literal experience and its poetic figuration become complements in the overall project of reconstructing Whitman's poetic identity.

19. Once again, I think that Whitman's revisions of *Drum-Taps* reinforce the emergence of this confident poetic voice, primarily by rearranging the narrative of the poems. Thus the 1891–92 edition of *Leaves of Grass* puts together and in this order "By the Bivouac's Fitful Flame," "Come Up from the Fields Father," and "Vigil

Strange I Kept on the Field One Night." Read in this order, the three poems dramatize the transformation of the poet from mere observer of war ("By the Bivouac's Fitful Flame") to surrogate father ("Come Up from the Fields Father") to Christlike savior ("Vigil Strange I Kept on the Field One Night"). Such a reading depends crucially on treating the different voices of the dramatic monologues variously represented in the three poems as parts of the same overarching poetic voice.

20. Dougherty, *Walt Whitman and the Citizen's Eye,* 100, reads "Come Up from the Fields Father" as a conventional poem for its sentimentalization of the family's grief in the mother's death at the end of the poem. Yet when read as Whitman's substitution of his own generative powers for those either of the Union or the dead soldier's parents, then the poem escapes the sentimentality of such war elegies by problematizing our responsibility for the war dead. This does not by itself render the poem "better" on purely aesthetic grounds than Dougherty judges it, but it does make it far more *interesting* than the spate of conventional poems about Union dead from this period.

21. Sweet, *Traces of War,* 43. Sweet interprets the speaker in the poem as "the father of the dead soldier," a conclusion that if taken too literally distracts us from the Christological rhetoric of the poem—a rhetoric necessary for Whitman's poetic voice to claim to be both *father and son,* thereby achieving his own symbolic resurrection at the poem's conclusion.

22. Dougherty's reading of "Vigil Strange" in *Walt Whitman and the Citizen's Eye* also misses the rhetoric of poetic resurrection, but it does treat the poem as centrally concerned with the problem of voice: "'Vigil Strange' is striking for the reticence of its soldier-persona. His I stands mute and passive in the presence of a Not-Me that exceeds his capacity to respond; and Whitman's imagination embraces that emptiness, not filling its void as he did at the end of 'Come Up from the Fields'" (102). As Dougherty recognizes, this is not the only poem in *Drum-Taps* in which Whitman uses silence, the inability to find poetic voice, and just the poet's afflatus to remind us that his theme is at least as much the problem of rediscovering poetic voice as witnessing the War.

23. Sweet, *Traces of War,* 24.

John Johnston, "Jameson's Hyperspace, Heidegger's Rift, Frank Gehry's House"

1. Michel Foucault, "The Order of Discourse," in *Untying the Text,* trans. Ian McLeod and ed. Robert Young (Boston, 1981), 67 and 65, respectively.

2. See Gilles Deleuze, *Foucault* (Paris, 1986), 115–20.

3. Fredric Jameson, "Postmodernism, or, The Cultural Logic of Late Capitalism," *New Left Review,* No. 146 (July–August, 1984), 59–92, republished as a chap-

ter of Jameson's book, *Postmodernism, or, The Cultural Logic of Late Capitalism* (Durham, 1991). All citations will refer to the book and will be noted in the text with a *P* followed by the page number.

4. Jean Baudrillard, *The Mirror of Production,* trans. Mark Poster (St. Louis, 1973). See esp. pp. 17–20.

5. Jameson's interpretation of the Gehry house first appeared in "Spatial Equivalents: Postmodernist Architecture and the World System," in *The States of Theory,* ed. David Carroll (New York, 1990), 125–48, republished in Jameson's *Postmodernism, or, The Cultural Logic of Late Capitalism.*

6. "Interview with Frank Gehry," in Barbara Diamonstein, *American Architecture Now* (New York, 1980), 44.

7. Gavin Maccrae-Gibson, *The Secret Life of Buildings* (Cambridge, Mass., 1985), 13–14 (quoted by Jameson, *P,* 115–16).

8. Fredric Jameson, *The Political Unconscious* (Ithaca, 1981), 236–37.

9. Jameson's limits point up the need for an alternative formulation of cognitive or cultural mapping that would recognize the abstract nature of all semiotic processes, which can possess both positive and negative valences. The basis for such an alternative, I think, can be found in Gilles Deleuze and Felix Guattari's *A Thousand Plateaus,* trans. Brian Massumi (Minneapolis, 1987).

10. Martin Heidegger, "The Origin of the Work of Art," in *Poetry, Language, Thought,* trans. Albert Hofstadter (New York, 1971), 77. The original German text may be found in Martin Heidegger, *Holzwege, Gesamtausgabe* (Vittorio Klostermann, 1977), V, 1–74.

11. See especially "The Age of the World Picture," in *The Question Concerning Technology,* trans. William Lovitt (New York, 1977), 115–54, where Heidegger argues that the epoch of modernity commences with Descartes, who inaugurates the age of the world picture or image in which human being is reduced to a subject (that is, a subjected being) before which stand objects and representations. Descartes, of course, in the second and third Meditations, also established the oppositional parameters—language and truth versus vision (painting) and falsity—within which the hermeneutics of Heidegger and Jameson operate.

12. *The Speeches of Adolf Hitler,* ed. Norman H. Baynes (2 vols.; London, 1942), I, 584–92.

13. Heidegger, "The Origin of the Work of Art," 63–64.

14. Here I draw on Christopher Fynsk's discussion of Heidegger's "Origin of the Work of Art" in his book *Heidegger: Thought and Historicity* (Ithaca, 1986), esp. pp. 142–47.

15. Jacques Derrida, "White Mythology," in *Margins,* trans. Alan Bass (Chicago, 1978). All citations, including those of Fontanier, are taken from pp. 255–56.

16. I borrow this definition of "false work" from Gregory Rukavina, whose own series of photographic "false works" alerted me to the possibility of this reading.

The definition is taken from his article, "ADAMINUS/DESCO/GEORG/IO. ME/FECI/T." in *Tema Celeste*, No. 40 (Spring, 1993), 52.

Joseph G. Kronick, "Afterword: Joseph N. Riddel (1931–1991)"

1. Joseph Riddel, "The Hermeneutic Self—Notes Toward an 'American' Practice," *boundary 2*, XII/XIII (Spring/Fall, 1984), 77. Hereinafter cited in the text as *HS*. The following abbreviations will be used for citations from Riddel's works: *CE—The Clairvoyant Eye: The Poetry and Poetics of Wallace Stevens* (1965; 2nd ed., Baton Rouge, 1991); *IB—The Inverted Bell: Modernism and the Counterpoetics of William Carlos Williams* (1974; 2nd ed., Baton Rouge, 1991).

2. See Riddel's discussion of paleonymics in "To Perform—A Transitive Verb?" included as the first essay in this volume. "Paleonymy" refers to the conserving of the *"old name"* in the deconstruction of the opposition of metaphysical concepts. See Derrida, "Signature, Event, Context," in *Margins of Philosophy*, trans. Alan Bass (Chicago, 1982), 329. Also see *Positions*, trans. Alan Bass (Chicago, 1981), 71.

3. In addition to "The Hermeneutic Self," cited in *n* 1, see the companion essay "Reading America/American Readers," *MLN*, XCIX (September, 1984), 903–27.

4. See *The Structuralist Controversy: The Languages of Criticism and the Sciences of Man*, ed. Richard Macksey and Eugenio Donato (Baltimore, 1970), 155.

5. Ralph Waldo Emerson, *Journals*, ed. William H. Gilman (16 vols.; Cambridge, Mass., 1960–82), VII, 304.

6. See also Jacques Derrida, *Mémoires for Paul de Man* (1986; 2nd ed., New York, 1989): "Were I not so frequently associated with this adventure of deconstruction, I would risk, with a smile, the following hypothesis: America *is* deconstruction (l'Amérique, mais *c'est* la deconstruction). . . . Let us say instead: deconstruction and America are two open sets which intersect partially according to an allegorico-metonymic figure. In this fiction of truth, 'America' would be the title of a new novel on the history of deconstruction and the deconstruction of history" (18).

7. Joseph N. Riddel, *C. Day Lewis* (New York, 1971).

8. See "Différance," in Derrida, *Margins of Philosophy*, 13.

9. Before his death, Riddel selected these essays for a book to be titled "The Turning Word: Essays on Modernism, Literature, and Philosophy."

10. This book has since been published: *Purloined Letters: Originality and Repetition in American Literature*, ed. Mark Bauerlein (Baton Rouge, 1995).

Contributors

CHARLES ALTIERI is professor of English at the University of California at Berkeley and the author of numerous books on modernist poetry and philosophical criticism. His most recent publications are *Subjective Agency* and *Painterly Abstraction in Modernist American Poetry.*

MARK BAUERLEIN is associate professor of English at Emory University and the author of *Whitman and the American Idiom* and editor of Joseph N. Riddel, *Purloined Letters: Originality and Repetition in American Literature.*

MICHAEL BEEHLER is associate professor of English at Montana State University and the author of *T. S. Eliot, Wallace Stevens, and the Discourses of Difference.* His most recent publications are on Wallace Stevens and Michel de Certeau.

PAUL A. BOVÉ is editor of *boundary 2* and professor of English at the University of Pittsburgh. He is the author of *Mastering Discourse* and *In the Wake of Theory.*

JACQUES DERRIDA is director of studies at the Ecole des Hautes Etudes en Sciences Sociales and professor of humanities at the University of California, Irvine. His most recent publications in English are *Points . . . Interviews, 1974–1994; The Gift of Death;* and *Specters of Marx: The State of the Debt, the Work of Mourning, and the New International.*

EDGAR A. DRYDEN is editor of the *Arizona Quarterly* and professor of English at the University of Arizona. He is the author of *Melville's Thematics of Form; Nathaniel Hawthorne: The Poetics of Enchantment;* and *The Form of American Romance.*

JOHN JOHNSTON is associate professor of English at Emory University and the author of *Carnival of Repetition: Gaddis's "The Recognitions" and Postmodern Theory* and *Information Multiplicity: American Fiction in the Age of High Technology* (forthcoming).

JOSEPH G. KRONICK is professor of English at Louisiana State University and the author of *American Poetics of History: From Emerson to the Moderns* and coeditor of *Theorizing American Literature: Hegel, the Sign, and History.*

KATHRYNE V. LINDBERG is associate professor of English and adjunct in Africana Studies at Wayne State University and the author of *Reading Pound Reading: Modernism After Nietzsche.* Her most recent articles are on cultural criticism, W. E. B. Du Bois, Gwendolyn Brooks, Bob Kaufman, and Nietzsche.

MARGOT NORRIS is professor of English and comparative literature at the University of California, Irvine. She is the author of *Beasts of the Modern Imagination: Darwin, Nietzsche, Kafka, Ernst, and Lawrence* and *Joyce's Web: The Social Unraveling of Modernism.*

JOSEPH N. RIDDEL was born on September 11, 1931, in West Virginia and died September 7, 1991, in Los Angeles. At the time of his death, he was professor of English and director of the Critical Studies Program at the University of California, Los Angeles. Prior to going to UCLA, he taught at Duke University, the University of California at Riverside, and the State University of New York at Buffalo. He was the author of *The Inverted Bell: Modernism and the Counterpoetics of William Carlos Williams; The Clairvoyant Eye: The Poetry and Poetics of Wallace Stevens; C. Day Lewis;* and numerous essays on American literature and critical theory. *Purloined Letters: Originality and Repetition in American Literature* has been published posthumously.

JOHN CARLOS ROWE is professor of English and director of the Theory Institute, University of California, Irvine. He is the editor of *New Essays on "The Education of Henry Adams"* and the author of *At Emerson's Tomb: The Politics of Literary Modernism in the United States,* both forthcoming.

HENRY SUSSMAN is professor and chair of comparative literature at the State University of New York, Buffalo, and has most recently published *Psyche and Text: The Sublime and the Grandiose in Literature, Psychopathology, and Culture* and *Kafka's Unholy Trinity: "The Trial."*